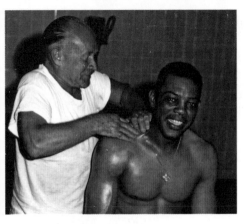

D0398744

24

24

Life Stories and Lessons from the Say Hey Kid

WILLIE MAYS

and JOHN SHEA

Foreword by Bob Costas

ST. MARTIN'S
PRESS
NEW YORK

First published in the United States by St. Martin's Press,
an imprint of St. Martin's Publishing Group

www.stmartins.com

Front cover endpaper photos by: at trophy case, San Francisco Giants; as a San Francisco Giant,
San Francisco Giants; with Mae Mays, collection of Willie Mays; with Queen Elizabeth and President
Reagan, collection of Willie Mays; with Barack and Michelle Obama, official White House photo by Pete
Souza; with Hank Aaron, National Baseball Hall of Fame and Museum; with Frank "Doc" Bowman,
collection of Rick Swig; with Giant the poodle, Jean Fruth/National Baseball Hall of Fame and Museum;
as a Birmingham Black Baron, Memphis and Shelby County Room, Memphis Public Libraries; with
Leo Durocher, Ron Riesterer; in a convertible, Brad Mangin; with Tiger Woods, Daniel Murphy; with
Frank Robinson, Earl Weaver, and Robin Yount, Rick Swig

Back cover endpaper photos by: with Orlando Cepeda, Juan Marichal, Gaylord Perry, and Willie McCovey,
San Francisco Giants; with photographers, San Francisco Giants; with Bobby Bonds and President Bill
Clinton, Daniel Murphy; with Ed Sullivan, collection of Willie Mays; with Dwight Clark, Michael
Zagaris; with Kareem Abdul-Jabbar and Tommy Lasorda, Rick Swig; at the White House podium, Rick
Swig; with President George W. Bush, Rick Swig; with Orlando Cepeda, Jim Davenport, and Felipe
Alou, Brad Mangin; with Bill Rigney, San Francisco Giants; as a New York Met, New York Mets; with
75th birthday cake, Brad Mangin; as a New York Giant, collection of Rick Swig

Editorial consulting by Kurt Aguilar

Photographic research by Brad Mangin

Designed by Steven Seighman

Library of Congress Cataloging-in-Publication Data

Names: Mays, Willie, 1931– author. | Shea, John, 1958– author.
Title: 24 : life stories and lessons from the Say Hey Kid / Willie Mays and John Shea.
Other titles: Twenty-four
Description: First edition. | New York, NY : St. Martin's Press, 2020. | Includes index.
Identifiers: LCCN 2019058386 | ISBN 9781250230423 (hardcover) |
    ISBN 9781250230430 (ebook)
Subjects: LCSH: Mays, Willie, 1931– | Baseball players—United States—Conduct of life. |
    Baseball players—United States—Biography.
Classification: LCC GV865.M38 A3 2020 | DDC 796.357092 [B]—dc23
LC record available at https://lccn.loc.gov/2019058386

First Edition: May 2020

10 9 8 7 6 5 4 3 2 1

To my father, Willie Howard Mays, Sr., who taught me about life,
and to the people of Fairfield, Alabama, who helped raise me.
—Willie Mays

To my daughter, Tereza, my wife, Zdena, and the memory of
my mother, Ann. Three generations of inspirations.
—John Shea

Contents

Foreword

SIX HUNDRED AND SIXTY career home runs. Two 50-home run seasons. Twelve Gold Gloves. A glance at Willie Mays' page on Baseball Reference reveals he led the league in one significant category or another 37 times. *Thirty-seven.*

And yet, none of that tells the whole story. Not even close. Impressive as they are, mere numbers could never do Willie Mays justice. Numbers are cold. They are instructive but, with few exceptions, not evocative.

How do you quantify the qualities of legend and romance? What is the metric for presence, charisma, and flair? How do you explain the intangible qualities that elevate craftsmanship to art? Excellence to true greatness?

It's been nearly half a century since Willie Mays hung 'em up. More than that since he was in his prime. Yet for those who saw him play, the memory does not fade. His place in the imagination is permanent.

The startlingly spectacular plays. The rush of excitement that filled the ballpark as Willie turned a double into a triple, his hat flying off as he rounded second. The way even the routine became distinctive: the basket catch at the hip, turning easy fly balls into personal signatures.

I always believed that if you took a nonfan to a Giants game—someone who didn't know a sacrifice fly from a squeeze play—he or she would naturally turn their attention to Willie. Whether climbing the wall for an impossible grab or just walking from the on-deck circle to the plate, the spotlight followed him.

A strong case can be made for Willie Mays as the greatest all-around player in baseball history. An equally strong case can be made for him as baseball's most entertaining player. He could do what others only dreamed of doing, and do it with a childlike joy everyone could feel and relate to. It's a cliché to say, "You had to be there." Or, "You had to have seen it to understand." But in Willie's case, it's absolutely true. He was so compelling, so distinctive, so flat-out wondrous that, well, you really did have to be there.

I am lucky enough to say I was. My first memory of the Say Hey Kid dates to 1957. The Giants' last season in New York. I am five years old, and my dad takes me to the Polo Grounds. We are in the grandstand down the right-field line. I don't remember any of the game's particulars. It's all atmospherics. The vivid colors of the playing field, a revelation when baseball previously had only come to me through the radio or in flickering images on a black-and-white TV. The buzz of the crowd. The swirling cigar smoke. The "beer here" and "get your scorecard" refrains of the vendors. And this: I am perched on my dad's shoulders, dazzled by the panorama of sights and sounds. The Giants are in the field when my dad says, "Look, Bobby, look at the player standing way out there in center field. No, not that guy, the one in the middle. That's Willie Mays." It was as if he were pointing out the Statue of Liberty or the Empire State Building. As if he were saying, "Take note, son, that's Willie Mays, you won't forget the first time you saw him." More than sixty years later, it's still true.

Decades later, Willie and I would become friends. I would interview him many times. He would cheerfully acknowledge that he purposely chose a cap a half size too small so it would fly off as he sped around the bases or across the outfield. "You have *got* to entertain the people." He is a natural storyteller. His high-pitched voice rising in volume as a favorite anecdote reaches its payoff. But all the natural enthusiasm, all the innate grace, shouldn't obscure the fact that Willie's baseball IQ was phenomenal. He routinely repositioned the fielders around him and seldom, if ever, took his cue from the third-base coach. His own sense of how a play would develop was all he needed.

Tim McCarver once told me that in a meeting before any series with the Giants, Cardinals manager Johnny Keane would remind his team that with the exception of the ninth inning or extra innings, with Mays on base and trying to score on a base hit, "never throw to the plate." Why? Because Mays was so smart, so aware, that he would purposely make the play appear close enough to draw the throw. But he would always be safe. Meanwhile, the trail runner (or runners) would take the extra base.

In 2006, on HBO, I asked him about Game 7 of the 1962 World Series at Candlestick Park. Yankees 1, Giants 0. Two out, bottom of the ninth. Matty Alou at first, Willie at the plate. He sent an opposite-field double down the right-field line. Roger Maris cut it off before the warning track, and Alou was stopped at third. After which Willie McCovey lined out. End of Series. Willie's recollection of every part of the game was spot-on. And here he grew emphatic. "If I had been the runner instead of the hitter, there wouldn't have been a stop sign. And if there was, I'd have run through it. Either I score, or I *make* them make a perfect play to get me."

One of the best broadcasting experiences I ever had came a few years later when Willie and Hank Aaron joined me for an hour-long conversation before a theater audience. The two greatest living players reveling in each other's company. The rivalry having mellowed into deeper friendship and mutual appreciation. The stories overflowed just as they do in this very welcoming book.

Willie Mays has been the subject of multiple biographies, documentaries, and print and broadcast appreciations. But Willie and John Shea have found a fresh way in, and here's how: Twenty-four chapters, each illuminating a chapter of Willie's remarkable career and life. Baseball history— the Giant-Dodger rivalry, through the eyes of those who lived it. Social history—Willie on his time in the Negro Leagues and his relationship with Barack Obama. Personal history—the influence of Willie's baseball-savvy dad. And new perspectives, including those of today's premier center fielder, Mike Trout, born in 1991 but destined to be part of the same conversation as Willie for decades to come. Entire chapters are devoted to Willie's four-homer game in Milwaukee and the 16-inning duel between Juan Marichal and Warren Spahn in 1963, scoreless until Willie homered off

Spahn to win it. And, of course, the 1954 back-to-the-plate World Series robbery of Vic Wertz, the most famous catch in baseball history.

Even if, like me, you thought you had pretty much read and heard all there was to read and hear about Willie Mays, this warmhearted book will inform and reward you. And besides, what true baseball fan can ever get enough of Willie Mays? Say Hey! Read on and enjoy.

—*Bob Costas*

1.

SET AN EXAMPLE

The Story of 24

"People judge you all kinds of ways. Let them say what they want.
Be your own judge. Trust your heart."

—Willie Mays

WILLIE MAYS WAS twenty-six years old and the most exciting player in
baseball when the Giants moved from New York to their new home in 1958.
San Francisco, however, was Joe DiMaggio's town.

DiMaggio was a native son born to Sicilian immigrants who settled in
the fishing community of Martinez before relocating across the bay to San
Francisco's North Beach neighborhood, where young Joe and his brothers
played ball on the sandlots.

After emerging as a local legend with the San Francisco Seals of the
old Pacific Coast League, especially amid his 61-game hit streak as an
eighteen-year-old in 1933, DiMaggio became a New York Yankee, the heir
to Babe Ruth, and hit in 56 straight games and won nine World Series. He
played through 1951, the year Mays broke into the big leagues.

After the Giants arrived in San Francisco, DiMaggio's celebrity didn't
vanish. Some locals welcomed the team but were unconvinced of Mays, who
had earned his claim to fame in New York. That Mays played DiMaggio's

position in DiMaggio's ballpark in DiMaggio's town made it difficult to be accepted at first.

They didn't know me. At that time, I felt they still wanted Joe to shine. He was from San Francisco and went on to play for the Yankees. They thought nobody else could play center field except him. That's what I got out of it. I think sometimes they wanted somebody else to be the leader of the ballclub.

Mays was learning what Mickey Mantle had gone through in New York. Following the great DiMaggio is no easy task. But unlike Mantle, who was DiMaggio's immediate successor on the Yankees, Mays appeared in San Francisco twenty-three years after DiMaggio last played for the Seals.

Still, a full generation later, Mays took the Seals Stadium field and wasn't fully appreciated. As wacky as it now seems, there were boos. Not always. Not rampant. Not consistent. But boos nonetheless. There were media criticisms. Not because he wasn't fantastic. Not because he wasn't the best player on the field. But because he wasn't DiMaggio, because he was the face of the franchise that displaced the beloved Seals, because there was hesitation to immediately adopt a New York star, because (at least for some) of his skin color.

And also because of Orlando Cepeda and other young players emerging from a rich and diverse minor-league system.

"Well, it's because they billed him so high," said Cepeda, who was named the National League's top rookie with the 1958 Giants. "San Francisco had been a Triple-A town, not a big-league town. They had never seen Willie play every day. But when they saw Willie play every day and saw him do the things he could do on the field, things changed. Because the things Willie did on the field in those days, nobody else did. Still today, I don't see players doing what Willie did."

Cepeda was the toast of San Francisco, having never played with the Giants in New York. He was twenty years old when breaking in, just like Willie. It was a strange dynamic, not everyone quick to embrace Mays, but most cynics eventually came to their senses and welcomed his one-of-a-kind talent. Cynics who didn't were ignored as contrarians who simply wanted attention.

Or, worse.

Race was a factor, of course. Before his first season in San Francisco, Mays and his wife tried to buy a house in an upscale San Francisco neighborhood and were denied because they were African American. After a storm of publicity and intervention from the mayor, they eventually bought the house, but a year and a half later, someone threw a bottle through the front window with a hate note inside.

Apparently, it was okay for the great Mays to tirelessly represent the city and region and delight thousands of fans every night so long as he didn't live in certain people's neighborhoods.

"That was 1958 when he came to San Francisco, and 1958 was 1958. We're past some things. We're not past everything," said Hall of Famer Joe Morgan, who grew up in Oakland and whose father took him to Giants games in those early years. "There were some writers who were critical and didn't want to give Mays his due because he was from New York. I didn't see DiMaggio play, but he was the golden boy of San Francisco. You've got to remember that. For a lot of people, Mays was the guy who was taking his spot."

Mays didn't see it that way. He had nothing against DiMaggio. In fact, as a kid growing up in Alabama, he idolized DiMaggio and wanted to emulate his all-around game.

I looked up to Stan Musial, Ted Williams, and Joe DiMaggio. I read about them in the papers. They were on the front page all the time, all over the headlines, Stan the Man, the Splendid Splinter, Joltin' Joe. Great outfielders, great ballplayers. This was before Jackie Robinson. I liked Joe and wanted to be like Joe, a guy who could do everything on a baseball field.

When I came out west in '58, they always talked about Joe being the San Francisco guy. There was no other center fielder except Joe. I didn't say anything or let it bother me. I just moved on and played. They didn't know that Joe was my guy, too. In the '51 World Series, he hit a home run, and I'm out there in center field clapping.

I don't remember doing too many things wrong, but what am I doing out there clapping for this man? I had to catch myself. I always wondered why nobody took that picture.

Over time, most if not all of San Francisco warmed to Mays, and why not? He no longer was in a New York uniform or playing home games in the Polo Grounds. He was in his prime and fully dedicated to San Francisco, where he lived year-round and was active in the community. He was inspiring a game, a nation, and many a generation and being called the greatest all-around player in the history of baseball, an American icon, a treasure, a hero.

What's not to love? Beyond the on-field athletic brilliance—no one was more gifted in so many areas or played with such artistic swagger—Mays, a major-leaguer just four years after Jackie Robinson broke the color barrier with the 1947 Brooklyn Dodgers, was known for his personal strength and integrity. While sports in general and baseball in particular have been plagued by scandals over the years, Mays' story is honorably refreshing. He gives his life to charitable causes, especially involving children and public safety, as a philanthropist through his Say Hey Foundation and other avenues, a calling that dates to his playing days—in 1971, he was the first recipient of what became known as the Roberto Clemente Award, a prestigious philanthropic honor named after the great ballplayer who died in a plane crash trying to aid victims of a Nicaragua earthquake.

Willie Mays' number 24 was retired by the Giants, whose ballpark is at 24 Willie Mays Plaza. (San Francisco Giants)

"I didn't dream about being president. I dreamed about being Willie Mays until I realized I couldn't hit. The presidency thing was the farthest thing from my mind. Being a ballplayer wasn't," said former president George W. Bush, who grew up in a baseball family and owned the Texas Rangers before becoming governor of Texas and then president. "I was an aspiring young kid. I collected baseball cards. I was just a baseball guy. I loved the game. Still do. When friends of mine and I bought the Rangers, it was like living the dream to be involved with Major League Baseball at that level. So Willie in many ways cemented my love of baseball. He was aspirational for me. I didn't know much about him other than the fact he was a great baseball player. And to think he came out of Alabama and battled his way through the segregation era and went into the Army, he's a man of remarkable talents but also remarkable drive."

Bush was born in the summer of 1946, as was former president Bill Clinton, the first two baby-boomer presidents, both with an early love and appreciation for baseball and both captivated by Mays, an immensely popular celebrity among the first generation that emerged after World War II. The country turned its attention to leisurely activities just as the Golden Age of baseball arrived, and Mays was at the forefront not just as the game's premier overall player but the most entertaining.

"I loved watching Stan Musial and the Cardinals, and I liked the Brooklyn Dodgers because of Jackie Robinson. They had a great roster in the '50s," said Clinton, who grew up in Arkansas listening to Harry Caray calling Cardinals games, "but my favorite player from the beginning was Willie Mays. He played with so much joy, and he had so many skills. I just liked him. He could do everything well. The Polo Grounds was a tough place to play baseball because it was so deep to center field, but the way he ran around out there was something to behold."

Mays' cumulative accomplishments are unparalleled—660 home runs, 3,283 hits, 338 stolen bases, 12 straight Gold Glove awards, 24 All-Star Game appearances—as well as his five-tool proficiency: hitting for average and power, fielding, throwing, and baserunning. Perhaps more than any player in history, a case can be made that any one of Mays' tools is as elite as the next. He runs as well as he hits as well as he defends. There's no clear answer as to which is his best tool. Or worst, for that matter.

Snapshot moments include the basket catch that he perfected in the

Army, the cap flying off his head as he raced from first to third, the World Series catch shown for eternity in black-and-white, the four-home-run day at Hank Aaron's park in Milwaukee, the 16th-inning homer to beat Warren Spahn 1–0, and the eighth-inning homer in the 1962 finale that led to a playoff with the Dodgers.

Generations have admired Mays' ability and determination along with his charm and flair. His honorable life has stood the test of time. Mays' fitting nickname—the Say Hey Kid—depicts a youthful exuberance that never went away. In his early days with the Giants, he didn't know everyone's name, so he'd just say "hey," usually in his distinctive and energetic high-pitched voice that lit up a room or dugout, and a sportswriter named Barney Kremenko was credited with naming him the Say Hey Kid. These days, Mays attends nearly every Giants home game, was a constant during the team's three World Series championship runs in 2010, 2012, and 2014, and engages in lively clubhouse banter as if he were still kicking it in his twenties and thirties.

"Willie's the greatest all-around player of all time," said Dodgers manager Dave Roberts, the majors' only African-American manager in 2019. "You listen to his stories, you learn so much. The details, the color, the humor. Nobody tells stories like Willie. If anyone has a right to walk around with a big head, it's Willie Mays. But he's so humble, so funny. He's one of the guys. He has a great love for the game. The ballpark is his second home, maybe his first home, and when he tells his stories, he inspires us all."

And from Hall of Fame outfielder Dave Winfield: "Watch his highlights. Always hustling. Look at his body. Dude was chiseled. He could fly and catch the ball, and he did it with a smile. Listen to the stories he tells. Always enjoying what he's doing, always with a sense of humor. If these young players were intelligent and bright and cared about the game, they'd learn from Willie. They should all go back and watch his highlights and listen to what he has to say."

Mays was listed at 5-foot-10 and anywhere between 170 and 180 pounds, though he swears 5-foot-11 is more accurate. Either way, it's not by any means the standard physical stature of a slugger. Ruth and DiMaggio were 6-foot-2. While Mickey Mantle, Reggie Jackson, and Harmon Killebrew were close to Mays in height, newer-generation hitters Ken

Griffey, Jr., Barry Bonds, and Alex Rodriguez all tower over Mays. Mel Ott, at 5-foot-9, is the only member of the 500-homers club shorter than Mays.

I have been blessed to be in the game. A lot of my love for baseball comes from my dad. We'd sit and talk baseball all day. I played football and basketball. Baseball was my third sport. You don't have to be a big guy to play baseball. You can be regular size as long as you can hit and throw and run and all that kind of stuff.

Mays' retired uniform number—24—is one of the most recognized and iconic in sports. He has a nine-foot bronzed statue in his likeness at 24 Willie Mays Plaza, home of the Giants' ballpark along the San Francisco Bay, where 24 palm trees surround the statue and the right-field brick wall stands roughly 24 feet high. On his eighty-fifth birthday, Willie was honored when a San Francisco cable car was dedicated to him. Car 24.

Willie Mays played twenty-two seasons in the big leagues and batted .302 with 660 home runs for the New York Giants, San Francisco Giants, and New York Mets. (San Francisco Giants)

The Giants retired the number long ago, but others have worn it in Mays' honor. Rickey Henderson, for example. The all-time stolen base king played for nine teams over his 25-year career and wore 24 on six of them, including his hometown Oakland A's. No one ever again will wear the number with either Bay Area team. Like the Giants, the A's retired 24.

"I take a lot of pride in that number," Henderson said. "I met Willie when I was a young man, at a kids' clinic. I was probably thirteen. You looked up to him and wanted to be like him. You better be good to wear that number. You don't just put that number on and not represent."

Tony Pérez grew up in Cuba and, through the influence of his father, José Manuel, idolized Robinson and Mays. Pérez wore 24 as the run-producing first baseman on Cincinnati's mighty Big Red Machine of the 1970s.

"When I got to the big leagues, they gave me 24, and I said, 'Wow, I've got Willie Mays' number,'" Pérez said. "I never forgot that moment. He was the most complete player in the game. He could do it all. When I played against Willie, I felt like a fan. Maybe some players were faster, but I've never seen anybody run the bases like Willie. When he hit the ball in the gap, I watched him go by me at first base, and when he rounded second, he wasn't even watching the coach. He was watching the ball and outfielder. He never missed a step. I couldn't believe it."

Among the Hall of Famers who wore 24: Mays, Henderson, Pérez, managers Walt Alston and Whitey Herzog, and Griffey, who wore it for Rickey, who wore it for Willie. That was Barry Bonds' number in Pittsburgh before he signed in San Francisco, where he wore 25, the same number of his dad, Bobby Bonds. Talk of the younger Bonds getting 24 with the Giants—because of Mays, his godfather—quickly got nixed.

It's not just a baseball thing. Basketball Hall of Famer Rick Barry, who led the Golden State Warriors to the 1974–75 NBA championship, grew up in New Jersey, where his father, Richard, taught his son the basket catch, the unique glove-at-the-waist method of catching fly balls that Mays popularized. Barry watched Mays plenty of times at the Polo Grounds.

"That's my boyhood hero," Barry said. "When I started playing sports, I wanted 24. I wore it all the way until I got to the Houston Rockets. I couldn't wear it there because Moses Malone had it. So I wore 2 at home and 4 on the road. I just told them that's what I want to do. Nobody said anything. I did it for two years."

One day, Barry cut school to see Mays at the Polo Grounds. "After the game was over, I jumped the left-field fence, dropped on the field, and sprinted to catch Willie before he went up the stairs to the clubhouse," Barry said. "I shook his hand, ran back, and got on the bus to head home. My mom and dad were both working, and my brother said, 'How was the game today?' 'I said, 'What are you talking about? I was at school.' He said, 'No, you weren't, you were at the game. I saw you on TV. The cameraman was on this kid who jumped over the wall and sprinted out to Willie Mays. It was you.' I said, 'Oh, my God, don't tell mom or dad, please.'"

Like the basket catch, Barry's free-throw style was unconventional. One of the all-time great free-throw shooters, he shot underhanded. Most everyone else shoots with the arms raised. Just like most everyone else catches fly balls with the arms raised.

"The similarities are there," Barry said. "I've become friends with my boyhood hero, and we both did things that have gone out like the dinosaur even though we were successful doing it."

Mays briefly wore 14 when getting called up in 1951 before settling on 24, which had been worn by an outfielder named Jack Maguire, whose claim to fame was giving Lawrence Peter Berra his nickname: Yogi. Maguire played 16 games that season for the Giants and was claimed by the Pirates about the time Mays arrived.

It was the number the Giants gave me. A lot of our outfielders wore higher numbers back then, mostly in the 20s. Monte Irvin. Don Mueller. Bobby Thomson, who was the center fielder before I came along. I had worn other numbers before coming up and didn't think a lot of it, but I enjoyed wearing 24, and a lot of guys over the years have liked wearing it. It's nice to know that.

Mays continued putting on 24 after his spring 1972 trade to the New York Mets, where owner Joan Payson had a great fondness and appreciation for the center fielder, dating to her minority ownership of the New

York Giants. Mays recalls Payson saying no Met would wear 24 again. She died in 1975 and never officially retired the number.

For the most part, the Mets have granted Payson's wish. There was a blunder in 1990 when Kelvin Torve, a late-season call-up, was given 24, a mistake that led to a backlash and quickly got fixed—Torve was given 39. Rickey Henderson wore 24 as a Met in 1999 and part of 2000 but only after checking with Mays.

"I had to call him and get his permission," Henderson said. "He said I could wear the number. That was a blessing to me."

Mays had imagined the Mets keeping his number out of circulation but admires Henderson as a person and player, including Rickey's combination of power and speed. That was supposed to be the lone exception, but the Mets, amid a front-office overhaul, gave 24 to Robinson Cano in 2019 after acquiring the infielder in a trade with Seattle. Cano had worn 24 with the Yankees but couldn't wear it in Seattle because it was retired for Griffey.

"My dad told me all the things Jackie Robinson went through, the barriers he broke for future generations," said Cano, who was named after Robinson and likes 24 because it's the reverse of Jackie's 42, which is retired throughout baseball. "But every time you think about number 24, you go back and think about Willie Mays. He was the one who gave real value to the number. I mean, he's a legend. There is no other word for him. That is what 24 represents for me."

While it would seem unusual to retire someone's number after just two seasons with a team, it's exactly what happened with another celebrated player, Hank Aaron. Like Mays, Aaron played for a team (Milwaukee Braves) that relocated to another city (Atlanta) and was traded late in his career to a different franchise in his original city (Milwaukee Brewers). Naturally, the Braves retired Aaron's number, 44, but so did the Brewers, who used him as a designated hitter in 1975 and 1976.

Regardless, Mays has moved on. He's happy the Mets retired the number of one of his favorite teammates, Tom Seaver, and appreciates that 24 is such an important part of the Giants' and the city of San Francisco's fabric.

"A lot of guys wanted 24, and no doubt some did 24 very proud," said

Morgan, who was a teammate of Pérez and Griffey's dad, Ken Griffey, Sr., in Cincinnati. "Willie Mays is the only 24 I recognize, to be honest with you."

Mays' legacy goes well beyond what number he wore. Or what numbers he put up. He has touched countless lives, and he has been touched by a long list of people who have helped shape his own life. His father, Willie Howard Mays, Sr. His Negro League manager, Piper Davis. His New York Giants teammate, Monte Irvin. His first big-league manager, Leo Durocher. And others who helped prepare and inspire him after he retired as a player, including the younger generation, whether it's current players or America's youth.

And, as always, the fans.

I was always aware that you play baseball for people who paid money to come see you play. You play for those people. You want to make them smile, have a good time. I would make a hard play look easy and an easy play look hard. Sometimes I'd hesitate, count to three, then I'd get there just in time to make the play. You'd hear the crowd. Sometimes you had to do that in order for people to come back the next day.

They often did.

"Willie Mays was, in my view, the greatest all-around baseball player in the history of the game," said John Thorn, Major League Baseball's official historian, who grew up in the Bronx a Dodger fan. "What could he not do? Not the greatest hitter, or fielder, or thrower, or base runner . . . but the greatest combination of all those skills."

Through it all, despite his vast talents and accomplishments, Mays remained a man of humility, according to Negro League teammate Bill Greason, who says, "Yessir. He's a humble spirit, believing in helping people, helping children. He's always been that way. You don't need to be a bragger even if you hit over 600 home runs. We both learned that at an early age."

Mays played in the Golden Age of New York baseball when Hall of Fame center fielders played for all three teams, including Mantle and Duke Snider, leading to heated debates throughout the boroughs as to who was the best. After the 1994 players' strike led to the cancellation of the World Series,

A 9-foot Willie Mays statue in front of the Giants' ballpark is a popular meeting place for fans. (Brad Mangin)

the New York Chapter of the Baseball Writers' Association of America sought a showstopper that could help draw folks to their prominent annual banquet and invited the three long-retired center fielders.

"The chapter inaugurated the Willie, Mickey and the Duke Award that evening to honor those inextricably linked in the game and awarded the first to those three gents," said Claire Smith, who received the J. G. Taylor Spink Award during the 2017 Hall of Fame induction weekend for her trailblazing writing career. "Willie was overcome with emotion when he spoke. I was chair of the event, so I sat right next to the podium and was stunned as I watched him cry, his tears hitting the podium. He said he never thought he was loved enough for the game to name a trophy after him. He spoke after Duke. Had people in the audience weeping. Then Mickey spoke. He said he'd been asked thousands of times which center fielder was the best. He turned to Willie and said, 'Willie, you were the best, but I don't mind being tied for second with you, Duke.' Everyone was in tears. It was magical."

Major League Baseball has its own award in Mays' name. On the 63rd anniversary of his famous catch that robbed Vic Wertz in Game 1 of the 1954 World Series, igniting the Giants to a sweep of the Indians, Commissioner Rob Manfred announced that the World Series MVP Award would be called the Willie Mays World Series MVP Award. The award goes back to 1955, and Mays' name was attached beginning in 2017.

That's a wonderful honor, and I'll always appreciate Major League Baseball for attaching my name to the award. I was proud to lend my name.

The trophy is given out every year, and it's always somebody new who steps up and has a big series. I'm grateful.

The first winner was Houston's George Springer, who keeps his trophy in his living room so he could see it every time he leaves for the ballpark. In another room, he has a framed congratulatory letter from Mays, who wrote that it was nice a fellow center fielder won the award.

"I've always been a huge Mays admirer," Springer said. "My grandfather came over from Panama and introduced the game to my dad as a kid, and my dad's favorite player was Willie Mays with all his greatness, all his glory, doing stuff that nobody had done. That's how I was raised, by watching the plays he made, the way he played the game, like the way my dad taught me. I don't think there was one instance where my dad hadn't compared something in my games to what Willie Mays did or what he could do. He was arguably the first of his kind in many ways. I wore his number. I've got plenty of old 24 jerseys. I tried to play like Willie Mays because that's all I knew."

Well, that's all Willie knew, too.

My father said the more you can do, the more you can help your team and the longer you can play. As far back as I remember, I wanted to do all the things in the game. That's why I looked up to Joe DiMaggio. I liked Joe because he could do everything. Hit, play defense, good base runner. I thought that was the way you should play, how I wanted to play. I worked on all parts of the game with my dad, one by one.

A writer would ask about being a five-tool player. I didn't like talking about it. It sounded like bragging. It's not the same as just going out and doing it and letting people see what you can do and let 'em make up their own minds. I felt everything in baseball, I could do. So I set out to be top five in everything. I didn't want to talk about a lot of that stuff as a player. I'll talk about it now.

2.

PLAY CATCH WITH YOUR DAD

The Story of Willie Howard Mays, Sr.

"Be open to learning from your parents and understanding where they're coming from. They can help you if you let them."

—*Willie Mays*

WHEN WILLIE MAYS was a kid, the major leagues were for whites only. Then came Jackie Robinson.

And my dad said, "Now you have a chance." What the hell do you mean I have a chance? He said, "You've got a chance to get to the major leagues now." My world changed.

Willie Howard Mays, Sr., was the most influential and inspirational person in his son's life. Managers, teammates, and friends in and out of baseball were instrumental in shaping the younger Mays through the years. But there was no one like his father.

No one made him believe in himself more than his dad.

He wasn't just my father, he was my friend. He always supported me and never hollered at me. He was a positive influence and always had

an upbeat attitude on life, and I've always strived for those things. He wasn't always around, but he taught me about life and baseball. I was so far ahead of the other kids because of what my dad gave me.

They played catch, but it wasn't just catch. It was class, and it always was in session. Dad the teacher and Willie the student. The games were lively, like the conversations. Back and forth the ball went, back and forth the chatter went.

Man, I loved that. I thought my dad knew everything about baseball, and I wanted to learn it all. We talked about the game as much as we played the game. I learned about every position. If it was Monday, we'd talk about pitching. If it was Tuesday, we'd talk catching. The next day, first base. All around the field. What to do at every position. Second base, third base, shortstop, the outfield. Ball down the line in left, two men on, who takes the cut? Ball up the middle, who covers second?

I learned more about baseball playing catch with my dad than any other time in my life. By the time I got to the majors, I figured I knew all about the game.

Born on May 6, 1931, Willie grew up in Alabama in the Jim Crow South during the Great Depression, just outside Birmingham in Westfield, a company town, and nearby Fairfield. Mays the elder worked in the mills and provided what he could for his son. The family had little. But in Willie's mind, plenty.

Willie's parents had him when they were very young and never married. His mother, Annie Satterwhite, wasn't a part of his life like his father, but Willie always kept a special place in his heart for her. Willie's dad worked multiple jobs and was gone for long stretches of time—aside from working in the mills, he was a Pullman porter on the Detroit-bound passenger trains—so Willie's two aunts took on the major responsibility of helping to raise him.

His mother's younger sisters, Sarah and Ernestine, though youngsters themselves, were pivotal in his early upbringing and provided a positive environment in tough times, a big reason Mays recalls his childhood in glowing terms with enough food and clothes to keep him satisfied, enough friends and family to keep him busy, and enough sports and games to quench his competitive appetite. It was a land of poverty, not that young Willie realized it. He always claimed to have what he needed. A roof, a family, a school, friends, and nearby open fields.

Shotgun houses, narrow buildings with rooms one behind the other, were the norm. In Willie's youth, his dad moved from Westfield, a town that was run by the Tennessee Coal, Iron and Railroad Company (with company-owned houses and stores) and which no longer exists, to nearby Fairfield, where the neighborhood, schools, and public services were superior. Willie lived with his father and aunts at 216 57th Street, and his

Willie Howard Mays, Sr., right, and his son flank Herman Franks, who was a Giants manager and coach. (Associated Press)

dad eventually built his own home nearby at 5507 Avenue G, across the street from Miles College.

Willie's father was a ballplayer, a tad smaller than the size his son became, but was so quick and deceptive on the field, displaying a feline-like presence, that he was known as Cat, a gifted and headsy outfielder and leadoff man.

Cat Mays was the son of Walter Mays, a sharecropper and prominent pitcher from Tuscaloosa, sixty miles southwest of Birmingham. Cat played for any team that would put a few bucks in his pocket, including on Fairfield's wire mill team in the Tennessee Coal and Iron League. These company-sponsored teams in Alabama, some black and some white, played in highly competitive industrial leagues that not only served as a vehicle to promote company loyalty and unity and provide community entertainment but were a feeder system to the major leagues for whites and the Negro Leagues for blacks.

Cat died in 1999 at eighty-nine. The memories of his father remain fresh in Willie's mind, some that explain his dad's influence on Willie's life, some that explain Cat's athletic prowess, and some that would prompt a listener to do a double-take.

Some of my best memories are watching my dad play ball and later playing with my dad on his mill team. My dad did things on the field that made you think. He was a smart ballplayer and always observant, a leadoff hitter who could bunt and a left fielder who could run.

How fast? I was the batboy when I saw him do something I never saw anyone do before or since. Instead of hitting the ball and running to first and then second, my dad hit the ball and ran straight across the mound and slid into second. Like he'd already been to first. No one seemed to notice. It may seem odd, but that's how I remember it. He was that fast.

Willie's dad wasn't a strict disciplinarian but a man who got his point across. He encouraged Willie to tell the truth and be true to himself and taught him about character, respect, and positive thinking, lessons Willie never took for granted.

There was the time a kid at school routinely bullied Willie and took his sandwich, and Willie's dad would tell him to turn the other cheek. It continued to happen. Willie wanted to go after the kid, and his dad said no. One day, Willie's dad told him to give the kid his sandwich and ask for half of it back, thinking the kid wasn't as much of a bully as he was hungry. Willie tried it. The kid gave him back half the sandwich, and they became friends.

Through it all, Mays maintained a never-ending love and admiration for his father and cared for him in his later years, always making sure he was nearby whether it was in New York or the Bay Area. Mays never forgot his childhood memories of his dad, the care his dad provided and the sacrifices he made, sometimes from a great distance, whatever it took during the Depression.

I had a happy childhood. I didn't feel deprived. My dad always wanted to make sure I was okay, and I had everything I needed. Aunt Sarah was like a mother to me, and Aunt Steen worked as a bartender and waitress and brought home tips for me, a few dollars, all in change. I would put that in my pocket for school.

My dad made money in the mills, as a porter, and playing ball. I never felt poor. I seemed to have enough clothes. I don't know how he did it, but my dad got me a few suits and knew I'd take care of them, and I let other kids borrow them. If they had a date, I told them, "You can come in and put the suit on, but you better clean it and have it back the next day so someone else could wear it. Or you'll never get another suit out of my house."

Willie's mother was a tremendous athlete who excelled in basketball and track, and she died delivering her eleventh child. She was thirty-seven. Annie had married a man named Frank McMorris and lived a few miles from Willie, her eldest child. Despite the family size, she'd find time to see Willie play ball, including when he started playing for the hometown Negro League team, the Birmingham Black Barons.

Willie Mays was raised in this house on 57th Street in Fairfield, Alabama. (John Shea)

My mother lived in a neighborhood called Powderly, and I used to go there a lot. In the South, you just don't take everything away from your kid. If I went there, my plate was on the table. She used to give me a couple dollars to put in my pocket. She was a good lady, strong-willed, a fighter, too. She had to be, with eleven kids.

Family always was Willie's foundation and backbone, from his childhood through the forty-one-year marriage with his beloved wife, Mae, who died in 2013 of Alzheimer's. Mae Louise Allen graduated from the University of Pittsburgh with a sociology degree and earned her master's degree in social work at Howard University. They were a perfect couple, both independent yet both respectful of each other's needs. Mae was kind and generous and, though they never had children of their own, shared her husband's love for kids, working with adoptions for the city of San Francisco and a pioneer in recruiting African-American families to adopt African-American children from foster care.

In 1971, Willie Mays married Mae Louise Allen. His beloved wife of forty-one years was a pioneering social worker for the city of San Francisco. (Collection of Rick Swig)

I knew Mae's mother before I knew Mae. She'd go to the Red Rooster and tell me she had a daughter in Pittsburgh she'd like me to meet, one of those type things. "Okay, I'll be down there when we play there." When we got to Pittsburgh, I called her. "My name is Willie Mays." She said, "Yeah, I'm Martha Washington." She thought I was lying. She came out to a game, and we got together later.

We had a lot of fun. Mae liked California. She liked what I liked. She liked baseball. Oh, did she. She worked with children at the Booker T. Washington center in San Francisco. She was very good at that. She took care of the kids and would bring them to games, sometimes ten at a time. She knew all about child psychology.

Mae's social work was so influential that the San Francisco Foster Youth Fund, which raises money to provide children with resources otherwise not available through the Human Services Agency, has used her name in its signature fundraiser event: the Mae Louise Mays Softball Tournament, in which dozens of adult teams (mostly from city government departments) compete to benefit the most vulnerable kids. Years after she died, social workers continue to build on her work.

Mae was Willie's second wife. He married his first wife, Marghuerite, in 1956, and they divorced in 1962. They had adopted a son, Michael, now a sports field producer based in New York.

When Marghuerite and I broke up, Mae took in Michael and treated him to what he needed. Mae took care of me in all kinds of ways. She would smile at what I'd say. She'd come get me at the airport—they let her come on the runway, which you can't do now. She was tall and strong, a good lady, a *good* lady.

Michael said Mae was "like the rock, the organizer, a source of information. She was really amazing" and said of Willie and Marghuerite, "Two Type A personalities in the same room could be volatile. Sometimes you need two different kinds of personalities." Michael speaks highly of the man he called Grandad, Cat Mays, who was a childhood inspiration. "Grandad was the great life coach," Michael said. "He's a big part of my existence. Everything out of his mouth was pretty much profound." Michael said of Willie, "He's the most generous man I've ever seen, especially with his time and attention. He always told me, 'You play for the twenty-fifth guy.'"

When it came to sports, Cat Mays was the first and major inspiration for Willie, who took to baseball not because he had to but because he wanted to. Pressure to play? No. Passion to play? Absolutely.

My dad didn't force me to play baseball, but he did open the door. When I was one or two, he rolled a ball around the room, and I'd go get it and roll it back. Different games like that. He told me later about how I always chased the ball, like it was a natural thing for me to do. Maybe that has something to do with why I was always pretty good on defense as a kid but couldn't always hit early on. I always loved defense while hitting was something I had to learn.

Willie Mays and his first wife, Marghuerite (married in 1956), adopted Michael, now a sports field producer in New York. (San Francisco Giants)

By the time I was ten, I played with guys who were fifteen. When I was fifteen, I played with guys who were twenty-five. I didn't play so much with kids my age. That's because my dad got me ready at a young age. He taught me how to pivot at second base, how to throw a curve, how to use shin guards when catching to protect my legs on a play at the plate.

But he didn't want me pitching or catching. He always tried to make sure I didn't get hurt, and he wanted me to play every day. You can't play every day if you pitch or catch. You might be able to catch, but your legs are going to feel it. So I played shortstop.

Kids around Birmingham saw the influence Willie's dad had on him. Childhood friend Charles Willis, who was with Willie at Robinson School and Fairfield Industrial High School, recalls how Cat passed on life lessons while teaching the finer points of baseball.

"By bringing Willie to games and showing him different techniques, Willie learned from that and took off," Willis said in an interview at his Fairfield home, the same house he lived in as a child. "In fact, I picked up a few pointers from Willie that he got from his dad. Willie's dad encouraged him and motivated him."

Remember, baseball was Willie's third best sport in high school. He was the quarterback on the football team and a high-scoring guard on the basketball team. Fairfield Industrial didn't have a baseball team, so he and his buddies played on community teams, giving Willie an opportunity to showcase his advanced skills against other high-school-aged teams throughout the region.

Charles Willis, Willie Mays' childhood friend and schoolmate, in front of his house in Fairfield, Alabama. (John Shea)

"There were good athletes, but Willie was the best," Willis said, noting Willie wasn't just superior to the high school kids but good enough to play pro ball and make money to help support his family.

One time, Willie climbed a tree near Miles College in Fairfield to watch a football game, but he fell and broke his right arm, which was set in a cast. "I was standing right there when he broke his arm," Willis said. "Willie climbed the tree. I can still see him landing on the ground. We were worried because he was such a good athlete." It was a temporary setback. Willie eventually healed but still proudly shows a lasting effect of the injury, a knot on the top of his hand. By high school, he could throw a football most of the length of the field, and after the fall, he began throwing with a sidearm motion that he later utilized in the big leagues.

In baseball, Willie had the arm, athleticism, and mind-set to play anywhere on the diamond. In his mid-teens, he was too good to be restricted to playing with high school kids and played for teams such as the Fairfield Gray Sox (a local sandlot team), Chattanooga Choo-Choos (a farm team in the Negro Leagues), and his father's mill team. Eventually, he was good enough to play for the Black Barons, one of the most prominent Negro League teams.

Playing with my dad, I started getting into games at first base and then center field. When my dad was near the end of his playing days, we played together for one year. It wasn't a whole year because every time a ball went up in the air, he looked at me. He wanted me to catch everything. I'm thinking, "If you can't catch that ball, you gotta quit, man. I can't catch all these damn balls."

He might have been testing me. A ball would go up, and he'd look at me, dare me to catch it. I got tired, man. But I learned how to run to the gaps to chase down every ball. Maybe he was trying to teach me something, making sure I was thinking and moving.

College wasn't realistic for a lot of kids in the area, and Fairfield Industrial provided job training. Willie's emphasis was cleaning, dyeing, and pressing. Charles' was shoe repair. "We all had a trade," Willis said. "You had automotive, welding, upholstery, cosmetology, food services. Many others. They had all kinds of vocations at that time. You pick what you want to do. It was there for you, whether you did it or not, that's your choice. If you didn't take a trade, they had you go straight to academics. Many of the boys went right to the trades. We had a lot of kids who finished school and would walk right over there and go to work in the steel mill."

There are no stories of Willie going down the wrong road, appearing on police blotters, or making news for the wrong reasons. Throughout his years, he wasn't known for drinking, smoking, or carousing and feels privileged that he always seemed to have people looking out for him, starting with his dad.

Because of my dad's guidance and the guidance of so many others, trouble didn't find me. My dad taught me the basics from childhood,

including keeping me away from drinking and smoking. He caught me one day, but he never hollered at me. He said, "If this is what you want to do, do it." And he gave me a White Owl cigar and some moonshine. I was sick for about three weeks, and he said, "You want more?" "No, no." I learned my lesson.

Since then, I had, let's see, one, two, three, four drinks. Champagne from 1951, 1954, 1962, and 1973. The World Series years. That's all I've had, and each time it didn't do well with me. One time, I was drinking it like water and passed out. When I came to, I remembered all the warnings my dad used to tell me about this stuff, and that was it.

One of Willie's teachers at Fairfield Industrial was a woman who married a fellow teacher at the school, John Rice, and they had a daughter in 1954. Sixty years after Angelina Rice taught Mays, he and her daughter hung out at a 2007 Giants game. She was a guest of the team and later wrote Mays a personal note that said in part: "I always admired you and I'm proud to say

Willie Mays Park is in Fairfield, Alabama, where Mays was raised, just outside Birmingham.
(John Shea)

that my mom taught you" and "all the best to you and the Giants." It was signed Condoleezza Rice, who had become secretary of state for President George W. Bush.

Condoleezza's mother was really a nice lady. I had a lot of good teachers. I had it good as a kid. I thought it was a nice area. For me, sports was our biggest thing. That's what I wanted to do. My dad wouldn't let me go in the mines. He didn't want that in my life. I never did have a job out of sports. Well, I did for one day. At a cafeteria, they wanted me to wash dishes, take the food out. That wasn't for me. I had to quit, man. I told my dad I wanted to go back and play ball. He was behind me. I didn't even go back for the money.

Cat Mays knew his son was good enough to make it in sports, and if Willie was going to devote himself, his father would support him. Willie played ball for the love of it. Yes, he was gifted, but his passion, determination, and hard work got him to a higher level. By the time Willie's dad told him he had a chance to play in the big leagues, Willie had every reason to trust him.

Reaching the majors was never a possibility when I was young. Baseball wasn't always my game anyway. I was better in football and basketball. There were no blacks in the majors, but guys were making money in the Negro Leagues, including with the Black Barons. I always listened to my dad, and when he told me I had a chance to play in the majors because the Dodgers signed Jackie, it became real.

I was still in high school, about fifteen, when Jackie played his first year in Montreal. When he got to the majors in 1947, I was three years from signing with the Giants, but I was playing enough ball to know why my dad had all that faith in me. When he said I had a chance, I believed him. He made it possible to believe.

3.

REMEMBER YOUR HISTORY

The Story of the Birmingham Black Barons

"We can't forget what got us here. The Negro Leagues are long gone, but we need to keep them alive, keep them in our classrooms, an important part of the fight for integration."

—*Willie Mays*

IT'S A NATIONAL treasure, a gorgeous ballpark that was a hub for the Negro Leagues, where some dreams began but other dreams died, the final stop for too many players who couldn't play in the major leagues because of their skin color.

Rickwood Field sits in an old neighborhood a few miles west of downtown Birmingham, the oldest professional ballpark in America, opening in 1910, two years before Fenway Park and four years before Wrigley Field. It's Willie Mays' only home ballpark that's still standing. The Polo Grounds, gone. Seals Stadium, gone. Candlestick Park, gone. Shea Stadium, gone.

Mays' professional career began in earnest at Rickwood Field, where the teenager played with men a decade older, where he not only belonged but blossomed with the Birmingham Black Barons, a team deep in talent, tradition, and pride.

While in high school, Willie Mays played in the Negro Leagues for the Birmingham Black Barons. (Memphis and Shelby County Room, Memphis Public Libraries)

I can still picture Rickwood Field. The big scoreboard over my shoulder, up against the wall in left-center. The dugout on the first-base side. The sound of the train passing by. It was one of the biggest parks. You've got to hit the ball good to get it out. We had a good team and big crowds, and fans would get all dressed up, especially on Sundays because they were coming from church.

The dugouts were small, but we didn't have a lot of extra guys. We didn't have many guys who sat on the bench all the time. If you couldn't play, you had to go somewhere else. It was my dream to play for the Black Barons. I thought that'd be the highest level I'd reach. My dad used to take me to the games, so Rickwood Field meant a lot to me.

Piper Davis was the Black Barons' manager and second baseman and the man responsible for giving young Willie the platform to turn into a Negro League star. Davis was a legend in the Negro Leagues and in Birmingham, where he played throughout the 1940s and managed the Black Barons to the final Negro League World Series in 1948. His center fielder was a seventeen-year-old who would go on to become the greatest all-around player who ever lived.

I was a young kid when I started playing for Birmingham. Piper Davis was like a father to me. He was good to me. He was a big, tall guy, and we sat and talked all the time about baseball. He never hollered at me. If I did something wrong, he just explained things to me. Piper taught me a lot about life, too. Piper took care of me. So did my teammates.

My dad knew Piper. He played with him in the Industrial League, and he'd call ahead to Piper and Artie Wilson, our shortstop, and had them look out for me and keep me out of trouble. That stuck with me. They didn't want me to go out by myself or spend all my money. They made sure I kept it in my pocket, and Piper had me room with the starting pitchers. If a guy was going to pitch the next day, he'd stay in the night before, and Piper figured I'd be safe if I roomed with him. I never went out alone or stayed by myself.

Davis, fourteen years older than Mays, attended Fairfield Industrial High School, where Willie graduated, and knew Cat Mays from playing on company teams in the area. Davis had known about Cat's son through his father and word of mouth. Willie was playing for the Chattanooga Choo-Choos, a lower-level Negro League team, when the sixteen-year-old ran into Davis in a Chattanooga hotel lobby. Always looking to deepen his roster, Davis was willing to try out the local kid.

I didn't play for Chattanooga long. I went up there. It rained a lot. I must've gotten hungry. I called my dad and said, "We ain't playing enough games. I ain't making no money. I've got to come home." I came home, and my dad said, "You're going to Birmingham Sunday." I said, "Why?" He said, "You're having a tryout with the Black Barons."

I didn't know my father had talked with Piper. I showed up Sunday to Rickwood Field, and Piper said, "Here's your uniform, but you're not going to play until the second game." Second game, he puts me in left field. I get a couple of hits, and Piper tells me I'm on the team.

This was no ordinary team. Several players on the roster should have been in the majors. It was one year after Jackie Robinson broke the color barrier with the Brooklyn Dodgers, and most other teams were slow to integrate. The Negro Leagues, of course, were loaded with talent, including in Birmingham. Davis was thirty-one and one of the best versatile players in the game.

Wilson won the 1948 batting crown and later became a legend in the

The 1948 Birmingham Black Barons. Front row: Willie Mays, far left; Bill Greason, second from left; Jimmie Newberry, fourth from left. Second row: Artie Wilson, far left; Piper Davis, far right. Back row: Jim Zapp, third from left; Alonzo Perry, fourth from left; Norman Robinson, sixth from left; Ed Steele, far right. (Memphis and Shelby County Room, Memphis Public Libraries)

old Pacific Coast League after a 19-game stint with the 1951 New York Giants—he was replaced on the roster in late May by a hotshot named Willie Mays. Alonzo Perry was a star pitcher and power-hitting first baseman. Jim Zapp and Ed Steele were gifted corner outfielders. Another rookie besides Mays was Bill Greason, who was seven years Willie's elder, a lifetime friend, and the first African American to pitch for the St. Louis Cardinals.

"That's one of the greatest group of guys I ever played with in my professional career, the Birmingham Black Barons," Greason said. "Piper Davis was a great inspiration as a manager with his leadership, discipline, and knowledge and could play all the positions. When he was at second and Artie Wilson was at short, we had one of the best double-play combinations in the league. And with Willie in center, I just had to make them hit it up the middle. If they hit it on the ground, Artie and Piper were going to get it. In the air, Willie would get it.

"Piper told the other outfielders that he didn't want them going for anything in left-center or right-center because Willie would go get everything in between. Willie could catch it, throw it, he was amazing. I've never seen another player like him."

Some teammates resented the teenager taking their playing time, but Mays eventually won them over and found a permanent home in center field. That was his destiny, and when the regular center fielder, Norman Robinson, broke his leg, it accelerated Willie's move to the position. His speed, arm, and instincts, even as a boy among men, turned him into a must-see attraction. Back then, long before he was the Say Hey Kid, his nickname was Buck Duck. Or Buck, which longtime friends still call him.

"Fantastic, just fantastic," said Faye Davis, Piper's daughter, who was a child in the Black Barons' late 1940s heyday. "If we needed anything, whether it was a hit or bunt or a fantastic catch, Willie had it all, the total package. He could cover the whole outfield if he had to. He would take off on the crack of the bat. It was uncanny to me."

They put me in center field when Robinson got hurt, and I had to catch all those balls in left-center and right-center and toward the lines. It got to the point Piper called the guys in and said, "Hey, you gotta help Willie out there." It wasn't any problem for me.

Davis helped Mays mature not only as a player but a person. They had conversations on the field and off, on the long bus rides to big and small towns throughout the South, where they played official Negro League games but also made many stops for exhibitions on barnstorming tours to showcase their talents and, of course, make a few extra bucks along the way. One telltale day, Mays had a memorable duel with Chet Brewer, a 6-foot-4 Cleveland Buckeyes pitcher.

I hit a home run off the guy, so next time up, Chet Brewer flattens me. I'm on the ground crying. So Piper comes out, kicks me, and says, "There ain't no damn crying in this game." I'm walking down to first base, and he says, "What you do now, you steal second, you steal third." So I steal

Piper Davis, a well-respected manager of the Birmingham Black Barons, was a father figure to Willie Mays. (Negro Leagues Baseball Museum)

second and third, and I score. We win the game, and Piper comes over to me afterward and says, "Now that's the way you play baseball." I had no fear after that.

Davis' teachings helped jump-start Mays' career, but sometimes the young player was overmatched. Then again, it was no sin to be over-matched by Satchel Paige, the celebrated pitcher who seemed to have played forever. He was in his forties when blacks began playing in the majors, but he still joined the Cleveland Indians and flourished for two seasons. He spent three more seasons with the old St. Louis Browns and even pitched a game for the Kansas City A's in 1965 when he was fifty-eight. Perhaps he was older. His age, which wasn't always clear, was part of his one-of-a-kind legend.

Paige preceded Mays in Birmingham, pitching for the Black Barons in the late 1920s. By the time Mays arrived two decades later, Paige had become known as one of the best pitchers—if not *the* best—in all of baseball and later became the first African-American pitcher inducted into the Hall of Fame. The first time they faced each other, Mays knew something of Paige. Paige couldn't say the same of the young Mays.

We're in Memphis. Satch doesn't know me. He sees a little boy coming to the plate. He throws a breaking ball, and I hit a double off the wall. He tells his third baseman to let him know when that little boy is coming back up. He's talking about me. Couple innings later, I come up, and I hear the third baseman say "They he is." Satch looks at me and says,

"Little boy." I say, "Yes sir." "I'm not gonna trick you. I'm gonna throw you three fastballs, and you're gonna go sit down."

I'm thinking, "If you throw me three fastballs, I ain't sitting down right now." First one, he does his windmill windup with his arms moving back and forth. "Whoosh." I've still got the bat on my shoulder. I don't swing. He does it three times. "Whoosh, whoosh, whoosh." "Now little boy, go sit down." "Yes sir."

Mays quickly evolved into an integral player the Black Barons needed to win the Negro American League playoff series in 1948. They played the renowned Kansas City Monarchs, managed by Buck O'Neil and featuring Hall of Famer Willard Brown and Hank Thompson, who later was Mays' teammate with the New York Giants—Brown and Thompson broke the St. Louis Browns' color barrier a year earlier but shamefully were released—and nineteen-year-old Elston Howard, who became the Yankees' first black player in 1955. This was Jackie Robinson's team in 1945 before the Dodgers called. Paige was a Monarch for much of the decade.

The first two playoff games were at Rickwood Field, which Faye Davis adored. "This is no exaggeration," she says. "If you wanted to get a seat at Rickwood for a doubleheader on a Sunday, you had to leave church before the minister preached." Dozens and dozens of Hall of Famers played at Rickwood, whether it was exhibitions, barnstorming, spring training games, minor-league games, or Negro League games. For example, Babe Ruth, Shoeless Joe Jackson, Ted Williams, and Joe DiMaggio, along with Jackie Robinson, Satchel Paige, and many other Negro League greats. Now it was the young Mays' turn. He hit a bases-loaded, walk-off single in the 11th inning for a Game 1 victory and an RBI double in a ninth-inning rally that sent Game 2 into extra innings. The Black Barons won in the 10th on another walk-off single, this one by Davis.

The Black Barons won Game 3 at a neutral site in Memphis, which wasn't strange at the time. It was an opportunity for players to showcase themselves in other cities and for owners to benefit in other markets. Still, it was another walk-off victory for the Black Barons, who famously were captured in a photograph moments after, players bunched together celebrating

The Birmingham Black Barons played in the final Negro League World Series in 1948. Willie Mays, pictured in the upper left, pops his head through his celebrating teammates. (Negro Leagues Baseball Museum)

and posing in the corner of a room with a serene and innocent Mays seen in the upper left.

The Monarchs tied the series at three wins apiece, and in the deciding game, Greason pitched all nine innings in a 5–1 Birmingham victory, sending the Black Barons to the Negro League World Series against the mighty Homestead Grays, who had been to the World Series four of the previous six years and won twice, both times over the Black Barons.

Mays' best World Series moments came in Game 3, when he displayed his multiple gifts. At one point, he chased down Bob Thurman's fly to the outfield's deepest regions. He also threw out Hall of Famer Buck Leonard trying to go first to third. The capper was his ninth-inning single that scored Greason with the deciding run in the only win for the Black Barons, who lost in five games.

With an increasing number of the top players and gate attractions moving to big-league organizations and interest in the Negro Leagues beginning to wane, it proved to be the last Negro League World Series. Mays played two more seasons for the Black Barons, 1949 and 1950, continuing to develop all the tools he'd showcase throughout the rest of his career, but 1948 was the most memorable.

Playing a few miles from his home in Fairfield and fitting his travel schedule and home games around his high school obligations made it feasible, but Mays didn't receive full support at Fairfield Industrial High School, where principal E. J. Oliver preferred he stay eligible for school athletics. Davis had warned Mays when they met in Chattanooga about losing eligibility, but Willie dominated high school sports and figured he'd improve dramatically quicker playing with the pros.

It was a problem because I wasn't eligible. I couldn't play in high school if I was getting paid by the Black Barons. Earlier, I played some games, and they might've used different names for me, but when I was getting paid, it was for something I loved to do. Because of the Black Barons, I knew about life before I even got out of high school.

I'd take a week and go on the road with these guys, and when I came back, I'd teach the class. When I say teach the class, I'd explain what I did, what I saw in the different cities, and everyone had to write a paper based on what I told them. My last report card when I got out of high school was all As and Bs, and I don't know how I got that. I guess the teachers were okay with me.

The travel was grueling. Playing during the day and driving at night was typical. The same players who were celebrated for their wonderful athletic talents found it demeaning when they weren't accepted at hotels and restaurants throughout the segregated South because of their race. The heat and humidity took a toll. Good nutrition, good sleep, and good medical attention weren't always realistic expectations.

For Mays, he still was living the dream. Playing baseball at a high level, away from a future life of working in the mills, he was willing to accept the hardships if it meant playing ball, getting paid, and enjoying the camaraderie of teammates who were much older but, once the game started, all dependent on him.

We did a lot of talking and sleeping. They were long trips, but I learned so much from those guys. They were like family. We talked about the game and about life. The experiences, they were something other kids weren't getting. Life-lasting experiences. I brought them home and told the class about the experiences, the Liberty Bell in Philadelphia, the Holland Tunnel in New York.

It wasn't the tunnel itself that was memorable but what transpired within its confines. The Black Barons were in town to play the New York Cubans and the semipro Brooklyn Bushwicks.

We were going through the Holland Tunnel when our bus caught fire. Our equipment was gone, and we had to borrow uniforms. I rushed back in and got my clothes because my father had just bought me some suits, and I wasn't going to let them go before the bus blew up.

Faye Davis remembers the bus stories well. Faithfully driven by Charlie Rudd, the bus would be parked in front of Bob's Savoy, where players gathered for the next excursion. It was one of the most popular black hangouts in Birmingham, a restaurant, bar, and dance hall, and it wasn't uncommon for the evening's entertainment to feature Count Basie, Duke Ellington, or Cab Calloway. Through the bus rides, Mays was forced to learn the importance of punctuality, though there's the famous story of Willie losing track of time while shooting pool only to discover the bus had taken off without him.

"My dad was a straight shooter," Faye Davis said. "If he said the bus was leaving at 2:30, the bus left at 2:30. You had to make sure you were on the bus. If you weren't, you got left. The bus would line up on Fourth Avenue between 17th and 18th Streets near Bob's Savoy. When it was time to go, my dad said, 'Okay, Rudd.' They'd say, 'Hey, Pipe, so and so's not here.' My dad would say, 'Okay, Rudd.' That meant go.

"I mean, I saw ballplayers flying down Fourth Avenue trying to catch that bus. Of course, after a block or two, Mr. Rudd would pull over and let them get on the bus. If they weren't fast, they were left. Sometimes ballplayers had to grab a cab in front of the Savoy and pay the cab fare to catch the bus. That's what happened with Willie. It was the funniest story I have heard."

Back home, the Black Barons shared Rickwood Field with the Southern Association's Birmingham Barons, the white team that owned the ballpark. The Barons were a Double-A affiliate of the Boston Red Sox, the last major-league team to integrate, a full twelve years after Robinson's rookie year. The Black Barons played at Rickwood Field when the Barons were out of town.

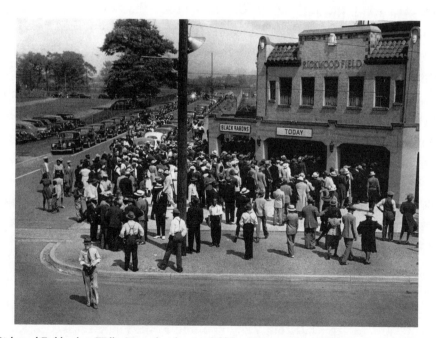

Rickwood Field, where Willie Mays played center field for the Birmingham Black Barons, opened in 1911 and is America's oldest professional ballpark. (Memphis and Shelby County Room, Memphis Public Libraries)

They had a thing at Rickwood where blacks and whites couldn't stay together. The white team played when we were on the road, and when they were on the road, we'd come in and play. They had an area down in right field. The whites sat out there for our games, and the blacks sat out there for their games. It's the way it was.

Rickwood Field was segregated just like all of Birmingham, which maintained the South's longest-standing racial zoning law from 1926 through 1951, when it was declared unconstitutional by the U.S. Supreme Court, overlapping Mays' entire childhood and three seasons with the Black Barons. Martin Luther King, Jr., called Birmingham "probably the most thoroughly segregated city in the United States." Blacks tried to buy homes in off-limit neighborhoods, and city officials stepped in, igniting racial tension and often leading to violence. Bombings became common, the most publicized and one of the most horrific coming on a Sunday morning in 1963 at the 16th Street Baptist Church that killed four African-American girls.

The Black Barons and white Barons coexisted at Rickwood Field from 1940 to 1962 but were worlds apart. In fact, it was a former Barons radio play-by-play broadcaster, white supremacist Bull Connor, who enforced legal segregation and opposed civil rights as Birmingham's public safety commissioner, maintaining administrative authority over police and fire departments. In 1963, Connor ordered the use of fire hoses and police dogs to subdue demonstrators calling for desegregation, some of them kids, and the national attention his actions received helped ignite the civil rights movement and brought social change and the passage of the landmark Civil Rights Act of 1964.

Not until the 1964 season was pro baseball in Birmingham integrated. By then, the Barons were a farm club of Charlie Finley's Kansas City A's and eventually became a feeder club for the Oakland championship teams of the 1970s. Reggie Jackson, Vida Blue, and Rollie Fingers played at Rickwood Field.

In Willie's time in Birmingham, baseball could be considered a diversion not only for black players but for the black community. Playing ball provided hope for equality on the field and off.

It was a different time. We were playing for ourselves but also for people in the community who'd come watch a game and get their minds away from any hardships. I was seventeen and surrounded by strong men and great ballplayers. Greason, Alonzo Perry, Artie Wilson, Jim Zapp, Ed Steele, Jimmie Newberry, Sammy C. Williams, Piper Davis. For me, when I look back, these were the guys who taught me things I carried with me throughout my life. I wouldn't have done what I did without those guys.

If Mays' Birmingham teammates reached the majors, their time was limited. Only Willie got a fair shake. The racist ways of white baseball were slow to change. Thanks to racial quotas and the belief black players needed to be stars and not role players, many deserving Negro Leaguers never reached the majors and were stuck in the minors or left out completely. Meantime, with baseball integrating, the Negro Leagues faded. In fact, the Negro National League, featuring the 1948 World Series champion Homestead Grays, disbanded after the season.

Mays and Hank Aaron are the last living Hall of Famers to come out of the Negro Leagues, which began in 1920 under the leadership of Rube Foster.

"When we think about Willie Mays and in the same context Hank Aaron, they are two of the guys who validate how good the Negro Leagues were," said Bob Kendrick, president of the Negro Leagues Museum in Kansas City. "As I give people tours of this museum and tell the stories of Josh Gibson and Cool Papa Bell and all these great stars who preceded Willie Mays, people are always respectful. But you could tell there's this air of skepticism. And then we come across this photograph of a seventeen-year-old Willie Mays in that great picture of the Birmingham Black Barons celebrating. All of a sudden, he validates all those other players.

"That, to me, is the testament of what Mays meant to the Negro Leagues.

When you heard the Buck O'Neils and Monte Irvins talk about the Oscar Charlestons and Josh Gibsons, they'd say, 'Willie was great, but you should've seen these guys.' To me, that's scary. You talk about Willie Mays being arguably the greatest major-league player of all time. And to think there may have been guys we never got a chance to see who were better is absolutely frightening and hard to conceive because that's how good Willie Mays was. It makes you wonder what you missed. This helps you understand how important the Negro Leagues were.

"All these guys were pulling for these young players to succeed. Contrary to the belief that they were jealous or envious of Willie Mays and others, no. They all wanted to see these young players who left the Negro Leagues be successful. It not only created the opportunity for others, but for those who never got the opportunity, it was a badge of honor to see how great Willie Mays and Hank Aaron were. They validated those other players."

That included Greason, Mays' teammate on the 1948 Black Barons and an American hero three times over. Not only was Greason a trailblazing ballplayer, but he served two terms with the Marines—in World War II and the Korean War—and has spent much of his life as a minister in Birmingham. Reverend Greason still preaches at his beloved Bethel Baptist Church.

In World War II, Greason was part of the 66th Supply Platoon, an all-black unit, during the five-week Battle of Iwo Jima in 1945. "That was an awful place. It taught me to really pray," Greason said. "There were over 20,000 causalities. Two of my best buddies right near me got it. I asked God if he got me off that island, whatever he wanted me to do, I'd do it. I didn't know he'd have me preaching, but I have no regrets. I've been blessed."

It's June 2019, and the ninety-four-year-old reverend is between sermons at his church, where he has an office and private room containing a lifetime of wonderful mementos from baseball, the ministry, and the military, including a Congressional Gold Medal, which he received during a Washington ceremony in 2012. He was a parishioner at the 16th Street Baptist Church in 1963, not present the day of the bombing. Martin Luther King, Jr., Greason's childhood neighbor from their days in Atlanta, would visit the church, which also served as a meeting point for civil rights activists.

Greason has dealt with racism, wars, and other hardships and, in his exemplary life, inspired countless people, including youth, through his sermons and community work. Through it all, he fondly remembers his time with the Black Barons, including his relationship with Mays.

"At that time, age didn't matter. They looked at ability," Greason says. "He grew so fast it was a shame. He had all the tools to play ball. Run, catch, throw, good hands. He didn't exactly learn how to deal with some of those pitchers right away, but he did in time. Just an amazing athlete.

"His dad backed off and let him go. Piper took him under his wing. Piper kept a close eye on him. Willie was not so quick to go out and run around. I didn't either. We knew at that time we wanted to be good ballplayers. We didn't do no drinking, no smoking. That's the way it was. Thank God for him."

Two miles from Greason's church, Clarence Watkins works from the Rickwood Field conference room/museum/gift shop as the tireless executive director of the Friends of Rickwood, a group that keeps the 110-year-old facility afloat. In 1991, when Chicago's Comiskey Park was demolished, Rickwood Field became America's oldest professional ballpark. But the structure was in sorry shape, at least before two significant developments in the early 1990s: the forming of the Friends of Rickwood and the filming of *Cobb*, the Ty Cobb biopic.

Ron Shelton, director of *Bull Durham*, liked the site for his new movie and paid handsomely to revitalize the place while maintaining its vintage vibe. Suddenly, Rickwood Field was a destination point, and it served as a setting for the HBO baseball movie *Soul of the Game* and the Jackie Robinson biopic, *42*. Walk into Rickwood Field now, it's like walking into the past. In fact, if anything needs repair, it's fixed to resemble 1948, Mays' rookie year.

"When a building gets old," Watkins says, "we look at it at in terms of dollars and cents, and almost all the time it's cheaper to tear something down and rebuild it than to keep the original structure. With Rickwood

Field, you're not just preserving a ballpark but the history that goes with that ballpark."

Watkins oversees Rickwood Field's busy schedule. These days, it's home to the Division II Miles College Golden Bears, two area high schools, and youth showcases, camps, and tournaments, one that's named after Piper Davis. The biggest event is the Rickwood Classic, in which the Birmingham Barons, now the Chicago White Sox's Double-A affiliate, plays a home game away from its newer facility in downtown Birmingham, Regions Field.

Regions Field is three miles from Rickwood Field and opened in 2013, and a nine-foot bronze statue of Willie Mays, depicting him making a leaping catch, greets fans outside the 14th Street entrance. Just beyond Regions Field is the Negro Southern League Museum, which opened in 2015 and tells the history of the Negro Leagues and highlights the importance of Birmingham, including its Industrial League. Some days, local Negro Leaguers will drop by, including Jake Sanders, who's a few years younger than Mays, attended his high school, and played in the Negro Leagues in the late 1950s. Mays, of course, is featured in the museum along with his 1948 Black Barons.

On a memorable December evening in 2006, Mays joined Black Barons teammates Greason, Wilson, Zapp, and Williams in Beverly Hills at an annual fundraising dinner for baseball scouts, an extravaganza that always includes a star-studded cast. On this night, it was baseball royalty. Mays was seventy-five at the time, the others in their eighties. An award in Willie's honor was going to be given out, and he made sure his teammates would be the recipients. They were proud he embraced them. Nattily attired, the five pioneers appeared together onstage as Mays paid tribute to his mentors and friends by telling a packed ballroom what they meant to baseball, society, and himself. They received a standing ovation.

The best glimpse of the 1948 pennant winners came when they gathered in Willie's suite, where he ordered food and drinks for everyone. They told stories, laughed, ribbed one another, and recalled vivid details of nearly fifty-year-old games as if they had happened yesterday. In their conversations, they relived the miseries of segregated baseball and the triumphs of

Birmingham Black Barons teammates reunited at a 2006 fundraiser for baseball scouts: Willie Mays, Bill Greason, Artie Wilson, Jim Zapp, and Sammy Williams. (Rick Swig)

rising above the prejudices to bond, compete, and win. Decades had passed since they suited up together, but Greason, Wilson, Zapp, and Williams still were looking out for the young guy. "How you eating, Buck?" "'How's your health?" "You need anything?" "Willie, what can I do for you?" They straightened his collar and fixed his tie. They brought him drinks and fussed over him. He was their little brother, their champion. The event paid for the flights, hotel rooms, and hotel meals, but Willie gave each $500 so they could tip and make purchases outside the hotel. They knew Willie was the reason they were together. A marvelous reunion for the ages. They enjoyed each other's company as if they were ballplayers again and warming up at Rickwood Field with their lives ahead of them but only the upcoming game on their minds.

I played in the Negro Leagues just a few years. I thought it was just like the majors. We had guys good enough to play anywhere. My teammates

from the Birmingham Black Barons were really the ones who made me understand about life. We played at a time baseball was becoming open to everybody, so we were playing for generations of players who were held back. We had a lot to play for, not just us. They were glad I made it. They were glad we made it.

4.

TAKE ON A CHALLENGE

The Story of Breaking Down Barriers

"Nobody should be insulted or bullied. There's no place for that. We need to treat people right. It makes it better for everybody."

—*Willie Mays*

ONE BY ONE, representatives of major-league teams came to see Willie Mays play for the Birmingham Black Barons. One by one, they gave or were given reasons not to sign him.

Picture Mays and Ted Williams in the same Boston Red Sox outfield. How about Mays and Hank Aaron together in the lineup for the Milwaukee Braves. The New York Yankees in center-field heaven with both Mays and Mickey Mantle? The thought of Mays as a Brooklyn/Los Angeles Dodger is too much for Giants fans to stomach. Even the White Sox were in the conversation, and imagine Mays and Ernie Banks in the same town.

All these teams scouted Mays. All these teams could have had the most promising prospect in the land. All these teams blew it. Either because scouts were interested and got the thumbs-down from ignorant management or because scouts filed flawed reports to their bosses.

It was either, "He's not our type of player." Or, "He wants too much money." Or, "He can't hit a curveball." Or, "We ain't signing no (whatever racist slur a particular narrow-minded team representative preferred)." All pathetic and inexcusable.

Somehow, Mays slipped to the Giants. Somehow, the Giants won the lottery. Somehow, no other team stepped up. All the others, with their lack of foresight and tolerance, forever would have on their conscience that they let Willie Mays get away.

It worked out. I liked the Giants. The Red Sox scouted me, too. They didn't like African-American guys back then so I didn't get a chance to play there. I came to the Giants because other teams didn't take me. The Red Sox, they finally brought in Pumpsie Green. Second baseman, slick-fielding. That wasn't until 1959. Other teams were slow, too. Maybe I was meant to be a Giant.

It was no secret Mays would play his final Negro League games in the spring of 1950. Jackie Robinson was in his fourth season with the Dodgers, who had four African Americans on their roster, and a few teams were trying to catch up. Scouts knew about Mays, but his father, Cat, had made it clear Willie was off limits until he graduated from Fairfield Industrial High School in late May, shortly after his nineteenth birthday.

Several teams had various levels of interest, but no team looked as ridiculous as the Red Sox. For starters, their Double-A team, the Birmingham Barons, played at Rickwood Field, so the access to Mays was unlimited. Of all the teams that whiffed on Mays, he mentions the Red Sox the most. In fact, he speaks of spending time on the roof at Rickwood Field with the Barons' brass, which included general manager Eddie Glennon, who had alerted the Red Sox about the talented kid on the Black Barons.

The Red Sox, however, had no interest in bringing a black player to Fenway Park. Apparently going through the motions, Larry Woodall was sent to scout Mays but told his bosses he wasn't their type of player. Later, Red Sox scout George Digby filed a glowing report on Mays, but too many decision-makers wanted no part of black baseball, starting with racist owner Tom Yawkey and general manager Joe Cronin, both of whom resisted integration.

In 1955, Pinky Higgins became the Red Sox's manager, the same Pinky Higgins who used a racist slur when insisting no blacks would ever play for the Red Sox if he had any say, according to Al Hirshberg's 1973 book, *What's the Matter with the Red Sox?* Well, guess who managed the Barons during Mays' final two seasons with the Black Barons. None other than Pinky Higgins. The Red Sox could have had Jackie Robinson and Mays, and got neither. In fact, they resisted blacks for such a long time, Robinson was two years retired before they finally integrated with Green.

Other teams had a variety of lame excuses for not signing Mays. Braves scout Bill Maughn targeted him the longest and tried to sign him before graduation but couldn't buy the player from Black Barons owner Tom Hayes for several reasons. The money wasn't all up front, and Hayes wanted to hold on to Mays longer. Plus, most white teams remained hesitant about signing black players and had racial quotas limiting the number of blacks in the organization. Unlike the other Boston team, the Braves (who eventually relocated to Milwaukee and then Atlanta) learned a lesson and signed Hank Aaron two years later. The Yankees were another slow team to integrate, waiting until 1955 to call up Elston Howard. Years earlier, Yankees management pooh-poohed pleas to sign Mays, including from part-time scout Joe Press, who expressed frustration that the team rejected his recommendations for top Negro League talent. Another Yankees scout, Bill McCorry, infamously concluded Mays couldn't hit a curveball.

Roy Campanella and Robinson, after barnstorming through Birmingham, pushed for the Dodgers to scout Mays, but Wid Matthews' lazy report was similar to McCorry's: couldn't hit a curve. Even if it were true, how many teenaged hitters master an accomplished pitcher's breaking pitches? The Dodgers sent another scout, but Ray Blades was late to the bidding. The White Sox were wise enough to hire the first full-time African-American scout but weren't wise enough to listen to John Donaldson, who recommended Mays. Along with Ernie Banks.

Eddie Montague was the scout employed by the Giants who signed a teenaged Willie Mays in May 1950. Mays reached the majors a year later. (Eddie Montague Family)

The guy from the Giants who signed me was Eddie Montague, the umpire's father, who came to Birmingham to scout Alonzo Perry. That's what I was told, the scout came to see Alonzo, who hit the ball all over with power. I guess he saw me, and things changed. He came by my house, met with my father and aunt, and signed me.

Montague, accompanied by fellow Giants scout Bill Harris, appeared at Rickwood Field and was wowed by the young Mays. Naturally, Mays remembers performing at a high level at that time. According to a letter penned to Giants scouting director Jack Schwarz on June 22, 1950, a couple of days after Mays signed, Montague wrote that other teams had been hot on Mays' trail, especially the Braves, and noted the Dodgers were ready to cut a deal. Strangely, Montague wrote that Mays had one flaw—"not knowing how to run"—and suggested the Giants hire Olympic legend Jesse Owens to teach mechanics. Of course, nobody needed to instruct this kid how to run.

A copy of the letter is in a scrapbook belonging to Montague's oldest son, also named Eddie, a major-league umpire for thirty-four years who lives in the Bay Area and is a regular at Giants games as a Major League Baseball umpire supervisor. His father shared his first thoughts of Mays in another letter dated November 1954, shortly after Willie's first MVP season: "When I arrived in Birmingham for the Sunday doubleheader, I had no inkling of Willie Mays on the club, but during batting and fielding practices, my eyes almost popped out of my head when I saw a young colored boy swing the bat with great speed and power, his hands had the quickness of a young Joe Lewis throwing punches. I also saw his great arm during fielding practice, and during the games his speed and fielding ability showed up. This was the greatest young ballplayer I had ever seen in my life or my scouting career."

The younger Montague recalled his dad telling the story: "Jack Schwarz had him go down to Birmingham to see a kid named Alonzo Perry. He didn't even know about Mays. He got there and forgot all about Alonzo Perry and went after Willie. He saw this young kid in the outfield and wanted to get him before all the other scouts and went to his Aunt Sarah's house for a fried chicken dinner."

That's where the deal was consummated, at 216 57th Street in Fairfield. Mays got $4,000 and a salary of $250 a month, the steal of the century. Tom Hayes, the Black Barons' owner, made out better than Mays and pocketed $10,000. Those were the times. Negro League players didn't exactly have much bargaining power, and it's not as if the other big-league teams engaged in much competition, taking turns bungling their opportunity to add a generational talent.

Alternative stories have been told, including in a 2009 book by John Klima, *Willie's Boys*, which reported that Giants officials had been aware of Mays because of the Black Barons' visits to the Polo Grounds in 1949 and 1950 to play the New York Cubans, owned by Alex Pompez, an ally of Giants owner Horace Stoneham. Pompez later joined their front office and helped sign Hall of Famers Juan Marichal, Orlando Cepeda, and Willie McCovey, among other stars.

Regardless, the elder Montague was the scout who signed Mays, and Mays got his wish to join a major-league franchise. His first assignment was the Trenton Giants of the Class B Interstate League, a team that played close enough to the Polo Grounds that the Giants' brass could closely monitor their newly signed center fielder. Mays didn't waste time packing and leaving Birmingham.

I couldn't go to my prom because Mr. Stoneham had already promised people at Trenton I'd be in Hagerstown for the next game. He didn't realize I had a prom. They gave me a couple of extra dollars to get on the

train to Hagerstown, and I gave it to my aunts to get a dress for the girl. Leaving all that was harder than playing.

Playing was the easy part. That's what Willie did best. He appeared in 81 games through the rest of Trenton's season and hit .353. The tough part was facing racism like never before, going from the comfort of an all-black team with veterans looking out for him to being the only African American not only on the team but in the league.

Mays had always enjoyed and flourished being around teammates, but when he reported to segregated Hagerstown, Maryland, he suddenly found himself crosstown at an all-black hotel, far removed from where the white players stayed. Hagerstown was a Braves affiliate and provided a rude welcome. It was the only team in the league below the Mason-Dixon Line, the traditional divide between the North and South, and the insults he heard each time he visited were impossible to forget.

They were calling me all the names you could imagine, pointing out my race. I remember from Piper (Davis) and all the guys in Birmingham, they said stay strong, ignore the name-calling, don't play their game, which is what Jackie was told to do his first two years with the Dodgers. My dad said focus on baseball, not on what people are saying or thinking, rise above all that. It wasn't easy.

I remember one series in Hagerstown, I got a lot of big hits the first two days. The final day, I was sitting in the dugout watching what the pitcher was throwing, trying to get a feel for what he had, when the announcer started calling out the names of the players. When he got to mine, he said, "Ladies and gentlemen. I know you don't like this kid, but *please* stop hollering at him. He's *killing* us." I started laughing. I didn't get a hit that day. I guess I relaxed so much I couldn't hit the ball.

Trenton second baseman Harry "Ace" Bell said Mays was a target of insults in other cities, including Sunbury, Pennsylvania, where the Philadelphia A's had a farm team. Many of these fans around the league hadn't seen an

African American play ball and were offended or even enraged by the notion of an integrated team. Mays turned heads with his elite performance and passion and began to soften some long-entrenched feelings of resistance and even hatred. Bell was impressed with how Willie rose above the abuse and focused on playing ball.

"Willie was such a nice kid," Bell said. "He was friendly with everybody, and he would praise everybody. He'd be your best fan. And you could tell right away he could hit. There wasn't anything that fooled Willie. I'm sure his Birmingham team had a better bunch of ballplayers than what Trenton had."

Despite the segregated towns and treatment from racist fans, Mays looks back fondly at his Trenton team and can recite the entire starting lineup. He also recalls his first night in Hagerstown when he was across town alone, separated from the rest of the team. There was a sign of solidarity that he appreciated and has stuck with him.

Three teammates climbed through my window. They came in and slept on the floor until the morning. They were looking out for me. It was a nice gesture from those guys. I don't think I needed help, but they wanted to help. You don't forget that.

The Giants tried to make Mays feel more at ease when adding another minority, José Fernández, but the experiment seemed forced and was short-lived. In large part, his teammates and manager, Chick Genovese, the brother of longtime Giants scout George Genovese, supported Mays and did what they could to make him feel comfortable.

"We had guys looking out for him, making sure he had a room and transportation," said Bell, who joined the team about the same time as Mays, after graduating from college. "A lot of places wouldn't accept a black person. Wilmington, Hagerstown. He had to go to a different part of the town. Three or four of the kids volunteered to find a place for him in those cities. They made sure he had a room. It was always in the black section. That's how Willie lived when we were on the road. That's the way it was at the time."

As the second baseman, Bell saw plenty of Mays' powerful arm. "I remember one of his first throws," he said. "There was a guy tagging up at third to go home. Willie was in deep center field and threw the ball over the catcher's head, if you can believe that. That's the kind of gun he had. Marvelous arm. His throws were so easy to handle. He had a great arm, but his ball came in lightly. Some throws from people are heavy. His were always light, easy to handle. Right where you wanted it."

Bell's claim to fame that season—"when I tried to explain to people I was really a good ballplayer"—was he outhomered Mays five to four. Bell played just one more season and became a longtime baseball coach at Springfield High School in Pennsylvania, where he tutored future big-league catcher and manager Mike Scioscia. Mays had other aspirations and opened the 1951 season at Triple-A Minneapolis, the Giants' top farm team.

Unlike in Trenton, Mays wasn't the only African American. The Millers had third baseman Ray Dandridge, who was inducted into the Hall of Fame in 1987, and pitcher Dave Barnhill, but both were in their late thirties and never reached the majors. Mays, who credits Dandridge for guidance at an important time in his life and career, dominated American Association pitchers even more than he dominated Interstate League pitchers and lasted just 35 games for the Millers.

When the Giants signed me, I found it much easier playing in their minor-league system than playing in the Negro Leagues because the level in the Negro Leagues was so much higher.

Mays hit a whopping .477 with eight homers for the Millers and continued to impress everyone with his defense and speed. The time had come. Mays was headed to the majors. In a short period, Millers fans fell in love with Mays and were disappointed when he got the call, so much so that Giants owner Horace Stoneham felt compelled to take out an ad in the *Minneapolis Tribune* explaining the move: "Mays is entitled to his promotion, and the chance to prove that he can play major-league baseball. It would be most unfair to deprive him of the opportunity he earned with his play."

Willie Mays played for two minor-league teams, including the Triple-A Minneapolis Millers, before the Giants promoted him to the big leagues in 1951. (Minnesota Historical Society)

I was in a movie house. We were on the way back to Minneapolis and were in Sioux City, Iowa, for an exhibition. During the movie, I see a message on the screen: WILLIE MAYS PLEASE REPORT TO THE LOBBY. I went out there, and the manager of the movie house told me to go back to the hotel. My manager, Tommy Heath, gave me the news. I talked to Leo (Durocher). I told him I liked it in Minneapolis and wanted to stay, but he wanted me in Philadelphia the next night with the Giants. I thought I could play with those guys. I didn't go back to Minneapolis. I went straight to Philadelphia.

On May 24, 1951, the twenty-year-old Mays got the call that generations of deserving Negro Leaguers never got. Including Piper Davis, his manager in Birmingham. And Oscar Charleston, an all-around talent who was considered Mays before Mays. Josh Gibson, Cool Papa Bell, Buck Leonard, Smokey Joe Williams, Ray Dandridge. And many, many others. Mays was carrying the weight of countless players who were overlooked because of their skin color. He was going to play for Leo Durocher. He was going to join Monte Irvin and Hank Thompson, who became the Giants' first two African Americans two years earlier. He was going to fulfill a dream that his father told him was possible after the Dodgers signed Robinson.

When I played in the Negro Leagues and then minor-league ball and then the Giants, my dad kept in contact. It seemed he called every night. "What are you doing?" I'd say, "What do you mean, what am I doing? I'm trying to play, man." He also kept in touch with Piper and Leo and Monte. If my dad couldn't be there with me, he made sure I was taken care of. He made sure I got in line with the right people, had the right roommates. If he felt something was wrong, he was there to make sure I got back on the right track.

Mays' journey to the majors was complete, a journey that seems hard to comprehend in today's world. Not just because of the racial barriers he and others broke down but because signing players mostly was a free-for-all before the amateur draft was implemented in 1965. Before that, teams with the most money and best scouting network often landed the prime players. Scouts would travel the country building relationships with players' families and searching for hidden gems. There were few rules. When pursuing Negro League players, there virtually were no rules.

What if Willie Mays were a high school senior today? First off, probably not as many teams would botch the process as in 1950.

"Every team would be on Willie Mays," said renowned scout Gary Hughes, who has worked for several teams, most recently the Diamondbacks. "Everybody in the country would know about him. As a freshman, he probably makes varsity, and here he comes. There's so much information out there, no one gets lost. Tournaments, showcases. You don't all of a sudden have a guy who comes out of nowhere. These guys are all known now. They don't get hidden. You can't say, 'Well, nobody knew about him.' All you can do is hope to have the first pick in the draft."

Hughes grew up in the Bay Area following the San Francisco Seals of the old Pacific Coast League and, when the Giants arrived in 1958, became an avid Mays fan. Hughes (even when unbiased) said he would give Mays a perfect 80 in the 20–80 scouting scale for each of the five tools: hitting, hitting for power, running, fielding, and throwing.

Judging players is far more scientific now than in Mays' day, but as recently as 2009, most of the industry blew it with Mike Trout, baseball's best all-around player since Mays and Mickey Mantle. Trout, who attended Millville Senior High School in New Jersey, didn't get drafted until 25th by the Angels.

Even if Mays were selected first in the modern draft, he would have two major bargaining chips to use in negotiations: college scholarship offers and other pro sports leagues. After all, Mays thought he was a better football and basketball player in high school.

Like Mays, Kyler Murray excelled in multiple sports as a sub-6-foot amateur and could throw a football a country mile. Murray was the ninth overall pick of the Oakland A's in 2018, but after winning the Heisman Trophy at Oklahoma, the quarterback committed to football and was taken first overall by the NFL's Arizona Cardinals. When Mays was young, black quarterbacks weren't given much hope beyond high school. The first high school player selected in the 2019 baseball draft was outfielder Riley Greene (fifth overall), who received a $6.18 million signing bonus from the Tigers.

"If Willie Mays is baseball's number one pick out of high school, he signs. You'll never be any higher than the first pick," said Hughes, who's known for drafting multisport athletes, including John Elway, John Lynch, Randy Winn, Delino DeShields, and Erick Strickland. "As for Kyler Murray, I don't see him being anywhere near Willie Mays. Well, we might never know, but there aren't too many Willie Mayses out there."

Mays' time in the minors was short, 116 games, but he made his mark as a trailblazer and, beyond the bigots, a fan favorite in the Interstate League and American Association, his final stops before the big leagues. Through the years, the camaraderie was impossible to forget, but so was the abuse, especially in Hagerstown, where he debuted. It wasn't the last time as a ballplayer he heard racial slurs or stayed and ate apart from white teammates, but it stung more than most because it was all new. Not until Hagerstown reached out fifty-four years later was he able to put it behind him and make peace.

Wanting to make amends, Hagerstown honored Mays in 2004 and apologized. He was paid homage in ceremonies at a downtown hotel and before a game played by the Hagerstown Suns, then a Giants affiliate, at Municipal Stadium, the very venue where Mays had been taunted. He received a standing ovation. His number 24 was retired by the team (though he wore 12 with Trenton), and Mayor William M. Breichner vowed to name a street outside the ballpark Willie Mays Way. Mays was teary-eyed and taken aback by the support. He gave his forgiveness.

Eight months later, however, the city council in the western Maryland town rejected Breichner's street-renaming plan amid protests from military veterans who said the street, Memorial Boulevard, was a tribute to them. No Willie Mays Way. Hagerstown struck again. In retrospect, Mays was more touched by the emotional outpouring during his visit than bothered by the change of plans regarding the street name.

They wanted to try making up for the sadness I felt all those years earlier. The way I figured it, I couldn't hold it against the whole town. I wasn't hurt by the town in 1950. I was hurt by the people. It was good that I went back.

5.

HONOR YOUR MENTORS

The Story of Leo Durocher and Monte Irvin

"It's important to have people you can look up to and trust. If you can listen and learn, it'll help forever."

—*Willie Mays*

WILLIE MAYS AND Leo Durocher were meant for each other. They needed each other, fed off each other, and most of all adored each other.

A gruff and combustible manager who was suspended in 1947 for associating with gamblers, which ruined his chance to manage the Dodgers in Jackie Robinson's rookie year, Durocher ran the New York Giants by 1951 and was seeking an upgrade to a team that got off to a rough start.

Mays, less than three weeks removed from his twentieth birthday and less than a year removed from his high school graduation, was seeking a smooth transition to the big leagues.

Their relationship began in earnest on May 25, 1951, when Mays made his major-league debut at Shibe Park in Philadelphia, and they remained close throughout their careers even as Durocher managed and coached elsewhere.

Leo was in my corner in '51. I was in the Army in '52 and '53, and after that, I was in my own corner. I was my own guy. I could play the way I wanted to play in the outfield. They didn't bother me. Leo was the right guy for me at that time, especially in '51. He was a good friend. He would cuss at other guys. He never cussed at me.

The Giants were scuffling with a losing record and in need of an identity. They hadn't finished first or second in the National League since the 1930s and opened the 1951 season 7–14. Durocher, after observing the extraordinary prospect in spring training, had wanted Mays to open the season in New York, but owner Horace Stoneham decided to ease him in.

Mays forced himself into the majors by hitting .477 in 35 games with Triple-A Minneapolis, and an elated Durocher, whose team rallied to get to 17–19 by the time Mays arrived, batted him third in the lineup for the first week, a spot reserved for a team's best hitter. Mays responded poorly with one hit in his first 26 at-bats including 0-for-12 in his first series in Philadelphia.

I was crying. I was upset. I wanted to go back to Minneapolis. I told Leo this league might be too fast for me. He said, "Son, you're my center fielder. You just go out and catch the ball. We'll hit for you." I was thinking too much. I was being called names. Philadelphia had good pitchers. Leo just told me to go home and get some rest.

Durocher was patient and knew what he had in Mays, whose only hit in those 26 at-bats was his first of 660 home runs, a blast over the left-field roof at the Polo Grounds off Warren Spahn, who became a 363-game winner and Hall of Famer.

I later joked with him that he grooved it so I could stay in the big leagues.

Mays began figuring it out, won Rookie of the Year honors, and helped the Giants overcome a 13½-game deficit on August 11 to win the pennant on the season's final day, courtesy of Bobby Thomson's home run off

Willie Mays is waved home in 1951 by Leo Durocher, his first big-league manager. (National Baseball Hall of Fame and Museum)

Ralph Branca, the celebrated Shot Heard 'Round the World.

"Leo guided Willie. Willie just loved Leo," said Bill Rigney, a backup infielder that season who succeeded Durocher as manager in 1956. "I have to give Leo a lot of credit for the development of Mays. Willie brought a pace to the '51 club that was all we needed. It was going to take a lot to catch the Dodgers, a real shot of energy. Even when he was going 0-for-12, the energy level was there every minute."

Chris Durocher, Leo's son, said more than six decades later, "I think my father could recognize Willie had talents but would need a little bit of time to take pressures off and go out and play ball. I don't think a lot of people realize what my father did for Willie and what Willie did for my father, the opportunities they both had working together. It was a perfect fit."

Mays often recognizes those who were at his side early in his career, and no teammate was more important and influential than Monte Irvin, his roommate and lifetime friend. Irvin was twelve years older than Mays, but they were as close as a teacher and student can be. Irvin and Hank Thompson, signed out of the Negro Leagues, became the Giants' first African-American players on July 8, 1949, and joined with Mays to form the majors' first all-black outfield in Game 1 of the 1951 World Series. A third baseman during the season, Thompson had taken over right field for injured Don Mueller.

A month younger than Jackie Robinson, Irvin was the choice of many of his Negro League peers to be the first African American in the majors.

Monte Irvin, one of the first two African Americans to play for the Giants, was Willie Mays' close friend and mentor. (San Francisco Giants)

Like Robinson, Irvin was college-educated and a military veteran and was a more established ballplayer than Robinson, but when he was contacted by the Dodgers' Branch Rickey after a three-year tour in the Army, he said he preferred to return to proper mental and physical condition before pursuing the majors. Also, the Newark Eagles wanted compensation for losing Irvin, and Rickey was hesitant to pay and turned to Robinson, signing him on October 23, 1945, seven weeks after Irvin was discharged.

Irvin did become the first African American appointed to a Major League Baseball executive position in 1968. Before he died in 2016 at age ninety-six, he expressed no regret he wasn't the first black major-leaguer and said, "It could've been (me), but I don't think about that. I think about Jackie getting a chance, setting a high standard, and making it possible for the rest of us to come along. Again, I want to pay tribute to Jackie for what he did. With Mays and (Hank) Aaron and Frank Robinson and Bob Gibson, it probably would've happened anyway in time, but he made it easier—and that much quicker for us by succeeding."

Mays was honored to be tutored by a noble and respected man. Irvin didn't reach the majors until he was thirty but still played spectacularly. In his second full season and first as Mays' teammate, Irvin hit .312 with 24 homers, a .415 on-base percentage, and a league-leading 121 RBIs. He was third in the MVP voting.

Irvin's greatest contribution was taking young players under his wing, including Mays. Four years after Robinson broke the color barrier, racism and discrimination remained prevalent in baseball and society, and Irvin preached to Mays the virtues of handling himself with class and dignity on and off the field.

It was very difficult that first year. At that time, in some cities, you couldn't stay with your team even though you're helping your team win. My father had warned me and told me to keep my mouth shut. Things began to progress after that, but the first year was tough. I am so thankful Monte came into my life and helped me when I came up.

We'd walk through a park near his home in New Jersey talking about baseball and life. He made sure I didn't go into the wrong crowd. You don't know as much as you think you know when you're young, and he was my mentor and made me aware of what I could and couldn't do.

It was like that through much of Mays' early time with the Giants, his teammates and manager constantly looking out for his well-being away from the ballpark, realizing a young player with no family nearby could succumb to society's temptations, especially in New York.

Monte taught me how to treat others and how to be treated. He played the game right and treated people right. He was a thinker. Everyone respected him. He made sure I didn't get into trouble.

He called ahead to restaurants and told them so that when I got there—I went to the Red Rooster and Smalls Paradise—they had a Coke with a cherry waiting for me. They said "no drinking." Monte had told them.

Even in 1954, when Mays was twenty-three with two years of military service to his name, Durocher went a long way to protect him, some suggest overprotecting him. On the road, Durocher sometimes had Chris Durocher, his nine-year-old son, room with Mays, partially to prevent Willie from going out at night.

"Willie was like a son to my father and like a big brother to me," said Chris Durocher, an adopted child of Leo Durocher and his wife, actress Laraine Day. "He was assigned to take care of me, and it was to keep him out of trouble. It was for both of our sakes. We'd go to the game on the bus, go out after the game, and get a bite to eat or have dinner in the room. It pretty much took up most of the day. He didn't drink or smoke. He was a baseball player on top of the world and a great role model, and I appreciate what he did for me in those years."

Mays always loved kids and welcomed the opportunity to look out for his manager's son.

Chris used to be my roommate on the road. Leo had faith in me, and he knew nothing would happen with Chris when I was with him. Chris and I became friends. I'd take him for soul food, and he didn't know what it was. Leo said, "What are you feeding my kid?" "I feed him what I eat. What's wrong?" Leo said, "What do you eat?" "Normal stuff, you know, greens with ham hocks, red beans and rice, sweet potatoes, cornbread, chitlins. *Food,* man." Leo said, "I can't have my kid eating that stuff." "What do you want me to do, Leo?" "You gotta give him real food, like steak." "Then you gotta give me steak money." So Leo gave me steak money from then on.

Mays overcame the slow start in 1951 to hit .300 through June, and the Giants pushed their record above .500 for good. Mays finished with a .274 average, .356 on-base percentage, 20 homers, and 68 RBIs, but it was the way he moved across the diamond with grace, purpose, and passion—in the outfield and on the bases—that captivated fans.

As the Giants were looking up at the first-place Dodgers, who were leading comfortably, Mays made two of the best plays of his career to provide hints of theatrics to come. On July 25, he caught a ball barehanded on the run, a drive to deep left-center by Rocky Nelson at Pittsburgh's Forbes Field. On August 15, Mays raced to right-center, stepped in front of Mueller, caught Carl Furillo's fly ball, spun around, and threw out speedy Billy Cox at the plate. Nobody would dare suggest Mays hogged the ball. In fact, those were his marching orders.

Leo said, "You have to catch balls line to line." I didn't know what the hell he was talking about. He said, "The ball goes to left, you gotta be

over there. The ball goes to right, you gotta be over there." I said, "Leo, what is that?" "Wherever the ball goes in the outfield, you gotta catch it." That was embarrassing to me, but the guys accepted it. I did it a lot in '54 when we had Dusty Rhodes in left and Don Mueller in right. They might not catch the ball, but they could hit it.

Irvin recalled a meeting upon Mays' 1951 arrival in which Durocher told everyone else to back off if Mays was close to a ball because of his superior range and arm. Like the others, Irvin deferred to Mays and came to the park every day expecting a magical moment from his understudy.

"I saw all the great center fielders. None could play like Willie," Irvin said. "He thought if the ball stayed in the ballpark, it was his solemn duty to catch it. Especially when the game really meant something, a catch to save the game, win the game. Everybody talks about Roberto Clemente, but Mays had a much better arm. He had a quicker release."

In the 1951 World Series, Monte Irvin, Willie Mays, and Hank Thompson formed the majors' first all-African-American outfield. (Osvaldo Salas/Collection of Rick Swig)

When the Giants beat the Dodgers in the game that Mays threw out Cox, they were five games into a 16-game win streak that was the genesis of a historic 37–7 finish, which pulled the Giants into an unlikely tie with Brooklyn after 154 games. The Giants won the pennant by beating the Dodgers in a best-of-three playoff, capped by Thomson's home run to end one of the most famous and debated games in history.

Mays was on deck when Thomson, the center fielder before Mays' arrival, was up with the Dodgers leading 4–2 and runners at second and third in the bottom of the ninth. Dodgers manager Charlie Dressen came to the mound to remove starter Don Newcombe. The relief options were right-handers Ralph Branca and Carl Erskine.

"Branca and I were throwing in the bullpen when Dressen called to see who was ready," Erskine said all these years later. "Ralph had only one day's rest after losing the opener at Ebbets Field. So I'm throwing alongside Ralph. I'm throwing everything straight overhand and bouncing my curveball some because you've got to keep it down. When Clyde Sukeforth, the coach, told Dressen on the phone they're both ready and Erskine's bouncing his curve, Dressen says, 'Let me have Branca.'

"That was a pivotal decision in that historic game. I pitched 12 seasons in the big leagues, and when people ask, 'Carl, what was your best pitch?,' I say, 'I think it was the curveball I bounced in the bullpen at the Polo Grounds.' I don't know if Branca appreciated that."

Branca threw Thomson a fastball up and in, and the rest is history. Mayhem immediately ensued for all the Giants except Mays, who momentarily seemed frozen in time.

I was happy it wasn't me. I was nervous. Bobby had hit a home run off Branca in the first game of the series, and I thought they'd walk Bobby to get to me. If you notice from the film, I was closest to Bobby, but I was the last guy to home plate. I didn't understand what was happening. Everyone's excited and running all around. I was so nervous.

If Dressen could be second-guessed for summoning Branca, certainly he could be second-guessed for not walking Thomson to get to Mays, who was 2-for-19 off Branca and in a terrible funk (3-for-his-previous-32), grounding into a double play his previous at-bat. Thomson was an accomplished veteran who had the team lead in homers and a 15-game hit streak. Walking Thomson would have put the Dodgers in position for a game-ending double play, but it also would have put the possible winning run on base, a no-no for managers at the time.

Then again, who's to say Mays wouldn't have channeled that nervous energy into a big moment himself? Over time, those were the at-bats he relished. For the record, Durocher said later he wouldn't have hit for the rookie.

Mays' first World Series seemed an afterthought in the wake of the most memorable pennant race in history. The Giants lost to the Yankees in six games, but it marked the beginning of an illustrious big-league career and reminder of a support group that helped make it happen. There was a time in that first season Mays believed he didn't belong. And another time he believed an at-bat was too big for him. After 1951, no longer was either the case.

I'm very thankful for Monte and Leo, and Piper Davis as well. They were all father figures to me. My dad wasn't around when I went off and played ball. He told me, "Don't try to embarrass nobody. Just play your game. If they like you, they'll cheer for you. If they don't like you, they don't like you. Move on. Just don't talk a lot."

I didn't talk a lot when I first came up. I just did what I had to do. I played. I'd hit the ball, run around the bases, come in the dugout, and sit down. I didn't do anything wrong. I just played.

6.

ACT LIKE YOU'VE BEEN THERE BEFORE

The Story of a Unique and Elegant Style

"Have fun with everything you do. Be comfortable. No need to act like you're somebody else. Be yourself. That's good enough."

—*Willie Mays*

BASEBALL DURING WILLIE Mays' playing career didn't involve bat flips. Or chest bumps. Or different celebratory greetings for every teammate. If you hit a home run, you didn't stand in the batter's box and admire the flight of the ball. You put your head down. You quickly ran the bases. You shook hands. You sat in the dugout.

Mays did all that. He played the game right, as it was supposed to be played in Willie's time. But he did a lot more.

He was more than a hitter, more than a fielder, more than a runner. More than someone who suited up and played nine innings. He was more than a ballplayer. Baseball's greatest star was baseball's greatest entertainer.

I just feel that when you're playing sports, you have to do more than catch the ball and throw it back in. You have to do something different.

You've got to improvise sometimes, you've got to create something for the fans. Make it fun. I tried to do something different at all times.

Mays is a product of the Negro Leagues. He learned the game from his father and refined it as a teenager with the Birmingham Black Barons while surrounded by older teammates and opponents who showcased flamboyant personalities and an up-tempo, all-out style of play—all of which was passed down to a young Willie, who created his own trademarks after signing with the New York Giants and working his way to big-league superstardom.

For example: For decades, outfielders were trained at an early age to raise their arms above their heads when catching a fly ball, keeping the glove hand above the bare hand, seeing the ball into the glove while closing it with both hands. Pushing the boundaries, Mays took a whole different and riskier approach. He held his glove at waist level, with his palms facing upward, and waited for the ball to drop to him.

Thus, the basket catch.

When I played, I made a game out of it. I was never uptight. The guys I played with, they couldn't be uptight. I tried to see to that. If they were uptight, they couldn't play like they should. If you don't understand that, I'll try to explain it to you a little bit more.

Baseball is a fun game. Say you go see a singer. If the guy is singing the same way every time, you're not going to like that. You want him to mix it up. You want to walk away saying, "Oh, he changed it up a little bit." That's a talking point. If you're a writer, are you going to write about the same damn thing every day? You've got to write so you know readers are going to enjoy reading you.

That's all part of being entertaining. You've got to relax and have fun. Show me a guy who's uptight, and I'll show you a guy who makes a lot of errors. I was just a guy who believed in doing things the right way, the simple way.

That meant having fun. You have to have fun out there, man. If you don't have fun, you can't play the game. You have fun, you'll try to hurry

Willie Mays delighted fans with his popular basket catch, holding his glove at waist level with the palms facing upward. (San Francisco Giants)

and get back to the field to play the next day. You have fun, now the fans are having fun. Now you're entertaining.

To succeed and survive in baseball, as Roy Campanella would remind us, "You've got to have a little boy in you." That's Mays to a T. Hall of Fame manager Joe Torre, who grew up in Brooklyn adoring Mays, said, "Willie thoroughly looked like he enjoyed himself when he played. He changed pressure into excitement." Legendary Dodgers broadcaster Vin Scully added, "He did everything with such an air of relaxation, confidence, and laughter. Yeah, he was a little bit of a showman, but it was as if he's saying to the world, 'God, I love this game.'"

Fans grew to expect Mays to make basket catches. When fly balls were directed toward center field, fans knew they weren't about to see anything routine. There was anticipation Mays would tap his glove, an indication to fans and a reassurance to teammates that the ball was his. There was anticipation he'd turn his left palm up to make his glove appear like a basket, with his right hand supporting the glove from underneath. There was anticipation he'd make a waist-high catch look a lot easier than it was.

Fans loved how Mays snagged the ball in a manner no one would or should teach, one of the reasons it was unwise to look away when he was on the field.

So how and why did the Say Hey Kid make basket catches?

If you normally catch the ball on your left side—as a right-hander, your glove is on your left hand and over your left shoulder—you've got to take

time to transfer the ball from way over here on the left side to way over here on the right side.

But think about it. If you catch it down here, at the middle of your body, you'll get rid of it more quickly. It takes less time to get the ball from glove to hand. When the ball is in your glove down here, you don't have to try to bring your body all around before throwing it. You're ready to throw.

The ball comes down quickly, so you've got to be ready, you've got to move your body to the ball. Your eyes are on the ball, and now you've got the ball in your glove. You keep going from there. You don't try to bring the ball back up and throw. You've already got it where you need it.

A note to kids: Don't try this at home, or in a game.

No, no, no. That's just me. The correct way to catch the ball is above your head with two hands. That's what I tell kids, over your head. Now, if you want to try the basket catch, that's your decision. But if you get hit in the head, remember I warned you.

I'm not going to tell kids to be like me. I'll try to help them, but I'll tell them, "Catch the ball the best way *you* can. Don't be like me, be like *you*."

Mays recalls feeling the desire to entertain as far back as high school. The desire heightened in the Negro Leagues and carried over to his minor-league stops in Trenton and Minneapolis and his rookie year with the Giants in 1951. His capacity as a showman reached a whole new level as part of a life-changing twist in 1952, in the second month of what would have been his first full season in the big leagues.

On May 28, Mays lined out to shortstop Pee Wee Reese in his final at-bat of the season in a 6–2 victory at Ebbets Field. Dodger fans respectfully stood and cheered Mays, knowing he was about to report for duty to Fort Eustis near Newport News, Virginia. Mays had been drafted into the Army, joining many other players who were called into duty after the United States entered the Korean War.

Willie Mays left the Giants early in the 1952 season to serve in the U.S. Army. (National Baseball Hall of Fame and Museum)

While Ted Williams, Jerry Coleman, and others distinguishedly engaged in combat, most players served stateside and played on service teams, including Whitey Ford, Don Newcombe, Johnny Antonelli, and Mays. Their official duties included using their athletic talents to entertain the troops, right in Mays' wheelhouse.

"People would be talking, 'How can he go play baseball when he's in the Army?' Well, it was more for morale than anything else," said Antonelli, who pitched for another Virginia-based service team and later became Mays' teammate with the Giants. "We would do regular duty until noon. We'd go fix up the field. At four o'clock, they would march the troops in. They were more or less stuck. They had to watch the ballgame. This is how it all happened. I think it was good for the morale. We thought we were doing something good for people."

In effect, Mays wasn't in the big leagues, but he still was able to delight people through baseball. He missed the rest of the 1952 season and all of 1953 but remained in his element, on the diamond showcasing his extraordinary skills and style. If he was going to get the opportunity to play ball while serving in the military, he vowed to make the best of it.

We played every day. I actually played seven days a week, for Fort Eustis and a team that played weekends in Newport News. In those two years, I got stronger. My power grew. I went in at 155, 160 pounds and came out at 180. I didn't have time to relax, but I wanted to learn something that was different, give 'em something to write about, and I tried catching the ball different ways.

The basket catch, I perfected that when I was in the Army. Bill Rigney, one of our infielders with the Giants, caught popups that way. I practiced it, first just messing around and then using it in games. I wanted people to know this was a new game. When I came out of the Army, Leo (Durocher) said you could do it, but don't miss the damn ball. I missed two. Ten years apart. Ernie Banks in the Polo Grounds and Donn Clendenon in Pittsburgh.

Fred Lovell was in the Army with Mays and recalled his old buddy was magnetic not just on the field but off.

"We took basic training together, about a six-week deal," Lovell said. "Willie was a hell of a nice guy and got along with everybody in the company. He would always come out and put a little show on for everybody, jive 'em up a bit. One time, he came out dancing with one boot untied, his pant leg up a little bit, and his hat turned sideways. Well, we had a new master sergeant come in, and the other sergeants said he'd give us hell when he got there. I actually knew him well before the Army, but he didn't know Willie and wasn't used to him.

"So when Willie comes out dancing around and putting on a show, the sergeant grabs him and throws him down. All the other cadets yelled, 'Lovell, get your friend off him, get your friend off him.' I tapped the master sergeant on the back and said, 'Willie's the only friend I have in the company, Sergeant, get off him.' He got off him, and it was all over with. Willie could've whipped the sergeant's rear end. He was in first-class shape when he was in the Army, but he didn't want to fight. After the sergeant got to know Willie, they were the best of friends."

Antonelli recalls Mays' on-field exploits. Before emerging as a five-time All-Star with the Giants, Antonelli honed his skills with his service team.

"I just thought he was a great ballplayer, a great guy who deserved everything he got in the game," Antonelli said. "I first saw Willie when we faced each other in the Army. It was just one game. I was at Fort Myer, Virginia, and he had just gotten in there. Our team was pretty good. We played some good ballclubs. We played Whitey Ford's team, Harvey Haddix's team. We beat these teams.

"I went 42–2 in two years in the Army. It was like my minor leagues. It got me ready for the big leagues. As it turned out, I got traded from the Braves to the Giants before the 1954 season and always wondered if Willie said something to get me to the Giants. I never did ask him that question."

Mays said it didn't happen, adding he was too young at the time to suggest such a transaction. Regardless, the trade significantly benefited the Giants, who swept Cleveland in the 1954 World Series. Not only was Mays the batting champion and National League MVP but Antonelli was the league's premier pitcher, winning 21 games and posting a league-low 2.30 ERA. He won Game 2 of the World Series and saved Game 4.

You've got to serve your country, and that's what I did. They called on a lot of players to do different things. I guess I was blessed to get to do what I did at Fort Eustis. I didn't rebel. They wanted me to be an enter-

Willie Mays, third row, second from the left, was stationed at Fort Eustis in Virginia and, like many other players drafted during the Korean War, played ball for his company team. (Collection of Willie Mays)

tainer for the troops, and that's what I did. We had some good teams in there, a lot of good players, a lot of major-league players.

Mays' work refining the basket catch in the Army helped him make his famous World Series catch, the one off Vic Wertz's bat in the 1954 opener. It was no ordinary basket catch because his back was to the plate in deep center field at the Polo Grounds, but his palms were up and the ball came down in his glove.

I messed around with all that kind of stuff. I could catch it up high, at my waist, one hand, two hands, behind my back, between my legs. I practiced that in spring training, catching the ball between the legs. That's how I got in shape, doing different things like that.

I'm not bragging. I never bragged. I just played the game, and every once in a while, I'd do something to keep the guys laughing. I would teach the guys to catch it behind their back, but I was scared to let them do it between their legs because they had no cup on.

The point is, you practice all these things, it becomes easy. You talk about the basket catch, I could do that because I practiced it. The entertainment comes with doing things the right way.

Rigney might have caught some infield popups with his glove turned around, but Mays was making those catches hundreds of feet from the plate. He popularized the basket catch and made it one of the most endearing qualities on his road to 7,095 outfield putouts, the most in history.

"Where do you think he learned the basket catch? He saw me," Rigney said with a wink decades later. "I never dropped one. Pitchers hated it. One said, 'If you ever drop one, I'm comin' after ya.' At Seals Stadium, one hit me in the chest but bounced into my glove."

Of course, it's not for everybody, even Angels center fielder Mike Trout, a generational talent who has been called a modern-day Mays (or Mickey Mantle) for his five-tool proficiency.

"I tried it during batting practice. It's pretty tough," Trout said. "It's amazing Willie was able to do that, pretty impressive. It was great to see his personality. That's the way the game's going now."

Part of Mays' charm was his daring willingness to do things others couldn't or wouldn't. They were usually simple things but pleasing to the eye, such as running so fast that his cap would fly off or throwing sidearm from all regions of the outfield.

They thought I used to knock my cap off. Nah. Eddie Logan, our equipment manager, used to give me one size too small, and when you look up, it's going to fall off anyway. People like that. They love all that kind of stuff. They want to see the hat fall off. No problem. I go back, pick it up, and put it back on.

I threw sidearm only when nobody was on base. If you look at film and I'm throwing sidearm, nothing is happening in the game. But if I have to make a throw to get a guy out, I go over the top because you want the ball to go straight. When you throw sidearm, the ball spins sideways.

Mays' flair and elegance were worshiped throughout the years, but he was more about substance than show. Flashy visuals aside, he seemed to always do the right thing, always be in the right position, always know what to expect. He has a one-of-a-kind style, but his actions were calculated because what mattered most was winning. He knew all eyes were on him, and while he would entertain with panache, he'd make sure to play with purpose.

"The Giants had five Hall of Famers, and we knew anytime we went into a town, the newspaper would say 'Willie Mays and Company,'" former teammate Felipe Alou said. "Everyone knew Willie was the guy, and he knew he was the guy. Some players probably didn't like that a whole lot, but Willie was leadership by example, a very responsible performer who played every day, hustled every day, and produced every day. We were proud of the company."

Fans flocked to ballparks around the country to see Mays play. In the 1960s, the Giants led the National League in annual road attendance eight times and again in 1971, Mays' last full season on the West Coast. In his fourteen full seasons in San Francisco, the Giants were first or second in road attendance thirteen times. In New York, they ranked second in 1954 and 1955, Mays' first two years out of the military.

"He was always a kid with that high voice and excitement level, always with a boyish enthusiasm. The Say Hey Kid and rightly named," said Roger Angell, the poet laureate of baseball, who has composed wonderfully vivid essays since the mid-twentieth century, especially for *The New Yorker*. "I can still see (Joe) DiMaggio with his long strides, never hurried, and I never remember him falling down or lunging for something. He was remarkable. But Willie would run faster and farther and make a great play. He engaged you. You'd go 'wow.' You'd never go 'wow' with DiMaggio, who had grace and style but kept you at a distance. Willie had tremendous speed. Deadly hitter. Great fielder. He caught the ball a new way, and all around the country, kids were trying basket catches."

Broadcaster Bob Costas recalled Mays as naturally stylish but not at the expense of efficiency and effectiveness.

"There are some athletes who go beyond talent, beyond craft, and they turn their game into an art form," Costas said. "Although the statistics attest to their greatness, the real abiding thought is just the images of watching them play.

"Instantly, if you walked into a ballpark and didn't know anything about baseball, your eye would go to Willie Mays. There was something so magnetic and so charismatic and so stylish and so artful about him that statistics only support him. You didn't have to look in the record book. You could feel it."

Or, as former teammate Joey Amalfitano said, "You never knew what the hell he was going to do. Movie stars have scripts. This guy had no script. You know what he had? Instincts. They were off the charts to perform like he did. Frank Sinatra had his own style. Well, this guy had his own style. Everything he did was poetry in motion. It was beautiful watching him hit a triple. You could take it to the bank that hat was falling off. No one had the style Willie had."

Mays' explanation:

I was me at all times. I don't try to tell guys to be like me. If a guy comes to me, I'll try to help him. But he's got to do it on his own.

7.

KEEP YOUR EYE ON THE BALL

The Story of The Catch

"Be confident you'll do what you set out to do because confidence is the key. Know you'll get it done. Never lose sight of your dream."

—*Willie Mays*

WILLIE MAYS' GLOVE. Where Vic Wertz's two-run triple in Game 1 of the 1954 World Series (to borrow and prolong a cliché) went to die.

If I missed that ball, we'd be down two runs. It was the eighth inning. Losing the opener to Cleveland, that would've been tough.

If I missed that ball? Good one, Willie.

Mays wasn't missing that ball. He had roamed the spacious outfield at the Polo Grounds enough to know what was in his grasp and what wasn't, and Wertz's momentous drive that sailed well beyond 400 feet was in the center fielder's grasp.

Yeah. I wasn't worried about catching that ball. I was worried about getting the ball back to the infield.

Such was the mind-set of a twenty-three-year-old budding superstar who made the most storied defensive play in baseball history. To understand Mays' frame of mind on September 29, 1954, it must be articulated how he got to that point. This was his first full big-league season. He had been called up to the majors in May 1951 and spent most of 1952 and all of 1953 in the Army. Then came 1954, the year he busted through as baseball's supreme all-around player. He won his first National League MVP award and inspired the Giants to a World Series sweep of the mighty Cleveland Indians, and he also would dominate winter ball, winning the batting crown in Puerto Rico and helping the Santurce Crabbers win the Caribbean Series.

The Indians had set the American League wins record with 111, back when the schedule was 154 games. The Giants knew them well because they played each other a whopping 21 times in spring training, including a barnstorming tour through the South before their seasons opened. Wertz hadn't joined Cleveland until he was traded from Baltimore in June, but the Giants had seen him in the spring, too, because the Orioles were part of the four-team Cactus League.

In the eighth inning of Game 1, Larry Doby, who integrated the American League three months after Jackie Robinson broke the color barrier in 1947, was on second base, and Al Rosen, who later became the Giants' general manager and built their 1989 World Series team, was on first. With no outs and a 2–2 score, Leo Durocher summoned a little left-hander named Don Liddle, whose lone batter that day was Wertz, a left-handed slugger who had three hits off right-hander Sal Maglie, including a two-run triple. Liddle featured an effective curve that produced ground balls, giving Mays further reason to creep in because he wanted a chance to throw out Doby at the plate, in the event of a single.

Liddle got ahead of Wertz one ball and two strikes, and catcher Wes Westrum signaled for an inside fastball to set up a curve with the ensuing pitch. But the fastball was delivered out over the plate, and Wertz smoked it to deep center, prompting Mays' celebrated toward-the-wall sprint, back-to-the-plate catch, and twirling, no-look throw that stunned the Indians and the crowd of 52,751 while establishing momentum for the Giants' four-game sweep.

We know it now as The Catch.

And we cannot overlook The Throw.

When Wertz hit that ball, I never doubted I would catch it. I was thinking I needed to get the ball back to the infield to prevent Cleveland from taking the lead. That's all I was thinking. I scored from second on fly balls like that. Easy. Doby was a very aggressive runner. He might be trying to tag and advance two bases. They told me he was halfway home and had to come back to second to tag up. I needed to keep him from scoring.

The ball was hit, and I ran toward the wall knowing I'm making the catch and thinking about how I'd get the ball back. I stopped in front of the wall and made a very quick U-turn. It was simple to me. You go back, you catch the ball, you spin, you turn, you throw it back to the infield. I don't like to exaggerate, but I was young and cocky enough to know I could catch any ball in the park. But the important thing was for the runners to stay on the bases. Doby got only one base, and Rosen went back to first.

The baseball world is blessed that the moment—a six-and-a-half-second sequence from Wertz's contact to Mays' release—was captured on black-and-white film, permitting generations of fans to witness a once-in-a-lifetime play that never will be duplicated. Big-league ballparks aren't Polo Grounds–sized anymore. The farthest to dead center in the majors is 420 feet at Detroit's Comerica Park. When Jack Brickhouse broadcast The Catch, he noted in his call the 483-foot marker in center at the back end of a recessed area and surmised with partner Russ Hodges that the ball must have traveled 460 feet.

That has been widely debated over the years. The play happened six decades before the arrival of Statcast, the technological tool that debuted in 2015 and uses cameras and radar to determine distances of

Willie Mays' famous World Series catch in 1954 is depicted in artist Thom Ross' series of life-sized paintings that were placed in front of the New York skyline. (Guy Watkins)

balls put in play. Bleachers were situated above and along both sides of the recessed area, and inside were steps up to the clubhouses and the Eddie Grant monument, which stood below the 483 marker and honored the former Giant killed in battle in World War I. Mays made the catch slightly to the right of dead center and in front of the large batter's eye (the wall that serves as the backdrop for hitters) that separated the field from the bleachers.

Longtime Giants broadcaster Jon Miller, a Polo Grounds historian who has a vast collection of Polo Grounds books and photos in his home office, reasons Wertz's ball traveled at least 450 feet.

"There wasn't much more room to go," Miller said. "Willie stopped on a dime, wheeled around, and heaved the throw back. If it's 483 to the memorial, I can't see the wall Willie was about to hit being any less than 460, and it could have been closer to 463 or 465. If that's correct, Willie would have caught that ball 450 to 455 feet from home plate. Using aerial shots, it's a good estimate that it was 18 to 20 feet from the front wall to the back wall. So I think it's a very safe assessment he's no closer than 450 when he caught that ball."

Author Arnold Hano, who was in the crowd that day and penned the critically acclaimed book *A Day in the Bleachers,* estimated the ball traveled 450 feet. Dodgers broadcaster Vin Scully, who knew the layout as well as anyone—he began attending games at the Polo Grounds as a child in the 1930s when he fell in love with Mel Ott, imitating his batting stance, high leg kick and all—suggested it might have been 440 feet, still a mighty poke. In the weekend of Scully's final career broadcast in 2016, fittingly at a Giants-Dodgers series in San Francisco, Mays dropped by his booth and engaged in a touching exchange. Scully told Mays, "I always remember Eddie Grant's monument at the foot of the clubhouse was 483. So that ball that you caught that Vic Wertz hit, that was probably 440, at least. I mean, that's how far out that was."

Perhaps no one ever will know exactly how far Wertz's ball sailed as we would now with Statcast, which could have calculated the metrics of the play, including Mays' jump, running speed, distance covered, and arm strength (in mph). His catch probability could have been determined based on the distance and direction he ran, the elapsed time, his proximity to the wall (to determine whether it was an impediment), and the ball's hang time.

A catch probability of zero to 25 percent gets five stars. All we had in 1951 was the eye test, but if Mays' play didn't warrant five stars, nothing did.

Unfortunately, Statcast can't judge the play based on the film. For starters, the film doesn't show Mays' location when the ball was hit. Or how far he ran. Even though it shows where the ball was caught, the exact spot would be an estimate. And even though it provides the time from the ball hitting bat to reaching glove, the film rate could be less than real time.

"There are a lot of unknowns there," said Tom Tango, senior data architect for MLB Advanced Media. "In order to figure out the distance covered, you have to know Willie's starting point. You can make the case that he had to cover 100 feet. Or 140 feet. That can be the difference between an easy catch and an impossible catch. But your ending point is a rough estimate, and your starting point is a blind estimate. Then you're taking the difference between these two estimated values. The uncertainty is just going to explode."

Sometimes it's okay not to know the exact data.

"There's something enjoyable with just letting it be the way it is," Tango said.

Whenever the play is brought up to Mays, his first thought is always the same, and that's what he expressed that day to Scully.

I tell everybody it's not the catch so much, it's the situation, getting the ball back to the infield.

Regardless of the distance of Wertz's clout, it would have been a home run in any of today's parks. It was the perfect environment for Mays because he had the speed to track down most any ball hit, the arm to throw from most any distance, and the ability to anticipate most any situation. "With all that ground to cover, I don't think people would have seen his true greatness if he hadn't played at the Polo Grounds," said Peter Magowan, who fell in love with Mays watching him as a nine-year-old at the Polo Grounds and in 1992 led a group that purchased the Giants, helping to prevent them from bolting San Francisco for Florida. Al Rosen, the runner forced to retreat to first base, said decades later, "I had a bad leg, a pulled hamstring, and I still would've scored, but he made the catch and set the tone for the Series. Nobody else could've made that play at that venue at that time. It was a catch for the ages."

Marv Grissom got the final two outs in the eighth, and the game went to the 10th when Mays walked and stole second to prompt the Indians to intentionally walk Hank Thompson. Dusty Rhodes hit a pinch walk-off homer, and the Giants won the opener 5–2. Epitomizing the unfairness of baseball and the wackiness of the Polo Grounds, on the day Wertz was robbed of extra bases on a ball hit halfway to the Harlem River, the game was won on a ball Rhodes barely popped over the right-field wall, a mere 260 feet from the plate.

World Series MVP awards weren't issued until the following year, but

Mays said there's no doubt the 1954 recipient would have been Rhodes, who pinch-hit for Monte Irvin in each of the first three games and finished the Series 4-for-6 with two homers and seven RBIs. Rhodes tied Game 2 with a pinch single and also homered in a 3–1 win. The Giants won the third game 6–2, again thanks to Rhodes, who hit a two-run single in the third. He wasn't needed in Game 4 as the Giants clinched with a 7–4 victory.

Mays hit .286 in four games, but The Catch was the defining moment of the Series and the standard by which all great catches have been measured. Those who witnessed it remained in awe through the years.

"I was in the bullpen when Willie made that catch. They needed an extra catcher to warm up the pitchers," recalled former teammate Joey Amalfitano, who was as close to Mays as anybody because the bullpen was in fair territory in right-center field. "I was just a young guy. I didn't know what the hell was going on. But I did know that when the ball was struck, Willie's body language indicated to me that this guy had the ball tracked, and what presence of mind to get the ball back to the infield so quickly. The good news is, every World Series, we get to see that play. In the clip, you can see him pivoting off his right foot, turning around, throwing the ball back to the middle of the infield and falling to the ground in position to do push-ups. Next time they show it, study it. It looks like he's doing push-ups. Fabulous."

Farther away in the Giants' dugout, pitcher Johnny Antonelli, who would start Game 2, also had confidence the catch would be made. "He tapped his glove. We knew whenever he tapped his glove, he was going to catch the ball. It didn't matter if it's hit 450 feet. This was a miraculous catch, perfect throw. Typical for Willie. I was 12–0 in the Polo Grounds that year before I finally got a loss. I let them hit it to center and then watched Willie run it down. He was amazing, the greatest I've seen. He could've played the whole outfield by himself. I really felt that way."

In his book, Arnold Hano chronicled with a vivid firsthand description his trek to the ballpark, the nuances of batting practice, the characters sitting nearby, and the famous play that inspired the project. Hano, then thirty-two, who paid $2.20 for a ticket, said he started writing *A Day in the Bleachers* three weeks after the World Series and tried to sell it as a magazine piece to *The New Yorker,* which rejected it. He turned it into a book and published it in 1955, and it's a highlight of his prominent career.

Hano sat in the bleachers a bit to the left of center field, nicely positioned to see all the particulars in the play: Liddle's misplaced fastball, Wertz's colossal swing, Rosen's and Doby's insecurity on the base paths, and, of course, the ball coming toward him and the Say Hey Kid chasing it down.

"You know what amazes me?" asked a ninety-six-year-old Hano. "When that ball was hit, the second it was hit, Willie turned and knew exactly where he was going to end up. How do these super athletes do that? I mean, he knew he would outrun that ball. It's just an incredible moment. I was in the perfect spot, a very lucky guy. I could've gone to a ballgame, and that ball could've landed behind him, and the Giants could've lost 4–2, and that would've been that. As luck would have it, I got up off my seat, my plank, and watched that ball coming. Well, the catch was pretty incredible, and then he whirled and made that great throw. He knew he was going to be throwing to second base to keep Rosen from advancing to second and stop Doby from trying to score from second. It was all in his head."

There's more to the story.

I played shallow anyway at the Polo Grounds, and now we've got Don Liddle coming in. People ask me how I play different hitters. It's not just the hitter, it's who's pitching. I was playing in. You could tell from the film. Because I ran a long way. Vic was hitting the ball hard that day. Still, I never thought a guy could hit it over my head. It didn't matter who's hitting. Wertz is a good hitter, but we needed to keep the game tied.

So I go back and make the catch. They say I tapped my glove. Usually when I do that, I got it. It's a matter of, "I could catch that." I threw the ball without looking because it's got to be quick. You've always got to be quick getting the ball back at the Polo Grounds.

You also see in the film no one came out for a cut. Alvin Dark and Davey Williams stayed in the infield. They knew I'd get it to 'em. I was told I threw a strike to Davey at second. I think the throw was the key to the play, and I think the play was the key to the whole World Series because if that ball gets past me, Cleveland has two runs in and Vic on third. Maybe we don't catch up.

Cleveland had a very good team, man. Four or five very good pitchers and many good hitters. Larry Doby, Al Smith, Bobby Avila, who won a batting title that year. Jim Hegan, the catcher. The infield was Rosen, George Strickland, Avila, and the guy who hit the ball I caught, Vic Wertz. I made other catches like that, but not all of them were televised or in the World Series.

If this was the crowning defensive moment in baseball history, surely it was the best in Mays' career, right? Wrong. Those who saw Mays the most say the World Series play doesn't compare with other illustrious highlights in his collection.

"The catch in the Polo Grounds was a masterpiece, but that wasn't his greatest catch," Vin Scully said in 2019, three years after retiring. "The greatest catch I saw was at Ebbets Field. The Dodgers were trailing by a run, and Bobby Morgan, a young third baseman from Oklahoma, came up and hit a ball in the gap in left-center. In those days, the Ebbets Field warning track was gravel and the wall concrete. It was a sinking liner, and in my mind, it would score two runs. But Willie runs as fast as he could and dives for it with his body parallel to the ground, fully stretched out. He catches the ball and literally bounces off the gravel and into the base of the wall, rolling over on his back with both hands on his chest. I'll never forget Henry Thompson, the left fielder for the Giants, walking over, bending down, taking the ball out of Willie's glove and showing everyone he made the catch. It was incredible."

This catch occurred April 18, 1952, eleven months after Mays' big-league debut and a few weeks before he entered the military. He preserved a 6–5 Giants lead by stranding two runners in the seventh inning. The Dodgers won in 12 on Andy Pafko's walk-off home run. Poor Andy Pafko. All that's remembered from the game is Mays sprawling across the warning track and landing on his belly with the ball in his glove.

Mays never liked to rank his catches and said he still stands by a clever line attributed to him from his playing days: "I don't rank 'em. I just catch 'em." He has been more revealing in recent years, and now it can be told that he not only puts the Morgan catch ahead of the Wertz catch but calls it the finest of his career.

That one was hard to explain because it happened so fast. You have to realize Ebbets Field was a small ballpark, and that ball was hit on a line over shortstop. I jump in the air to catch it and knock myself out when I hit the wall. When I came to, I can see Leo and Jackie. Leo wanted to see how I was doing, and Jackie wanted to see if I caught the ball. That was a good catch, better than the World Series catch. I believe my best catch.

Not that Morgan, from his home in Oklahoma, would disagree.

"Hanging curve up in the wheelhouse," Morgan recalled. "I understand the Vic Wertz catch was a piece of cake for Willie. He had that ball all the way. He's made hundreds of catches like that. I would say the ball he caught off me was better than the Vic Wertz catch. Jackie said it was the greatest catch he ever saw in his life. In fact, Jackie went out to see if Willie caught the ball or not."

Carl Erskine needn't be reminded. He pitched for the Dodgers that day and exited when Morgan pinch-hit. Had Morgan driven in the runs, the Dodgers would have taken the lead, and Erskine would have been in line for the win. It still irks him that he had a winning record against every National League club except the Giants and that he was denied that day by Mays.

"Bobby Morgan hits a shot up the alley in left-center. This had extra bases written all over it," Erskine said. "I'm counting it a win already, and out of nowhere comes Willie. He makes a headlong dive to catch the ball, and the inning's over. It cost me the game, but we got the win. They didn't film anything in those days. The Wertz catch, that was it, and you see it over and over again. You see how much room Willie had to run for the ball. At the Polo Grounds, he could run forever, and his arm was exceptional. It seemed like his instincts under all conditions were correct. Willie made plays over and over again that were unbelievable. Now, Willie never admitted until very recently that he thought the catch he made off Bobby Morgan was his best catch ever. I wrote Bobby Morgan a note: 'Willie finally admitted it. The game he stole from us, that was his best catch.'"

Erskine witnessed another gem in Willie's rookie year and in the early stages of the Giants' momentous surge to the 1951 pennant. On August 15, the Giants and Dodgers were tied 1–1 in the eighth inning at the Polo Grounds when Carl Furillo hit a long fly to right-center, between Mays and Don Mueller. Billy Cox tagged at third, and the Dodgers were about to pull ahead 2–1.

"It was going to be an extra-base hit," Erskine said. "You wouldn't believe Willie could catch it, but he did. Though that was sensational on its own, he just blindly threw in the direction of home plate, and he threw a strike. That was another play that was never filmed. If you were there, you were there. I was there, and both of them stand out for me, and both of them were better than the Wertz catch."

Roger Angell was there, too. He's as impressed today as he was in 1951 when he watched the play as a fan in a seat behind first base. Mays caught Furillo's ball and twirled to his left, as if he were performing a pirouette, before firing home.

"This was when he first arrived, and he was just amazing," said the ninety-eight-year-old Angell, who saw Babe Ruth in his prime. "I remember Willie running full tilt and turning around in midair and throwing the guy out at home plate on a fly. Everybody was saying, 'Oh my God, did you see that?' Even the Dodgers, coming out of their dugout, were saying, 'Did you see that? Did you see that?' Willie was the best. The best player ever."

The throw beat Cox at the plate to complete an inning-ending double play, and Mays singled to begin a two-run rally in the bottom half of the inning. The Giants triumphed 3–1 and went on to win 39 of their final 47 games, culminated by Bobby Thomson's pennant-winning homer off Ralph Branca.

That was the year Leo said I gotta play line to line and catch everything I could get. Mueller was behind me, and I knew once I caught the ball, I didn't have enough time to set my feet to throw. I knew they'd send the runner. The Dodgers were always aggressive like that. I caught the ball and threw all the way through to the catcher, Wes Westrum. Past Whitey Lockman, who was lined up on the infield. The ball didn't touch the ground. I had to make that play because that boy could run, Billy Cox.

Mays made another memorable catch the same year at Pittsburgh's Forbes Field, where the wall stood 457 feet from the plate. Rocky Nelson hit a bases-loaded laser that appeared to be sailing over Mays' head, but Willie caught it on the run. Barehanded. Later in life, both Irvin and Joe Garagiola, a Pirate that season, said it was superior to The Catch.

A few years before his 2016 death, Garagiola visited Mays in the Giants' spring training clubhouse and, with all the players out on the field, shared stories and laughs that were unforgettable for the lucky handful of people in the room. It's a little-known fact that Garagiola witnessed the Wertz catch from a window in the Giants' center-field clubhouse. He had been acquired that September but played only five games and wasn't on the World Series roster, so he watched through the window and clearly is seen in some photographs of The Catch. Garagiola kept a copy of a photo autographed by Mays with this inscription to the former catcher, "I'm glad you didn't call that pitch."

Garagiola favored the Nelson catch: "That one really sticks out for me." A left-handed batter, Nelson hit a deep fly that tailed away from Mays' glove side, so he snared it with his right hand. Branch Rickey, by then the Pirates' general manager, was in attendance and famously called it the finest catch he ever saw. Irvin ranked it No. 2 behind the Morgan catch.

"Willie ran and ran and ran and got to where he thought the ball would fall," Irvin said. "But the wind drifted around to his right. So instead of moving his glove across his body, he reached out and caught the damn thing barehanded. On the way in, Durocher says, 'Let's give Willie the silent treatment, have a little fun with him.' Willie gets to the dugout, and nobody says anything to him. Willie finally says, 'Hey, Leo, ain't you going to say something?' Leo says, 'What do you want me to say?' 'Well, I thought I made a pretty good catch out there.' So Durocher says, 'I missed it. What you have to do is go out the next inning and do it all over again.'"

Mays laughed when hearing Irvin's account of the story.

Yeah, that's what happened. Rocky sliced it. I was running for that ball but couldn't get my arm far enough out to catch it, so I reached out with my bare hand and caught it. I got to the dugout, and no one was saying anything. "Leo, you see what I did?" He said, "Go out and do it again, and then I'll congratulate you."

Mays also stole a two-run home run from Ted Williams in the 1955 All-Star Game in Milwaukee, backpedaling to the fence in right-center and perfectly timing his leap. The catch prevented the American League from extending its 5–0, seventh-inning lead, and Mays led off the bottom half with a single and scored the first run for the National League, which rallied to win in 12 innings on Stan Musial's game-ending homer. In retrospect, Mays downplays the Williams robbery as somewhat routine.

That wasn't that hard. It was a high fly ball. Look at it again. He hit it way up there. I caught it as it was going over the fence. But it was the All-Star Game, so they had to find something to write about, I guess.

There was no downplaying a catch Mays made at Candlestick Park less than a month before his thirty-ninth birthday. Cincinnati's Bobby Tolan hit a ball above the cyclone fence in right-center that Bobby Bonds was chasing, but at the last moment, Mays dashed to the scene, used his left foot to brace himself against the fence and leap over the 375-foot marker to make the catch over Bonds. Neither called for the ball. It wasn't that type of play. It wasn't known if either could snag it. Both extended their gloves above the fence, and it was Mays who came down with it.

The players collided and tumbled to the ground, still tangled. Mays fell on Bonds and lost his breath, and Bonds reached into Mays' glove, pulled out the ball, and showed it to the umpires. The catch saved the game for Gaylord Perry, who pitched all nine innings in a 2–1 win.

I knew Tolan could pull the ball, so I was able to get a good jump when he hit it in the gap. The only question was how I would catch the ball. We both went up for it. Bobby fell, I fell. I felt his knee in my stomach,

and I was out a couple of seconds. I think that was just as good as the catch in the World Series.

The game was televised nationally on NBC's Saturday *Game of the Week*. Bob Costas hadn't joined the broadcast crew by then but recalls being mesmerized with Mays' athleticism as the play unfolded. "I remember thinking, 'Wait a minute. This guy was thirty-eight, thirty-nine years old,'" Costas said. "It's not as storied as the World Series catch, but it was just a phenomenal play."

The World Series catch, though admittedly not on top of Mays' list, always will be the play for which he's revered.

"He did make better, and there were several other plays he regards as better," Costas said, "but you have to consider the stage. It's in the early days of the World Series being televised. The Polo Grounds was so massive that when the ball left the bat and people were watching on a black-and-white TV, it just didn't seem possible that someone could cover that much ground. As the ball left the bat, people were thinking, 'Is this a triple or is this an inside-the-park home run?' At that time, the play was a revelation, and it was on the biggest stage, the World Series.

"When a player is iconic, he needs a signature moment. We see (Hank) Aaron in our mind's eye between second and third when he hit his 715th. We see (Mickey) Mantle hitting the ball off the facade in Yankee Stadium. (Sandy) Koufax pitched four no-hitters, but it's the perfect game with Vin Scully's call that really sets him in the mind's eye. Ted Williams homering in his last at-bat. Those things capture the imagination more than raw statistics. Willie had many signature moments. But if you had to pick one, that's the one."

Mays made The Catch with a Rawlings glove, about which a heartwarming tale has surfaced. In the summer of 1955, on a team flight to St. Louis, Mays was sitting with pitcher Rubén Gómez in front of Liddle and Liddle's six-year-old son, Craig. As the story goes, the boy was talking to his father about playing Little League the following year and needing a glove, and the next day in the Sportsman's Park clubhouse, Willie gave the wide-eyed kid one of his gloves—the same one he used to catch the ball hit by Wertz. It was expendable because Willie had broken in a new glove. So the man who caught the ball handed over his glove to the son of the man who pitched the ball. Rather than holding on to it as a keepsake, Mays thought it was more important to give it to a kid who simply needed a glove.

At first, it was too big to use for the young boy, so he stashed it away until he was an older Little Leaguer and it became a better fit. These were the days when game-used gear wasn't valued as it is now, and Craig used the glove to play ball, left it out in the rain, all the things a kid that age would do with a glove. As the years went by, the glove was stored in a closet in his family home in Salem, Illinois. In adulthood, Craig realized the glove should be shared with the public, not hidden in a home. So he notified the Hall of Fame, which wasn't sold at first this was the glove used for The Catch. Once Mays confirmed he gave the glove to the Liddles, the Hall had its verification and was elated to include it in its Cooperstown collection.

Don Liddle died in 2000, and Craig Liddle died in 2010. Both of cancer. Craig left with his wife, Terry, extensive notes about the glove in case someone inquired for, say, a Willie Mays book. The glove is on loan to the Hall with one stipulation. It must remain on display and can't be rotated in and out. Otherwise, it must be offered back to the Liddles.

"It's quite an honor to be the caretaker and make sure it's out there where people can see it. I think that's important," said Terry Liddle, who like her husband was a teacher. "Right now, it's where Craig wanted it. When Willie gave Craig the glove, he told him, 'You take care of it, and it will take care of you.'"

Selling the glove is not an option for the family, though it could fetch a small fortune. "If we sold it, could you be guaranteed that whoever bought it would share it publicly? No," Terry Liddle said. "There's a lot of people who'd do the same thing, but a lot who'd put it in their own collection. That's not what Craig wanted. Willie's affection for kids was evident back in the '50s when he gave that glove to Craig. 'Here's a kid that needs something, and I have something to share with him.' That showed his good heart even then."

The glove has been on display in Cooperstown since 1992, a blessing because it's an extreme rarity for the Hall to accept items on loan. But this is Willie's glove.

"I'm not sure there are other defensive moments in the history of the game that are quite as famous or iconic as that one," curator Erik Strohl said. "In this case, the glove is of the utmost importance. It's really cool we're able to share it."

It often has been reported and accepted as fact that after Mays ran to the deepest depths of the Polo Grounds to make The Catch, Don Liddle walked off the mound wisecracking, "Well, I got my man." According to the Liddles, that's not quite what happened. "Craig's dad was always bothered by that statement," Terry Liddle said. "He said he would never have said that on the field during a game. I understand he said something like that later in the locker room after the game."

Much of Mays' career, including most of his best defensive work from his early years, wasn't captured on film, but he's comforted that this generation, especially the younger crowd born long after his playing days, can see significant footage from his career, including The Catch and The Throw, and absorb the everlasting stories from the Golden Era in which he and others flourished.

Mays doesn't have any of his old bats or gloves handy and donated some of his many artifacts to the Hall of Fame over the years, though the treasured glove he used in the 1954 World Series took a different course to Cooperstown, thanks to Craig Liddle. For Mays, that's the best of both worlds. It's on exhibit for all to see, and it was a useful resource for a lad during childhood.

I gave bats and gloves to kids all the time. After a while, what did I need them for? If it made a kid smile, that was better than me holding on to it.

8.

HONOR YOUR PEERS

The Story of Willie, Mickey, and the Duke

"Friends can mean everything. Have fun and laugh with them. You want to keep them close."

—*Willie Mays*

THE BALL WENT up, a high fly to right-center field at Yankee Stadium. When it came down, three Hall of Fame center fielders intersected forever. Willie Mays hit it. Joe DiMaggio caught it. Mickey Mantle regretted it.

The 1951 season marked a momentous changing of the guard in New York, baseball's epicenter. It was Mays' and Mantle's first year in the majors and DiMaggio's last. DiMaggio was winding down a legendary thirteen-year career that featured a remarkable ten World Series, nine that went in the Yankees' favor, and Mays and Mantle were beginning their concurrent paths to superstardom and front-row seats at Cooperstown.

All three suited up for the 1951 World Series, and Mays hit a seemingly routine fly ball to open the fifth inning of Game 2, in between DiMaggio and Mantle, the interim right fielder who would move to center once DiMaggio was gone. The ensuing moments were anything but routine. Manager Casey Stengel had told Mantle to go for anything he could because of DiMaggio's bad heel. But DiMaggio, playing center field, called for the ball, and Mantle deferred. Naturally. As any rookie would in the presence of the great DiMaggio. Mantle went from a full sprint to a sudden stop and collapsed as he caught his spikes on a drainage cover.

Mantle sprawled in pain on the outfield grass, his right leg bent gruesomely, and was carried off on a stretcher. His knee was blown out. He never again played pain-free.

Mickey told me the rule was, if Joe called for the ball, it didn't matter where it was, get out of the way. Joe called for it, and Mickey stepped in a hole trying to get out of the way rather than trying to get the ball. They had a drainage system in right field. They shouldn't have had it exposed like they did. They didn't even try to cover it up. In those days, they tried to cut corners. It was unfortunate.

These days, Mantle would have benefited from advanced surgical techniques and undoubtedly been properly diagnosed with an MRI exam, undergone arthroscopic surgery to fix the extensive damage to his ligaments and cartilage, and followed up with physical therapy and rehabilitation to return to the field near 100 percent. In those days, Mantle was diagnosed with a sprained knee and taken by his father, Mutt, to a nearby hospital, where they watched the rest of the World Series, won by the Yankees in six games.

Mantle underwent several surgeries over the years, none of which resolved all the problems, which included osteomyelitis, a bone infection he had in his ankle and shin since childhood. Author Jane Leavy, in her 2010 biography of Mantle, *The Last Boy*, reveals through research and the help of modern medicine that Mantle sustained a torn anterior cruciate ligament, torn medial collateral ligament, and torn meniscus. Miraculously, he played 18 seasons and hit 536 home runs, all but 13 coming after the disastrous injury in 1951. He still had incredible speed and stole 153 bases, but injuries and alcohol abuse took their toll and left the baseball world forever wondering what Mantle could have accomplished as a ballplayer with a clean and healthy life, a "what if" for the ages.

As is, the switch-hitting Mantle was one of the elite all-around players in history. He won the 1956 Triple Crown by hitting .353 with 52 home runs and 130 RBIs. Like Mays, he hit .300 10 times and 50 homers twice.

After DiMaggio retired, Mantle permanently patrolled center field at Yankee Stadium while Mays was across the Harlem River roaming the Polo Grounds. Their lives were intertwined from childhood with both growing up in the South during the Great Depression, Mays in Alabama, Mantle in Oklahoma, and both raised by fathers who worked in the mills, were exceptional ballplayers, and taught their sons the game. Both prodigies were born in 1931, Mantle five months after Mays. Both were given children's names, perfectly appropriate considering they were born to play a kid's game. Both were under six feet, both under 200 pounds. But with outstanding power. When both arrived in 1951, each scuffled at first but showed glimpses of five-tool prominence that was on display the next two decades.

And they were pals. One white, one black, and so much in common. From less-than-humble backgrounds to the top of the heap of New York baseball. They played the same position in different leagues but in the same town and against each other in All-Star Games, barnstorming tours, and two World Series. After their careers, both were suspended for their associations with Atlantic City casinos, a decision by Commissioner Bowie Kuhn that didn't warrant much praise or boost his legacy. During their playing days and after, the more Mays and Mantle came across each other, the closer they got and the more they would understand each other, perhaps like no one else could.

We were two kids from the South. We played together and enjoyed each other. He was one of those guys, if I needed something, whatever it was, I called him, and before I could put down the phone, it was at my house. Same with me. If he wanted something, he called me. "I need this, I need that." "Okay, you got it." We had a lot of fun together, so many laughs.

Mickey was funny, man. We were like kids whenever we were together. It was a good time in New York with the three clubs, the three center fielders. All of New York would talk about us, Willie, Mickey, and the Duke.

Willie Mays and Mickey Mantle had much in common beyond their five-tool talents. They were born in the same year and played the same position in the same town. (Collection of Rick Swig)

Otherwise known as the great debate. Willie, Mickey, and the Duke was more like Willie, Mickey, *or* the Duke, and legitimate arguments were heard from Manhattan to Brooklyn to the Bronx to everywhere else fans weighed in on the uniquely gifted trifecta. Duke Snider was five years older than the others and already an established All-Star with the Dodgers when Mays and Mantle arrived.

The Duke of Flatbush was one of the iconic Boys of Summer and hit .309 with 42 homers and a career-high 136 RBIs in 1955, the only year the Dodgers won a World Series in Brooklyn, thanks largely to Snider, who hit .320 with four homers to help sink the Yankees in seven games. He's the Dodgers' all-time homers leader with 389.

Duke came first. Then Mickey and I came along at the same time. We always tried to make each other feel good, though sometimes Mickey would kid Duke. "Hey, Duke, you're not getting paid what we're getting paid." We'd all laugh. Mickey said, "Willie, you talk about me, I'll talk about you." And Duke said, "What about me?" We had fun with Duke. It was a good relationship. We respected each other. Just good guys. We had fun.

The baseball community, at least off the field, can be a far cry from the cutthroat business world in which competitors try to crush each other without guilt or remorse. Willie, Mickey, and the Duke got along with one another while representing three teams vying for superiority in the same market.

We later did card shows together, and they didn't always want to pay Duke what they paid us. I said, "No, no, no. It don't work that way, sir. You gotta give him the same you give us." Mick says, "That's right." We got it. Duke made some good money with us. In baseball, you respect the team you play, the guys on the other side. That's how the game works. Play to win but appreciate the opposition. They're trying to make a living and get paid just like you.

Mays regularly crossed paths with Snider as National League foes and squared off with Mantle in the World Series in 1951 and 1962, the Yankees besting the Giants both times. Mays and Mantle were opponents in a whopping 18 All-Star Games while Mays teamed with Snider in four All-Star Games.

After 16 years as a Dodger and one as a Met, Snider played his final 91 games for the 1964 Giants, a thirty-seven-year-old playing out the string with the rivals. Duke served mostly as a pinch-hitter. When he was in the lineup, it was as a left fielder or right fielder.

He came to me and said, "Hey, you gotta play left and center now." I said, "What do you mean I gotta play left and center?" He laughed and said, "I may not be able to move." Duke was a funny guy. He was kind of quiet. He wasn't loud like Mickey and me.

Mays and Mantle converged in late 1959 for a memorable made-for-TV event, the original Home Run Derby, the precursor to the melodramatic extravaganza that's now part of All-Star festivities. It was filmed at a Pacific Coast League ballpark in Los Angeles called Wrigley Field, named after chewing gum mogul William Wrigley, Jr., as was Wrigley Field in Chicago. Back then, Home Run Derby featured twenty-six syndicated installments that were seen in black-and-white and hosted by announcer Mark Scott, who provided play-by-play of the batter's swings while playfully conversing with the opposing contestant.

It was a simple nine-inning format involving the game's top sluggers, including Frank Robinson, Ernie Banks, Hank Aaron, Gil Hodges, Al Kaline,

Eddie Mathews, and Snider, nineteen in all. Mays and Mantle went one-on-one in the first episode.

Oh, man, I had a big lead on Mickey. I hit four out in the first inning. I had him 8–2. The producers were telling me I've got to slow down for a minute. Slow down? I messed around, and Mickey caught me. He was killing the ball. He beat me 9–8. I said, "You cheatin' SOBs." They all wanted me to slow down. We all laughed. We were getting $2,000 if we won, $1,000 if we lost. That was pretty good for that time.

Mays and Mantle each appeared on the show five times, Mantle winning $10,000 and Mays $8,000 to finish behind Aaron, who won $13,500, including a $500 bonus for hitting three straight homers.

In those days for pro ballplayers, even the superstars, every dollar counted. Free agency didn't arrive until the 1970s, and six-figure contracts were extremely rare. DiMaggio made that much. Ted Williams and Stan Musial did, too. Mays' three favorite players growing up. Now Mays was entering the $100,000 club. Before the 1963 season, Mantle signed for $100,000, Mays for $105,000.

We had a little friendly thing going. If I hit 49 home runs, Mickey would want to hit 50. He'd want to make a dollar more than me. He'd say, "Hurry up and sign your contract so I can get my damn raise." We didn't do anything against each other. He was such a good guy. Most of the time, we just laughed when we were together.

Over the years, Mays and Mantle appeared in commercials and struck mutual endorsement deals, and one of the goofiest and unlikeliest in advertising history came in the early 1980s and involved both appearing in blue bonnets while eating corn on the cob and singing the praises of Blue Bonnet margarine, one of the most recognizable commercialized jingles of the time and performed by many of the day's celebrities.

In retrospect, the gig was ridiculous, but it paid a few bucks and was a blast. Plus, if heavyweight champ Joe Frazier agreed to peddle the product while wearing a bonnet, who'd second-guess Mays and Mantle? Mays proudly hangs a picture from the filming on his wall.

"Everything's better with Blue Bonnet on it." Wow. It seemed like it took us four or five hours to do four lines. I told Mickey, "Man, speak up, speak up." Okay, let's do it again. And again. "Everything's better with Blue Bonnet on it." If you were there, you'd be cracking up. We were just two dummies. We didn't know what the hell we were doing. They were paying us. That's all we knew.

It was a sign of the times. Not only were salaries limited because of owners' stranglehold on players, so, too, were pensions. Ballplayers had to fend for themselves after their playing days and accept odd jobs. Even the legends.

In 1979, Mays found a well-paying gig as a goodwill ambassador at Bally's Park Place Casino Hotel in Atlantic City, a ten-year contract for $100,000 annually, the beginning of a twenty-six-year relationship. But just months after Mays was inducted into the Hall of Fame, Kuhn suspended him and prohibited him from taking any salaried job in baseball. The industry that Mays not only dominated but enriched was turning its back on him even though gambling was legal in Atlantic City and licensed by the state and Mays' casino contract forbade him from wagering at his job site, where there was no sports betting.

In 1983, Mantle was hired by another Atlantic City outfit, Del Webb's Claridge Casino Hotel, and Kuhn suspended him, too. Kuhn argued that he didn't want two of the game's greats exposed to the misdeeds of gambling, though their duties involved little more than hobnobbing, playing golf with clients, and appearing at charity events. It's how they made their living.

"I can understand Bowie Kuhn was trying very hard to protect the best interests of baseball," Fay Vincent, commissioner from 1989 to 1992, says now. "Bowie thought it looked bad and reflected badly on baseball. But I think there's a certain amount of hypocrisy with all the history on gambling."

Kuhn didn't reprimand Yankees owner George Steinbrenner or Pirates owner John Galbreath for their connections with horse racing, an obvious case of double standards. Decades later, Major League Baseball cut a deal with DraftKings, a daily fantasy sports company, while teams began striking sponsorship deals with Native American tribes that run casinos. In the spring of 2018, the Supreme Court ruled that states could offer legalized sports wagering. Six months later, Major League Baseball announced an $80-million, four-year agreement with MGM Resorts International as its authorized gaming operator.

My wife, Mae, and I go to Bowie, and I tell him, "Bowie, I have a contract here that says I cannot gamble in Atlantic City. I'm not going to do it anyway, it'll hurt baseball." He says, "Well if you stay with it, you're out of baseball." I say, "Bowie, you mean to tell me after all the things I did in baseball, you're gonna throw me out?" I was upset. I didn't want to say too much. If I did, I knew I'd be in more trouble. I said, "C'mon, Mae, let's go." I don't think Bowie understood. He thought if he put us out, he'd look like a big guy. It went the other way around.

Enter Peter Ueberroth, the highly successful organizer of the 1984 Olympics in Los Angeles, who replaced Kuhn in late 1984. One of Ueberroth's first duties as commissioner was reexamining the Mays and Mantle suspensions. It didn't take long to reinstate them in a March 1985 announcement that served as a public relations boost for baseball and reprieve for Mays and Mantle, who still weren't permitted to be involved in gaming operations or promoting gambling.

A *Sports Illustrated* cover showed Ueberroth standing behind Mays and Mantle with the headline screaming, "WELCOME HOME!" Mays has that on his wall, too.

We both met with Peter individually. Mickey was saying, "I don't give a damn about getting back." I said, "Shut the hell up. I gotta get back in there." I know he was happy when they let us back in. Peter did good things by me and Mickey.

Ueberroth grew up in the Bay Area in the 1950s and went to San Jose State on a water polo scholarship. Once the Giants moved to San Francisco in 1958, he was well aware of Mays' exploits at Seals Stadium and Candlestick Park.

That, he now says, had nothing to do with his decision to rescind the ban. Nor did his association with then–Giants owner Bob Lurie, whom he befriended in 1981 when partnering with him in Pebble Beach at the Bing Crosby Pro-Am golf tournament. The friendship led Lurie to recommend Ueberroth to his fellow owners.

"Coming from the West Coast, I was obviously a fan and somebody who respected very much the way Willie played the game," Ueberroth said. "He was effortless when he ran to the fence at full speed and caught the ball. He provided fans with excitement because he cared a lot about the game. Every play, he gave his all."

While watching Mays play ball, Ueberroth couldn't have predicted one day he'd become commissioner and bring him and Mantle back into the game.

"Early on, I looked into this involvement, and frankly it was in my view inexcusable to ban these two players," Ueberroth said. "Pretty much all they did was go to golf tournaments. Baseball didn't provide pensions for either of them. It was a very easy and quick decision.

"I wanted to make sure it got attention because when they got punished, it got great attention by the press. It was a matter of exonerating them. I thought it was important the public knew about it, not just that they were forgiven but that they never should have in any way been given that kind of punishment. It was outrageous."

In 1986, a year after Mays was reinstated, the Giants took advantage of the opportunity to give him a front-office job as a special assistant, his first official gig in baseball since he last worked for the Mets in 1979, before the suspension. By then, Al Rosen, who had plenty of associations with Mays—he also had worked at Bally's and was stuck on base when Mays made his famous World Series catch—was the Giants' general manager.

Bob Lurie called me and said, "Hey man, it's time for you to come back home." It made me feel good. I needed to be back. The Giants are my family.

So what's the answer to the eternal question: Willie, Mickey, or the Duke? The Say Hey Kid, the Mick, or the Duke of Flatbush? Volumes have been written. Numbers have been crunched. Arguments have been ongoing. The debate started in 1951, the first year all three suited up in New York, and forever will be disputed in the annals of baseball lore.

"Great, great debate," said Peter Magowan, who watched Mays as a kid, only to become a Giants owner in the 1990s. "The guy who suffers is Snider, who was a great ballplayer, hit 40 home runs five years in a row, a wonderful defensive outfielder. I saw him make spectacular catches, and he benefited from being the only left-handed hitter in the Dodgers' lineup. But we all thought he was the third best center fielder in New York. Not everyone thought Willie was the best. I did. One reason, he was a much better base runner than Mantle."

Snider's supporters refer to a magnificent four-year stretch when the disputes in the boroughs were raging, from 1954 to 1957, from the time Mays returned from the service to the final year on the East Coast for the Giants and Dodgers.

Mays was MVP in 1954, Mantle in 1956 and 1957. In 1955, Snider finished second in the MVP voting to teammate Roy Campanella. During the four years, all three center fielders batted above .300 while averaging between 38 and 41 homers and 104 and 115 RBIs. The Giants, Dodgers, and Yankees were champions in back-to-back-to-back years. Snider didn't run like Mays and Mantle, obviously, but over those years, he was no less a hitter.

Once the Dodgers moved to Los Angeles, Snider's power numbers dramatically tailed off. He was in his early thirties. Similarly, Mantle's last big year was 1964, at age thirty-two, as health issues, whether they were on-field or self-inflicted, took their toll. Mays' long career was a difference-maker. He won his second MVP award at thirty-four. When he was forty, he hit 18 homers and led the league in walks and on-base percentage, the only year Mays drew at least 100 walks.

While Mantle struck out a lot more (17.3 percent of plate appearances compared with Mays' 12.2 percent), Mantle walked far more (17.5 percent to Mays' 11.7 percent). Mantle drew 100-plus walks in 10 seasons, which

In the 1950s, New York was blessed with three Hall of Fame center fielders. The Giants featured Willie Mays; the Dodgers had Duke Snider. (William Jacobellis/Kidwiler Collection/Diamond Images)

helps explain his .421 career on-base percentage. Since Mantle retired, only Barry Bonds and Joey Votto (through 2019) had higher career OBPs. Mays' was .384.

It's a reason why some advanced stats are kinder to Mantle. Both he and Mays finished with a .557 slugging percentage while Mantle had a higher OPS (on-base percentage plus slugging percentage), .977 to .941. Mantle also was an excellent bunter and hit into fewer double plays (113 to Mays' 251) and stole bases with a slightly higher success rate (80 percent to Mays' 77 percent), though Mays stole far more bags (338 to 153).

Author and historian Bill James, godfather of the modern analytic movement, uses his own Win Shares metric to calculate a player's worth and determined Mantle's peak seasons were more impactful than Mays'. While Mays' high for a season in Win Shares was 43, Mantle had seasons with Win Shares of 51, 49, and 48. In fact, James concluded two other center fielders also had superior peak seasons: Ty Cobb (48, 47, 46, 45, and 44) and Tris Speaker (51 and 45).

"At the same time," James said, "if the issue is 'Who is the greater player?,' there is no doubt that Mays was a greater player over the course of his career than Mantle or Speaker, and I would also rate him ahead of Cobb. I think most people would. What is remarkable about Mays is that he is *so* close to the top of the scale in so many different areas. But the *most* remarkable of those is consistency."

James pointed out the gap in Win Shares between Mays' best season and 15th best season isn't large and is significantly tinier than the gaps between the first and 15th seasons in the careers of Mantle, Speaker, and Cobb.

"What I am saying, without the numbers, is that Willie Mays' best season is . . . every year," James said. "Just pick one. They're all great. Whereas Mantle had a few absolutely tremendous seasons, Mays performed at the top of his game from the beginning of his career to the end in a way that only a few other players ever have. The Mantle pattern is actually the common one. Most great players have a few years that stick out, and then in other years they have injuries or other issues.

"That's true of Ted Williams or Barry Bonds or Joe Morgan or George Brett or Roberto Clemente or Frank Robinson or most other great players. There are only a few guys like Mays who were just great every year—Mays, Musial, and Aaron, really. I'm not sure there is a fourth one for that group. That's what makes Mays, in my mind, pretty clearly the greatest center fielder of all time."

Wins Above Replacement, a popular modern metric that measures a player's offensive, defensive, and baserunning contributions against a replacement-level player's, is figured somewhat differently by Baseball Reference, FanGraphs, and Baseball Prospectus. Regardless, a 10-plus WAR season is extremely rare, just 60 in history, according to Baseball Reference, and Mays had six, twice as many as Mantle. Mays' best stretch via WAR in seven straight seasons topped Mantle's, 70.5 to 64.3, and the 10-year comparison showed a much wider margin of 96.9 to 83.5.

From 1954 to 1968, Mantle's swan song, Mays had better WAR numbers in 11 of 15 years, and Mays' career WAR—third all time behind Babe Ruth and Barry Bonds according to FanGraphs, fifth all time according to Baseball Reference, which ranks pitchers Walter Johnson and Cy Young in the top four—was significantly higher than Mantle's and more than double Snider's.

"That's three good ones," former Yankees second baseman Bobby Richardson said of Mays, Mantle, and Snider. "I'd vote for Mickey. Mays can do everything Mantle could do, but Mantle hit home runs from both sides of the plate. Mays, that play against Cleveland in the World Series, was the best play I've ever seen. All three of them were tremendous defensive players, and all were team leaders. When they played well, the Yankees, Dodgers, and Giants won. I remember '62, Mantle missed 39 games, and we did not have a good record (20–19) without him. All three of those guys were winners."

Another Mantle teammate, pitcher Ralph Terry, said, "When I came up, I thought Mickey was the greatest thing I ever saw. If he had two good legs . . . well, he might've spent a few years in the Navy. You look at Willie (who did serve nearly two years in the military), he had the all-around ability and could play center field and run the bases. He might have been the best all-around player of our era."

Dennis Minogue favored Mays. Dennis Minogue? He's a former minor-league pitcher who took up a music career, changed his name to Terry Cashman, and wrote "Talkin' Baseball," the popular 1981 recording featuring the three center fielders that heightened the debate. Cashman grew up a few miles from the Polo Grounds in Washington Heights, and his lyrics revealed his allegiance: "Me, I always loved Willie Mays. Those were the days." The song ended, "Willie, Mickey, and the Duke. Say hey, say hey, say hey."

"He could do everything," Cashman says now. "I was at the Polo Grounds when he hit his first home run off Warren Spahn, over the roof in left field. I came to be a big fan. My whole family were Giants fans, except for my sister Kathy, a Dodger fan, a rebel. I was old enough to remember Bobby Thomson's home run and Willie coming up in '51 and being Rookie of the Year. I was ten years old. He came back from the Army and was the star of the '54 Giants. As the song says, I love Willie Mays and did throughout his career and still rooted for the Giants when they left and went to San Francisco.

"All three of them, Willie, Mickey, and Duke, really loved the song, and all loved being mentioned in the company of the other two, and all were very, very nice to me, very respectful."

In interviews late in life, Mantle said he had as much ability as Mays when healthy but called Mays the better player. Mays, who savored their relationship, heaped constant praise on Mantle.

Mickey could do a lot of things. He could hit, man. And he could run. Mickey and Vada Pinson, the kid from Cincinnati, the center fielder, those were the two fastest guys I saw when I came along. I had to tell Mickey, "Man, you can't beat me throwing." He could beat me hitting long balls. He didn't hit as many home runs, but he could hit a ball a long way. He almost hit a ball out of Yankee Stadium. He was so strong, a little heavier than I was. He had power from both sides. I'd hit the ball a couple of rows over the wall. He'd hit them above the bleachers. You didn't see people running faster or hitting the ball farther than Mickey.

Other factors are weighed in the conversation. Mays was a better defender and base runner with more durability and longevity. Mays had better instincts in the field and on the bases and got better jumps, though Mantle's knee issues always must be mentioned in this context.

Mays played at the Polo Grounds, where center field and the power alleys were so far away that they were a blur, and at Candlestick Park, where the cold and wind were not hitters' best friends. Also, Mays played in the National League, which not only was first to integrate but far more quickly filled its rosters with African-American and Latin players than the American League. Mays was facing a deeper level of competition.

"It's very rarely talked about, but one of the great undernoted stories of that era was that the National League was quite a lot better than the American League. That's been demonstrated pretty effectively. The National League's dominance in All-Star Games was not a coincidence," said Rob

Neyer, a prominent statistical analyst and author. "For me, the Mays-Mantle comparison isn't even that close. It's been argued, probably by me at some point, that Mantle still wins the peak comparison over six or seven years, but now I don't think even that's true. Mays was essentially better than Mantle for all the years."

One obvious difference was their nightlife. Mays didn't drink. Mantle drank up a storm and admitted in retirement that he wasted his colossal talent and that his alcoholism shortened his career. Mantle started drinking shortly after his rookie year, after his dad died of Hodgkin's disease at age thirty-nine. It was an easy escape for Mantle, and he was a heavy drinker the next forty-two years. Because the men in the Mantle family died young, he reasoned, he was going to live life to its fullest. Binges with teammates Billy Martin, Whitey Ford, Hank Bauer, and Moose Skowron were legendary and cost Mantle dearly in his career and life.

The Yankees had a reputation for not doing anything wrong on the field. Off the field was different. Mickey and Billy, three or four of them ran around together. They used to go to the Copacabana in New York. Those guys had good times, man. Me, I couldn't hang with those guys. They were in a different league anyway. But it got the best of Mickey. It was wonderful when he stopped drinking. He seemed to find peace. I was proud of him.

Mantle checked himself into the Betty Ford Center in January 1994 and completed treatment. His son, Billy, died at thirty-six that March, but Mantle was said to have remained sober. He received a liver transplant in June 1995 and established a foundation to promote organ donations. He also made amends with his estranged wife, Merlyn, and spent many of his final hours praying with Bobby Richardson, a devout Christian. In August, Mantle died of cancer. He was sixty-three. At the funeral, Bob Costas delivered the eulogy, Richardson the sermon.

Before Mickey passed, he called me in Palm Springs and said, "Oh, man, I don't know how long I'm going to be here, I just wanted to thank you

for all the things we did together." He just got out of the hospital before going back in. We didn't talk long. We would've started crying. I said, "Mickey thank you very much, man." He said, "We really had some good times together, man." Mickey was my good friend. He was right. They were good times.

9.

WHEN LIFE THROWS YOU A CURVE, GO WITH THE PITCH

The Story of the Polo Grounds and Candlestick Park

"Life takes you many places. Make the best of any situation.
Complaining doesn't help. You've gotta adjust and make it work
for you."

—*Willie Mays*

WILLIE MAYS PLAYED in two of the weirdest baseball facilities in history.

The Polo Grounds, which wasn't built for baseball.

And Candlestick Park, which never should have been built for baseball.

Or football. Or soccer. Or the pope's visit. Or the final Beatles concert. Or any other scheduled event during the four decades that the Giants made the concrete edifice their home.

Howling winds and near-freezing temperatures were constants at Candlestick, one of the worst spots imaginable for a baseball game. Situated alongside San Francisco Bay, it supposedly was designed to curtail the wind but instead intensified it.

Fans in the know would leave their sunny Bay Area neighborhoods with parkas and blankets, realizing conditions at the Stick would be significantly worse. The wind blew in the faces of fans and players, caused hot dog wrappers to swirl throughout the premises, and made every fly ball an adventure.

And there was Mays, coping with the elements in center field, in the batter's box, and on the base paths. Rather than whine that the ballpark served as a wind tunnel, which was a natural reaction for many players through the years, he took advantage of it.

I didn't want to complain because the seventeen other guys had to play there, too. You gotta remember, I'm just one guy. It was fun for me. I enjoyed it. A lot of guys didn't want to play at Candlestick because of the wind. It was cold, and the wind made it colder. Sometimes guys on the other team didn't want to play. It was good for me. That meant I didn't have to run the ball down so much.

The Say Hey Kid ran down his share.

I knew the wind. You didn't always go after the ball right away. You'd give it a one . . . two . . . three. Then you'd move. Sometimes the wind pushed the ball away from you. It was tricky. A lot of guys didn't like that. Some guys took the wrong first step, but you had to wait sometimes. I wouldn't count like that on the road. Just at Candlestick.

During his time with the Black Barons, Giants, and Mets, Mays made five ballparks his home.

From the Polo Grounds to Seals Stadium to Candlestick, Mays made himself an entirely different hitter because at the Stick, hard-hit balls to left field were knocked down by the wind, which whipped across the diamond from left field to right field. Balls that would be home runs in other parks turned into routine flies or even popups. It didn't help when the batter's hands were frosty and a cloud of dust blew in front of the plate just as the pitch was thrown.

Bill Rigney, the Giants' last manager in New York and first in San Francisco, said of Candlestick, "I remember saying to the players, 'This is our park. Make the most of it.' Mays never complained about it. Back then, none of the good players complained about it. Except the visiting guys."

The Polo Grounds, Willie Mays' first big-league baseball home, housed the Giants through 1957 and Casey Stengel's Mets in 1962 and 1963. (National Baseball Hall of Fame and Museum)

It was hard, man, but you've got to adjust. If I swung and kept the ball down and underneath the top of the bleachers, I could hit it out. If I hit it high, the wind brought it back. Balls I pulled for home runs on the road were outs at Candlestick.

So I hit a lot of balls to right field. I hit 'em and let 'em blow out in the jet stream. Don't try to pull it if they pitch you outside. Take it the other way. If they pitch you away or throw a curve, you go to right-center. Inside pitch, I'd hit it to right field, too. Inside-out swing.

I tried to hit it as best I could, as hard as I could. But you could hardly get it over the fence in left field, especially the first year.

The first year at Candlestick was 1960, after the Giants had spent 1958 and 1959 at Seals Stadium, located in the Mission District and home to the San Francisco Seals of the old Pacific Coast League. When Candlestick opened, the dimensions were 330 feet to left field and stunningly deeper than Seals Stadium's to the power alleys (397 feet) and center (420).

Seals Stadium had better weather than Candlestick. The Hamm's beer company was right there. The scoreboard was right behind me. There was a big fence in right field, and behind right field was a park. You could hit it out there and bounce it into the park.

Seals Stadium was all right. I remember it wasn't that easy to hit home runs there because pitchers kept the ball away from me. Actually, I liked Candlestick better. I could roam. I could go get the ball. The only thing was the wind and cold. The elements didn't bother me like they bothered other people. Especially coming back from playing in the heat and humidity on the road. You come home, and it's in the 60s. It kept me strong and fresh.

Mays' power numbers temporarily declined once he started playing in San Francisco, though his 1958 batting average was a career-high .347. After averaging 41 homers in his final four seasons in New York, he hit 29 and 34 in the Seals Stadium years and 29 the first year at Candlestick, just 12 of those at home. That didn't last.

The Giants realized the field was too massive and brought in the fences the following year to better align with other ballparks of the day—365 to left-center, 375 to right-center, and 410 to dead center. Aside from the dimensions becoming more prototypical (it still was a good poke in the wind), Mays made noticeable adjustments. After the Giants' first year at Candlestick, he averaged 44 homers in a six-year stretch from 1961, including 52 in 1965.

"I really admired Willie for adapting his swing to go to right field when he got to San Francisco," Hall of Famer Frank Robinson said, "because left field was like hitting into a net. The ball would leave the infield and, boy, you knew you had it—and the shortstop would catch it. You could not drive the ball out to left field with a cannon."

Offering somewhat of a rebuttal, Mays' former teammate Felipe Alou said, "Sometimes you saw Willie try to go to right field, but the majority of his home runs were to left field. He could fight the wind and still hit it out. Guys like Willie Mays, the ballpark doesn't make a difference."

Art Santo Domingo, who grew up in Westchester County in New York watching Mays play at the Polo Grounds and was a Giants executive in their early years in San Francisco, saw firsthand how his boyhood hero transitioned from one home ballpark to another.

"He was too smart to let a stadium get him down," Santo Domingo said. "Obviously, it would've helped him to play somewhere else just like it would've helped Ted Williams to play at Yankee Stadium. Willie became a different type of hitter at Candlestick and didn't pull the ball as much. The

Polo Grounds, it was really close if you pulled it, but left-center and right-center were miles away, and obviously the pitcher would pitch you away so you couldn't pull it. It could eat you up if you hit it to center. There was so much room out there."

Nobody knows more than Vin Scully, who grew up a fan of the Giants emulating Hall of Fame outfielder Mel Ott before he began his legendary sixty-seven-year broadcast career with the Dodgers.

"I always thought Duke Snider was a little cautious and afraid the ball would go to the wall at the Polo Grounds," Scully said. "A lot of center fielders, they'd almost put their knees together on a base hit. But Willie would charge every grounder like a shortstop who was throwing to first base. It was as normal as picking up a blade of grass.

"I thought, 'My gosh, two men on base, if he doesn't come up with that ball, it'll go all the way to the Eddie Grant memorial.' Willie never thought he'd make an error. I guess he never thought negatively, always thought he could catch the ball. There was no fear, no doubts, and he was thinking about getting the ball back as quickly as possible. Remarkable."

Mays doesn't list his favorite ballparks for hitting because he doesn't believe the ballpark was the biggest factor in succeeding at the plate.

It's not the ballpark. It's the pitcher. I don't care how big a ballpark is. If I get the right pitch, I could hit it out of any ballpark. I focused more on the pitcher than the stadium.

There was no bigger stadium than the Polo Grounds, at least when measuring the distance from the plate to center field. As Rigney recalled, "Boy oh boy. To see him play center field in the Polo Grounds with all that space, and then we came out (to San Francisco), he'd go back on balls at Seals Stadium, and the park was just too small for him. He'd come back after someone hit a home run and say, 'Skipper, I was going to catch that one.'"

The Polo Grounds was a big ballpark, but if you could pull it, it was a hitters' ballpark. I could pull the ball, but if you're just a one-way hitter,

you're hurting yourself. I moved the ball all around. I hit a lot of balls to right-center even then.

At the Polo Grounds, you needed a good center fielder. If the ball gets by you, it's a triple. Or inside-the-park homer. Most of the center fielders played way back. This is when Leo (Durocher) told me I had to play line to line. If a ball went up to left field, they looked at me. Right field, they looked at me.

It was so big, the bullpens were in the outfield. If a ball bounced in a bullpen, you had to go get it. They were in play, and those pitchers didn't help you out. The clubhouses were in center field, side by side. When the game was over, everybody walked to center field. I don't recall another clubhouse like that.

I had a little head start with the Polo Grounds because I played there when I was with Birmingham. We played two exhibitions at the Polo Grounds and one in Brooklyn against a semipro team called the Bushwicks. I remember hitting the ball pretty good on that trip.

Mays never homered in a game over the center-field wall at the Polo Grounds, but very few hit a ball that far after the stadium's 1923 remodeling. One was Hank Aaron, who did it off the Mets' Jay Hook on June 18, 1962. As chance would have it, it came one day after rookie Lou Brock did it off the Mets' Al Jackson. Brock was a Cub then, two years before he was dealt to St. Louis, where he became a stolen-base king.

Aaron's teammate in Milwaukee, Joe Adcock, homered to center off the Giants' Jim Hearn on April 29, 1953, one of the years Mays spent in the Army. The only other was Luke Easter of the Negro Leagues' Homestead Grays in a game against the New York Cubans on July 18, 1948, the year Easter's Grays played Mays' Black Barons in the final Negro Leagues World Series.

I could never get it in the center-field bleachers. People didn't want to see you hit it that way because they wanted to see you hit home runs. People were closer to the plate in left field, and they could get balls hit to them out there.

Willie Mays swung away in 1960 in the first game at Candlestick Park, the Giants' longtime cold and windy home. (San Francisco Giants)

Mays played 889 of his 2,992 career games at Candlestick—the Polo Grounds were a distant second at 399—and those who saw him regularly insisted he'd have hit far more than 660 home runs if he weren't challenged by the ballparks he played in, especially Candlestick.

"Willie hit in front of me, and he lost so many home runs," Hall of Famer Orlando Cepeda said. "Candlestick is a tough place to hit. Not only that, the mental preparation is so much tougher because it's so cold. I remember one foggy night, we're playing Pittsburgh. Elroy Face is pitching. Ninth inning. Willie tells me, 'I'm going to look for the fastball first pitch.' Because Face used to throw a fastball, then a splitter.

"Willie hits the ball to left-center, and the ball went out. And came back. Román Mejías caught it. The next day, Román tells me about it. That stuff happened all the time to Willie. He could have hit 750 home runs."

Felipe Alou has a similar story.

"I'll never forget a ball I caught against Cincinnati," he said. "I was in left field, and when Frank Robinson drove a ball, everybody knew it was to downtown San Francisco. So I turned around to see where the ball was going to land. You know where it landed? In my glove. With my back to the plate. Ridiculous. The Reds protested and said a fan threw the ball to me. That was Candlestick. Willie Mays, when we were teammates, lost dozens of home runs."

Giants coach and manager Herman Franks said Mays in any park but Candlestick would have topped 700 homers. "Easily. Nothing was insurmountable to Willie. But records weren't important to Willie. He just cared about winning," Franks said.

Hall of Fame baseball writer Bob Stevens, who covered the Giants during Mays' entire time in San Francisco, took it to another level: "In any other ballpark, Willie would have hit 800 home runs. He just never played in his type of ballpark."

Lon Simmons, a Hall of Fame broadcaster who witnessed nearly all of Mays' homers in the San Francisco years, went as far as saying Mays would have been the one to break Babe Ruth's record of 714 if not for Candlestick.

"If he played in the same stadiums as Hank Aaron, he would've hit more home runs than Hank Aaron," Simmons said. "I would say Candlestick took at least 50 homers away from him. And had he played in Atlanta or Milwaukee, imagine how many more he would have hit. They didn't call Atlanta the Launching Pad for nothing."

It must be noted that in Mays' career, he hit more home runs at home (335) than on the road (325), and that's true in his Candlestick years (202 at home, 194 on the road), which can be attributed to his familiarity with the playing conditions, his ability to adjust his approach to make the home park benefit him, and opposing pitchers' issues with the elements.

Mays isn't caught up in how many homers he lost at Candlestick. It can be debated all day but never quantified. On the other hand, missing two seasons in his early twenties for his military commitment absolutely put a significant dent in his career homers total. A similar argument could be

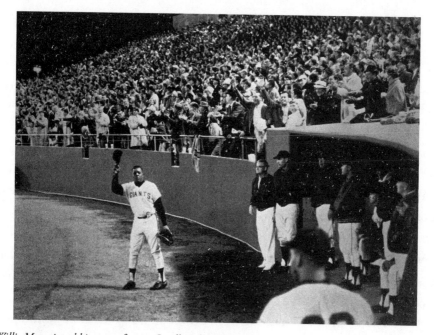

Willie Mays tipped his cap to fans at Candlestick Park in 1966 after hitting his 512th home run, breaking Mel Ott's National League record. (San Francisco Giants)

made for Ted Williams and a host of other elite players who served their country during wartime.

Mays missed most of the 1952 season and the entire 1953 season to serve during the Korean War. His first year out of the Army, he hit 41 homers. The next year, 51. So it's safe to suggest he might have hit another 60, 70, or 80 homers had he played those two seasons, which would have pushed him past Ruth.

On the other hand, Mays said he has no regrets about his home run total, which when he retired ranked third all time behind Ruth and Aaron. Nor does he express regret that Aaron was the one who broke the record.

I think I would've gotten the Babe without the two years in the Army, but a lot of us went in the service. You have to serve your country. I'm okay with 660. I'm proud of the accomplishment.

Behind Candlestick and the Polo Grounds, No. 3 on Mays' homers list is Wrigley Field, where he hit a blistering .342 with 54 homers in 179 games. In smaller sample sizes, he batted .403 at Montreal's Jarry Park and .367 and .355 at two of the Dodgers' facilities, the Los Angeles Coliseum and Ebbets Field, respectively.

All the parks were different. We didn't have as many as they have today. When I came up, we had eight teams in the league. If it was the Dodgers, you knew you'd see Don Drysdale and Sandy Koufax. Back in Brooklyn, Don Newcombe and Carl Erskine.

Forbes Field (Pittsburgh), we'd face Bob Friend, Vern Law, and a kid from Birmingham, a tall left-hander named Bobby Veale. Connie Mack Stadium (Philadelphia), it was Jim Bunning, another guy who knocked me down, but I got him a couple times. It wasn't too bad there.

Crosley Field (Cincinnati), it wasn't too big, but you still had to hit it pretty good to get it out of there. Sportsman's Park (St. Louis), County Stadium in Milwaukee. There was good pitching everywhere. Wrigley Field, the Cubs had good pitching as well, but I hit well there. There was a house beyond left field. I hit the top of the house, and Dave Kingman hit it over the house.

Mays closed out his career with the Mets, who played at the Polo Grounds when they came into the league in 1962 and were settled in at Shea Stadium by the time he returned to New York in 1972.

Shea Stadium was a big ballpark. I could hit it out of there, but I didn't hit it out that much. I was older when I played there. I got more base hits than anything.

For the most part, Mays always will be connected with the Polo Grounds and Candlestick. Before relocating to their downtown ballpark in 2000, the Giants played their final game at Candlestick in 1999, and afterward, Mays threw out the ceremonial last pitch. Barry Bonds, his godson, caught it.

Candlestick got old. They had to get out of there. It was a tough place to hit. Maybe I could have hit another 50 to 80 home runs if we didn't play there, I don't know, but I didn't mind it. I didn't have problems with the wind. Like I said, it's not the ballpark you've got to worry about, it's the pitcher.

10.

GIVE IT ALL YOU'VE GOT

The Story of a Four-Homer Day

"Push to get the most out of your ability in whatever you do and feel good about yourself for getting the job done every day."

—*Willie Mays*

WILLIE MAYS CONCLUDED early in his career that if he was going to suit up, he was going to play. Thirteen straight years, he appeared in more than 150 games, which remains a record, and most of that streak came when seasons lasted 154 games, not the current 162. He didn't miss more than three games in a season (excluding his time in the military) until 1963, 12 years after he debuted. Production was a major part of the equation. Equally important was durability.

The easiest three seconds of a manager's job was writing Mays' name on a lineup card.

My father worked weekdays in the steel mill, and then on Fridays, he would go work as a Pullman porter to Detroit and back. He made good money doing it. I never did see any wrongdoing in that, myself. I was taught if you can go out there and walk around, you could play. I played every day.

It was a brisk Sunday in Milwaukee on April 30, 1961. Some clouds, some wind. Mays hadn't been feeling good at the plate, going 0-for-7 with three strikeouts in the first two games of the Giants' series against Hank Aaron's Braves. Even the sight of Warren Spahn, the man he loved to face, didn't help. Mays' first big-league hit was a home run off Spahn, his first of 18 career homers against the Hall of Fame lefty, more than any other pitcher. But in Mays' first two at-bats in the Friday game, Spahn struck him out on the way to his second career no-hitter.

Hours after the Saturday game, in which Mays' roommate, Willie Mc-Covey, homered twice in a 7–3 Giants victory, they shared some ribs, nothing out of the ordinary in terms of meals on the road. But these ribs played a role, in a roundabout way, in the best game of Mays' career. It turned out to be a bad order of ribs, and Mays came down with a stomach illness and spent much of the night vomiting. By the time he got to County Stadium, he was in no position to play and was out of Alvin Dark's lineup. The Giants had no game Monday, conveniently, so he'd get a two-day break before they opened a series ninety minutes down Interstate 94 in Chicago. It would be just his seventh missed game since the Giants moved west in 1958. It was going to be a rare day off, and no one was going to put up a stink.

But then Joey Amalfitano, nicknamed "Louie" by Mays and three years younger, approached with some advice for which the baseball world forever will owe Amalfitano thanks. Mays played. He hit four home runs. He hit the ball hard enough the other time to make it five. He was denied a sixth at-bat because he was on deck when the top of the ninth ended.

Actually, Louie had something to do with that. He came over and said, "Willie, you gotta use this bat." I said, "What the hell am I going to use it for? I'm not playing." He said, "Go use it." It was an Adirondack, lighter than what I usually swing. I took it, and I hit five out of the ballpark right quick in batting practice, in six or seven swings. Okay, I gotta play then. I go talk to Alvin because he had someone else playing center field. He said, "Oh, you're going to play?" "Yeah, I can play. Let's go."

"That Adirondack was too light for him, too heavy for me: 35 inches, 32 ounces," said Amalfitano, noting the bat actually was one of the Willie Mays models that Amalfitano had been using. "The barrel had two big knots in it. It was heavier than my bat, and I'd use it in BP to get my hands moving. Willie's hands were mammoth, and he didn't like lighter bats. He usually swung 34 ounces."

Oh, I could tell the difference. Every now and then, when I get tired, I swing a 32, 33 maybe for a week and a half or two weeks and then I go back to my bat.

"So he went out to dinner with McCovey, got ill and was up all night," Amalfitano said. "He gets to the ballpark, and our lockers are together. I don't know how that happened. My number was 12, his was 24. He said he wasn't going to play."

I just didn't feel good when I got to the ballpark the next day after I ate those ribs. Louie was a good kid. He asked me how I felt and to give him a number from 1 to 100. I said 75.

"I said, 'Really? Let me tell you something, your 75 is better than some-body else's 100,'" Amalfitano said. "I said, 'Why don't you go out there and use that bat in BP.' So he did. He put on quite a show in BP, and it pleased him. He went to Alvin, and he played. The rest is history. That's when I really knew I was going to be a coach someday."

Mays became the ninth player in history with a four-homer game, and the Giants whipped the Braves 14–4. So much for a day off. He wound up playing all 154 games in the final year of the 154-game schedule and hit .308 with 40 homers, 123 RBIs, and a league-high 129 runs. It was run-of-the-mill Willie. Play at an elite level, do it every day. Or at least make that the objective. This was a demanding era in which starting pitchers expected to last nine innings. Position players anticipated four at-bats. Everyone's aim was durability, but few were as sturdy as Mays, whose first trip to the disabled list came in his 22nd and final season. Managers and teammates relied on

In 1961, Willie Mays became the ninth player in major-league history to hit four home runs in a game. The next player to accomplish the feat was Mike Schmidt in 1976. (San Francisco Giants)

Mays' production and leadership, knowing they were better off with him in the lineup. He welcomed and cherished the responsibility.

On the other hand, over the years, Mays experienced mental and physical exhaustion that sapped his strength, led to hospital visits, and prompted questions about whether he should be pushing his body or resting it. Mays usually chose to push it, and no one would dare tell the team's driving force, the meal ticket, the best player in the game, to sit down. It's not as if Mays volunteered. He simply dealt with it, sometimes to his detriment. In retrospect, he has no regrets. He knew his value to the team, and it was important to show loyalty to fans, teammates, and ownership. To the Say Hey Kid, that meant setting a good example by taking the field every day.

Sometimes you've got to push yourself when you're not 100 percent. You don't know what you can do unless you give your best. There were many times in my career I wasn't at my best, but I pushed myself and tried to get the best out of what I had that day.

These days, players rest more than we did, and that could be a good thing on the body. But when you get in there, there's no excuse for half speed. You might not feel right, but you've got to push yourself to be productive. Part of it for me came down to feeling confident that we had a better chance to win if I played.

Center field is a grueling position, especially at the expansive Polo Grounds and glacial Candlestick Park, and Mays figured his duty, no matter the circumstances, was to go all out not only on the bases but in the field. He directed where his teammates should play, backed them up, and ran after every ball. He usually was the highest-paid player on the team, if not the league, and took his leadership role personally. That the Giants averaged 21 doubleheaders annually in the 1950s and 11 in the 1960s, and he usually was seen on both ends, shows the man's strength and endurance.

"If I was a manager and had to make a lineup card and pick between Mays and Mantle as my center fielder, what would I do?" asked former Dodgers pitcher Carl Erskine, who saw plenty of both, Mays in the National League and Mantle in the World Series. "Mantle could do everything, but he might be hobbling with a bad back or bad knee. I gotta go with Willie because he's durable. Willie was a complete player and never seemed to make a mistake. He's always been my answer to who's the greatest player I played with or against."

Mays had no chronic injuries but had his share of aches and pains, especially in his final years. He experienced his first serious injury during spring training in 1959, on the eve of the Giants' second season in San Francisco. A collision at the plate left Mays with a gash on his right leg that required thirty-five stitches to close.

Spring training games are meaningless, especially for faces of the franchise with guaranteed roster spots. In those days, winning exhibitions was emphasized more than today, and when Mays saw a roller to Red Sox shortstop Don Buddin, he felt obligated to try to score all the way from second base. Flying around third and performing a hook slide at the plate, Mays was called safe. But nobody cared. Buddin's throw was high, and Mays' leg caught the shin guard of 6-foot-3 catcher Sammy White, tearing open his skin and shelving him for two weeks.

That was at the old Scottsdale Stadium. I was on second, and Daryl Spencer hit a roller, and I knew the guy couldn't get me so I said, "I'm gonna score." When I came home, the catcher was just standing there. I hit him, and something sharp on the shin guard got me. They took me straight to the hospital.

Mays still was in the Opening Day lineup, which was no surprise. On the all-time list of games played, despite missing nearly two full years in the Army, he's ninth at 2,992, nine behind ironman Cal Ripken, Jr. The leg injury was easy to diagnose, of course, as was the shoulder injury that shelved Mays for part of his swan song season. What wasn't easy to detect in those days was why he collapsed, blacked out, or even fainted during games. It happened a few times in his career, and it wasn't uncommon for him to spend time in a hospital to regain strength. But nobody, including doctors and trainers, could explain why this happened. All they said was that Willie was exhausted and needed rest.

One of Mays' episodes came in the heat of the 1962 pennant race. A year after his four-homer display, Willie had intended to play every game again even though the National League schedule beefed up by eight games as two expansion teams were welcomed, the New York Mets and Houston Colt .45s. Mays played the first 145 games through September 11, when the Giants were a half game behind the Dodgers and embarking on their final scheduled trip of the season, an 11-gamer through four cities. Though he was beginning to feel signs of fatigue, Mays figured it was no time to rest, not with a pennant at stake. It wasn't just about him but his team. Mays was so concerned about other players that he was known to play cards into the night with teammates just to keep them from carousing. That the Giants had lost 14 of the first 21 games he missed in his career (from 1951 through 1962, excluding his time in the military) provided more motivation to keep playing.

On a hot and humid night in Cincinnati, in the opener of the trip, Mays finally ran out of energy. He struck out in his first at-bat, and when preparing to bat in the third, he fainted and collapsed in the dugout. Teammates rushed to his side along with the manager, Alvin Dark, and trainer, Frank Bowman. Mays was taken away on a stretcher and driven to nearby Christ Hospital for tests and rest. Indeed, if he were to miss games in the prime of his career at thirty-one, he had to be carried off the field. And he was. At least he finally found a spot where he could take a breather, because he wasn't getting one on the field.

Mays was released after two nights, and doctors and trainers never determined the cause of his condition. Just a simple case of exhaustion, they said. He'll be back on the field in no time, they said. No big deal, they said. Others were suspicious of the diagnosis and suspected it was something more serious, maybe some sort of mysterious ailment. When Mays looks back at the times he blacked out, he recalls being genuinely fatigued, and why not? During his time with the Giants from 1951 to 1962, he appeared in 1,534 of 1,555 games, a 99 percent attendance record.

When I fell out in Cincinnati and went to the hospital, I was tired, man. They saw me going down and called timeout. They got me out of there. We played a lot of doubleheaders in those days and didn't take days off. I needed to rest a bit. As it turned out, when I did fall out, it usually happened before an off day so I wouldn't miss much time. I'd get out of the hospital and play right away. You didn't doubt yourself at the time because you wanted to play and the team needed you. There was nothing wrong with me.

That was the judgment in November 1962 from San Francisco's Mount Zion Hospital, where Mays was more fully examined after the expanded regular season, seven-game World Series, and barnstorming tour to which he committed during the summer. Mays went through three days of extensive tests, and doctors declared he was fine and that his fainting was due to exhaustion.

Similar conclusions were reached after Mays suffered consequences from other episodes in May 1957, June 1958, and September 1963, when he fell to his knees at the plate, was escorted off the field, spent two nights at Mount Zion Hospital and missed four games. In both 1957 and 1958, he was admitted to the Harkness Pavilion, a hospital in New York. In large part, he missed time on the field only because his body wouldn't allow it, not because a manager was being proactive and preserving the perennial MVP candidate's strength for the season-long grind. On the other hand, it happened in the offseason, too. In December 1965, in the wake of his second MVP season, the highly coveted Mays had a fainting spell in Salt Lake City during one of many of his appearances and wound up resting for several days at the Utah home of Herman Franks, who not only was Mays' manager in the second half of the 1960s but became one of his trusted financial advisers.

All these years later, a group of doctors shed light through the lens of the latest medical developments on Mays' condition during his playing days. Dr. Elliott Schwartz, medical director at the Northern California Institute for Bone Health Inc., who's also associated with the UC San Francisco Medical Center, and several of his peers studied Mays' episodes that were reported at the time and rehashed in books and other publications over the years. Schwartz, who has worked for teams in Major League Baseball, the NBA, and the NFL, consulted with several other physicians and surmised it wasn't a chronic illness as much as being victimized by the standards of the time.

"Let's presume there was virtually no knowledge about nutrition and very little knowledge about hydration. I mean, there were no professional trainers coming out of Springfield College," said Schwartz, referencing a school known for developing athletic trainers. "My physician consultants and I agree there may have been exhaustion, and I would say it was probably multifactorial. Nutrition, hydration, sleep patterns. How was the nutrition on the trains in the '50s? In those days, people didn't know anything about sleep. Now we know 80 percent of bone healing takes place while you're asleep. You don't see teams traveling late after games as much if they can get a good night's sleep and travel the next day. Sleep patterns are less disturbed. Teams now have many consultants dealing with all this stuff.

"Willie may have played to the point he couldn't play anymore. It was so different that we have trouble conceiving how different it was. I know from books and movies about the abuse Jackie Robinson dealt with. The mental fatigue and abuse probably contributed to Jackie's early demise, though he had a chronic disease, diabetes, and was fifty-three when he died. I'm sure Willie as a black player in those days didn't complain about an ache and pain that would cause these guys today to sit out for three days. They played because they thought somebody would take their job, not that anyone was taking Willie's job.

"I'm sure all these things built up and caused Willie's exhaustion, and they didn't really know what to do about it other than to say rest for a day or two. They didn't send them to minor-league rehab in those days. Willie got out of the hospital and played the next afternoon. That's the way it was. Yogi Berra caught 117 doubleheaders. The stories of Mickey Mantle out all night drinking are legendary. When Casey Stengel was asked his thoughts about players having sex before the game, he said it's not the sex before the game that bothers me, it's the staying out all night looking for it. It was a different time."

Aside from the physicians, a San Francisco–based psychologist has assessed what might have led to Mays' setbacks. Paul Watsky cited the significant load Mays was carrying as the team leader and the era's best player. Like Schwartz, Watsky said dehydration along with the aforementioned other deficiencies could have played a role, along with Mays' protracted divorce proceedings (with his wife, Marghuerite) and resultant financial woes.

"My theory would be that he was a guy who always felt he had to carry the team, so if he would feel himself slipping or tiring a bit at the time the team's needs are high, that may send the pressure on him through the roof," Watsky said. "Having to be in the public eye all the time could wear on him, and obviously a divorce would be one more source of pressure. They're trying to win a pennant, and he feels he needs to carry the team, and now he has to miss some games.

"Another thing I'd be curious about is how solid was his social support system. When he came up and struggled to get a hit and felt upset about it, he kind of lucked out because Durocher, an impossible manager for most people, really took Willie under his wing and said, 'You're going to be my center fielder forever, don't pressure yourself.' Willie came around, and Durocher remained supportive of him those first few years when he truly was a kid and trying to get himself sorted out.

"You've got a convergence of hard-to-identify physical factors and emotional stuff. If he's feeling tense, it's a hot day, he's not hydrating enough, is distracted, nervous, maybe not sleeping so well the night before, all these things clump together and cause those things to happen."

Mays appeared rejuvenated from his September 1962 hospital visit and hit .373 with six homers in the final 16 regular-season games. The Giants had won seven straight before Mays fainted but began a six-game skid in his absence. They were four games out of first place with seven to play, and Mays hit a game-winning homer in the finale as the Giants pulled into a 162-game tie with the Dodgers and forced a best-of-three series to determine the pennant. Mays homered twice in the opener (once off Sandy Koufax) and hit an RBI single in a ninth-inning rally in the third game that eliminated the Dodgers and catapulted the Giants to the World Series.

In retrospect, Mays said the workhorse mind-set was supported by all his early managers, starting with Durocher.

He wouldn't let me rest. In '54, I played darn near every game, then the World Series, then winter ball, then the Caribbean Series. I didn't miss games in spring training in those years, either. I said, "Leo, I'm tired, man." He said, "They came to see you play." I was already in shape. I told him, "Okay, let's make a deal. Every time I hit a home run, I could leave." So I'd hit a home run, go around the bases and keep walking. Every time we went to Tucson, I'd hit a home run in the first inning and leave. Get in my car and go home. Leo would get upset. He tapped me on the shoulder and said, "Uh-uh, no more. People are getting mad. You gotta play. If I gotta stay here, you gotta stay here."

So I got my breaks some kind of way, but I played every game, man. Let me put it like this. When you're going into a city, they always want to see you play. If you have a passion about playing, you play. What happened, and I had fun with this, people would come out early to watch us take batting practice, sometimes 30,000 in places like St. Louis. Just for batting practice. We had to do something for these fans. So (Orlando) Cepeda and I would play Mac (Willie McCovey) and Tom Haller in a little home run contest. Haller hit left-handed like Mac. There were so many people in some of these places. I felt I had to go out there every day and let the people see you.

I didn't get hurt too much. I hurt my arm later in my career and still have pain right now. I tried to keep that quiet back then. For a while, it was killing me, but I didn't want the other team to know. So I'd come out before the game during infield practice and throw two to third and two to home. My arm was hanging, but if the other team is watching infield practice, they don't know that. I limited my throwing so I could save it for the game. I go back in the clubhouse and the trainer would rub it and get it back in order. Nobody knew that. It didn't affect my hitting, just throwing.

Meanwhile, back in 1961, the baseball world was abuzz about Mays hitting four home runs in Milwaukee, two off Lew Burdette and one each off Seth

The day Willie Mays hit four home runs, he wasn't supposed to play because he got sick from a bad order of ribs. After the historic game, he felt so good that he helped himself to ribs while addressing the media. (Associated Press)

Morehead and Don McMahon. Mays drove in eight runs, and the Giants cruised 14–4. Ten homers were hit in that game, eight by the Giants and two by Aaron. With two outs in the ninth, Jim Davenport grounded out. Had he reached base, Mays, the next hitter, would have had a chance to become the only player in history with five homers in a game.

Davvy made the last out, and they booed him in Milwaukee because the ninth inning ended with me on deck. I teased him about that. "Man, we should've switched. You should've hit third, I should've hit second, I could've gotten another at-bat." Looking back, I should've had five anyway, but Hank made a great play at the fence. He was playing center field that day. I remember the whole game, I hit the ball very well.

Thank you, Joey Amalfitano.

"After the third home run, Willie says, 'Don't let anyone take that bat.' I say, 'Don't worry about it, I got it covered,'" Amalfitano said. "After Milwaukee, we go to Chicago. Willie's first time up, he cracks the bat. He tells me, 'Get that bat and put it upstairs,' and I do. I put it in my locker, but I come up after the game, and it's gone. It was terrible. Willie said, 'Don't worry about it.' I felt bad about it and learned a valuable lesson from that. Anything with value from a game, whatever it was, I'd disguise it and hide it because of that experience of someone taking Willie's bat.

"Well, a few years ago, we were sitting in the dugout at Scottsdale Stadium and talking about the four home runs in Milwaukee, and he said, 'You know what I was going to do with that bat?' I said, 'Give it to Cooperstown?' He said, 'No, I was going to give it to you.' Oh my. I don't know who took the bat. If it was one of the kids in the clubhouse, he probably took it home, pounded some nails into it, and used it. What the hell? Something to play with. Who thought later on it would be worth something?"

Now the truth can be told. The bat wasn't snatched by a clubhouse kid. It wasn't lost forever, as had been reported over the years in various publications. It was secured by a Giants employee, Eddie Brannick, the traveling secretary. Unbeknownst to Amalfitano, the director of the Hall of Fame, Sid Keener, had sent a letter to Brannick on May 3, a day after the bat broke, asking for the bat. Keener followed up with another letter on May 18, and Brannick phoned the Hall of Fame on May 22 and said he was mailing the bat to Cooperstown.

It was added to the museum's inventory on May 31 and has been in the Hall's possession all this time, with Willie's signature engraved in the barrel and the crack clearly noticeable between the Adirondack label and handle. Mays was thrilled to hear the bat is in good hands in Cooperstown.

Oh, is that right? It's still there? That's good they have it. It had to be somewhere, I guess. That's a good bat.

For decades, Amalfitano had been fretting over the loss of the bat. When informed about its whereabouts, he said, "Oh, for God's sakes. I'll be dog-gone. I had pictured some kid in Chicago playing with it. Willie said he was gonna give it to me, so tell the Hall I've got half ownership of that thing."

The bat is in an exhibit called "One for the Books," which tells stories behind some of baseball's greatest records. Mays has a bunch of other artifacts in the Hall, notably the bats he used for his 512th home run to set the National League record, 600th home run, and 3,000th hit, the ball he hit for No. 3,000, and the glove he used for his famous catch in Game 1 of the 1954 World Series. Counting his four-homer bat and World Series glove, Cooperstown contains the two most legendary mementos from Willie's career.

"We as a society, the people who love baseball, obviously place a lot of emphasis on home runs," curator Erik Strohl said of Mays' 1961 performance in Milwaukee. "Anyone who's an observer of the game, a lover of the game, knows that home runs are just one part of the game, but they're loud and brash and instant gratification so people find them exciting. Obviously, a four-home-run game is the pinnacle of all of that, so it's something we memorialize and give credit to here in the Hall."

Accompanying the bat is a note reminding that Mays was "feeling sick from a midnight snack and spare ribs" when he hit his four home runs. No one duplicated the feat until Mike Schmidt in 1976. "Milwaukee had great barbecue ribs, and Willie got sick," Orlando Cepeda said, "but you didn't see him miss games. Willie played every day, every game, every inning. Nobody was like Willie. Even spring training games, he went all out. He was a great teammate because he came to play every single day." McCovey, the cleanup hitter, added, "It turned out to be a pretty good day considering the circumstances and how sick he was feeling all night. I shook his hand at the plate four times. I was busy."

As was the other Willie.

It was the best game of my career, and the main thing is, we won. If we lost that game, the four home runs wouldn't have mattered. I think it's a lesson for kids. You don't have to be 100 percent to have a big day. You can still accomplish a lot.

11.

LIFE AND BASEBALL AREN'T FAIR

The Story of a Game of Inches

"If you give your best effort, don't get down on yourself if things
don't work out. Be happy with yourself and move on."

—*Willie Mays*

MATTY ALOU RACED around second base representing the tying run in
Game 7 of the World Series. He had no intention of trying to score, especially with third-base coach Whitey Lockman throwing both arms in the
air to signify a stop sign.

I wouldn't have paid Whitey no attention. I would've passed right by him.

Maybe the Giants would have won the 1962 World Series if the base runner had been the hitter.

Maybe they would have been champs if Mays had been the guy running,
not the guy hitting.

That's the beauty of the '62 Series, won by the Yankees in seven games.
There were enough twists, turns, and subplots crammed into the final moments of Game 7 to last generations.

When Mays reflects on the fateful ninth inning, he doesn't blame Alou for not trying to score and admits Felipe's younger brother would have been out. Nor does Mays harp on losing to the Yankees 1–0 in the capper. He always lived by the credo that you can't change the past, so why worry about it?

What intrigues Mays, what gets his competitive juices flowing decades later, is wondering what would have happened if he, and not Alou, had been the runner. It was Mays who hit a two-out double down the right-field line that sent Alou to third just before Willie McCovey hit a scream-ing line drive to second baseman Bobby Richardson for the final out, setting off a Yankees celebration at Candlestick Park.

We know now that Mays, as the lead runner, would have blown by Lockman's stop sign even with Hall of Famers McCovey and Orlando Cepeda the next scheduled hitters. But we can't know if Mays would have been safe or tagged out by catcher Elston Howard. With a season on the line and unwavering confidence in his abilities to make things happen, even on the biggest stage, the Say Hey Kid was willing to take the chance.

If he tried to stop me, I would've hit Elston. That's the way it was back then. He was a good guy, a very strong guy. Matty might've been a little nervous about running. He didn't want to make the last out. Leo (Durocher) told me, "Hey, do what you want to do. Steal what you want to steal." If I had been running, I would have had to try to score. I would've taken a chance.

In retrospect, the Yankees knew that.

"I know he wouldn't have stopped at third, that's for sure," said Richardson, who took the cutoff throw from Roger Maris and threw a one-hopper to the plate that bounced a bit high. "I saw Willie in New York several years ago. He says, 'I would've scored. We would've won the World Series.'"

Richardson chuckled, then recalled another moment he had with Mc-Covey, forty-five years after the latter lined out to the former.

"He says to me, 'I bet your hand is still hurting,'" Richardson said. "I told him, 'You hit it hard.'"

Mays' teams won just one World Series, the four-game sweep over Cleveland in 1954. He was in a World Series four other times, his Giants losing to the Yankees in 1951 and 1962 and his Mets falling to the A's in 1973. Also, his Birmingham Black Barons fell to the Homestead Grays in the final Negro League World Series in 1948.

The toughest loss was 1962. It would have been the Giants' first World Series triumph in San Francisco, in their fifth year away from New York, maybe a precursor to more championships in the '60s. Instead, their first came in 2010 in their fifty-third year on the West Coast, the first of three titles in five years.

These Yankees were on the tail end of a dynasty in which they won 10 titles in 16 years. They wouldn't win another until 1977. Ralph Terry,

The Giants had a good time in their 1962 pennant-winning season, as demonstrated by Felipe Alou, Jim Davenport, Willie Mays, Juan Marichal, and Orlando Cepeda, all All-Stars that season. (San Francisco History Center, San Francisco Public Library)

a 23-game winner, and Hall of Famer Whitey Ford anchored the rotation. Mickey Mantle and Maris, a year after engaging in an epic home run chase, Maris breaking Babe Ruth's single-season record, remained a formidable 1–2 punch. They didn't hit well in the World Series, but the Yankees received enough contributions from the rest of the roster to win their 20th title.

Rather than bemoan the plight of a lost World Series that could have gone either way, Mays moved on and tried not to let it weigh on him.

It's over. What are you gonna say? I wish we could've won because everybody wanted to celebrate. I wish we would've done this, could've done that. I didn't let it bother me at that time. I never did do all that, get all upset about something. Getting to the World Series, that's a good thing on its own. If you feel sorry for yourself, then you've got four or five months feeling sorry for yourself. I never did that. You've got to keep going. I just went on home and got into bed.

Now consider Ralph Terry.

Terry won the game, pitching all nine innings and claiming the World Series MVP award, but he was oh so close to taking the loss. If McCovey's liner had reached the outfield, Terry would have been victimized by two walk-off hits to end World Series Game 7s in three years. It happened in 1960 when Pittsburgh's Bill Mazeroski hit his career-defining home run at Forbes Field, complete with his memorable helmet-waving gestures around the bases, that sunk Terry and the Yankees.

"That was Casey Stengel's last year managing the Yankees, and I felt bad for him," recalled Terry. "I went in his office, and he's sitting there with his pants to his ankles, shirt open, with a beer, taking his Yankees uniform off for the last time. He said, 'What's up, kid?' I said, 'I feel bad. I'm sorry it ended like this.' He said, 'How did you pitch him?' I said, 'I tried to pitch low and away. I know he's a high-ball hitter. I couldn't get the ball down.' He said, 'If you can't get the ball where you want it, that's a physical mistake, not a mental mistake. Forget it, kid. Come back next year and have a great year.'

"That was great advice. The next year, I ended up 16–3. Casey could've gotten on me. He could've put the blame on me. He didn't. Casey was fantastic, maybe the greatest manager of all time. I got another chance in a Game 7 in '62, and it was the best game I ever pitched. If I lost that game, I'd have thought about losing my identity."

The point is, Terry coped with the 1960 World Series loss his way, and Mays coped with the 1962 World Series loss his way. Both refused to let it beat them up. Both let it go and kept flourishing.

I always tried to stay positive when I played. I never looked back negatively at things like that. That would be a waste of time. That's just wishing. We weren't even supposed to get to the World Series. It was a great playoff with the Dodgers. They had us beat in the third game of that series. They had us beat in the ninth inning.

Oh, the Dodgers. Always the Dodgers. Long before the wild Game 7 theatrics at Candlestick, the Giants had to overcome a four-game deficit with seven to play to finish the 162-game season at 101–61, same as their pals from Los Angeles. On the final day, while the Dodgers lost 1–0 to St. Louis, Mays hit an eighth-inning home run that beat Houston 2–1, one of the most significant homers in his career.

A best-of-three tiebreaker was to settle the National League pennant, just like in 1951 when Bobby Thomson danced off into Giant-Dodger lore. Eleven years later, the Giants had to do it all over again. Except this time, Mays wasn't a nervous rookie in New York waiting on deck as Thomson homered off Ralph Branca. He was a thirty-one-year-old enjoying another career year as the leader of a determined group on the other coast.

In the opener at Candlestick, Mays hit two home runs, and the Giants cruised 8–0. The series moved to Los Angeles, and the Dodgers won the second game 8–7 when Maury Wills scored on Ron Fairly's game-ending sacrifice fly. The Dodgers held a 4–2 lead in the ninth inning of the finale, and the Giants responded the same way they did in the ninth inning of the 1951 finale.

With a four-run rally. This one was a tad less dramatic. Mays' infield single, a liner off the pitcher's glove, scored the first run, and the rally included a sacrifice fly, bases-loaded walk, and error. The Giants won 6–4 for the right to play in the World Series against the Yankees, who already were in San Francisco wondering if they would face the Giants or need to fly to Los Angeles.

Game 1 was scheduled at Candlestick a day after the Giants won the pennant at Dodger Stadium.

Didn't need a break. Let's play. I didn't drink, and I wouldn't let the guys drink. "Hey guys, gotta wait, gotta wait." I'm sure some guys had a drink. They can't win the pennant and not have a drink.

We flew into San Francisco and had 50,000 people waiting for us at the airport. Fans were running all over. It was an exciting time for the city. We had to find an alternate runway to land the plane. People who came to pick up players couldn't get close, and a lot of the guys had to hitchhike. Russ Hodges, our announcer, and I were lucky to find a cab.

Mays had three hits in the World Series opener, but the Giants lost 6–2. McCovey homered off Terry in the second game (hold that thought), and Jack Sanford spun a three-hitter in a 2–0 Giants win. The Series moved to Yankee Stadium for the next three games and returned to San Francisco to a tremendous rainstorm and the Yankees holding a 3–2 lead. Candlestick was unplayable, so flooded that helicopters were deployed to help dry the field, and four days elapsed between Games 5 and 6. The Giants and Yankees traveled an hour and a half east to hold workouts in Modesto.

When play resumed, Orlando Cepeda's three hits led the Giants to a 5–2 win in Game 6, but the rain proved costly to the Giants in the finale. Not only were the Yankees able to reshuffle their rotation and pitch Terry, the Game 5 winner, but they benefited from the soggy grounds as the momentous ninth inning unfolded.

The 1962 season ended with a star-studded World Series that went seven games and pitted Willie Mays against Roger Maris, left, and Mickey Mantle. (National Baseball Hall of Fame and Museum)

Matty Alou opened the inning with a beautiful drag bunt toward Richardson, who had no play. Alvin Dark, the manager, had each of the next two hitters try to bunt, but Felipe Alou and Chuck Hiller both failed to put bunts down and eventually struck out. It was one of several strategies in the inning, by both teams, that were second-guessed. Felipe Alou had a terrific year—.316 batting average, 25 homers, 98 RBIs, but only two sacrifice bunts—and now he was asked to bunt? Visualize the social-media outrage if that had happened in today's world.

Through the decades, the botched bunt remained one of Alou's regrets in life. When he became a manager, first with the Montreal Expos and then the Giants, he emphasized fundamentals and tried to make sure his players were prepared to bunt in any situation. He admits he was not.

"It kills me that I could not bunt Matty Alou to second, a nightmare for me that I didn't get him over," Felipe Alou said. "The bunt is an offensive maneuver, an obligation. The wind from the storm was blowing in forty miles an hour. It was a game to bunt the ball to move the runner, not try for a home run. I should've been able to bunt, and then Willie's hit ties the game. When you have a good runner at first base, your bunt doesn't have to be perfect. It went foul. Next pitch, Alvin puts on a hit-and-run, and it's up and in, and I couldn't do anything with it. Now it's 0–2, and Ralph Terry struck me out with a nasty fastball."

No, I wouldn't have had Felipe bunt. He wasn't a bunter. He had a good year, put up big numbers, but he wasn't asked to bunt a lot. It wasn't a bunting team.

Sacrifice bunts are frowned upon nowadays because the numbers show the expectancy of scoring a run with a man on first and no outs is greater than with a man on second and one out. Therefore, bunting a runner over reduces the expectancy to score.

To which Mays says hogwash.

I disagree. I'm not sure how they calculate that, but if I'm on second with one out, I have a little more advantage to score than if I'm on first and no outs. I could steal third easier than I could steal second. I could get a bigger lead. I'm behind the pitcher. A lot of things can happen when you're on second base.

With two outs in the bottom of the ninth inning in Game 7 of the 1962 World Series, Mays stepped to the plate.

"I tried to go inside on Willie the first two pitches," Terry said. "Ball one. Ball two. They looked like brushback pitches. I had only one three-ball count the whole game, to (Jim) Davenport, and I thought I struck him out on ball three. The umpire didn't think so. So anyway, I throw the first two pitches to Willie inside, and it's pretty obvious what I'm trying to do next. Low and away on the black, knee high. Willie opened up, threw the bat at it and hit it into right field."

That's when the soaked grounds played a role.

The only reason Matty didn't score was because it was wet out there. It rained for seven, eight days, and we had to go down to Modesto to take batting practice because we couldn't go to Candlestick. I saw the ball hit that wet spot, preventing it from going to the fence. It would've been a triple. If Matty had scored, I would've made it to third easily. Roger was able to get to the ball before it got to the fence because of the wet field. That's why he got to it so quickly. It slowed down the ball.

Longtime Giants broadcaster Lon Simmons noted, "If it hadn't been raining, Mays' ball would've gone all the way to the fence, and they would've scored. Mays might've scored himself. Things just conspired against them."

Instead of a tie game, the Giants still trailed 1–0. McCovey was the next hitter. He had homered off Terry in Game 2. In the seventh inning of Game 7, he hit a two-out triple to center off Terry but was stranded as Cepeda struck out.

Easy call to walk McCovey, right? The left-handed slugger saw the ball well off the right-handed Terry. When Yankees manager Ralph Houk walked to the mound, it seemed clear he'd pull Terry for a lefty. In today's game of constant lefty-righty matchups, the strategy would have been predetermined. Instead, Houk let Terry decide. Face McCovey or walk him to face Cepeda, a right-handed batter who hit .158 in the Series but had three hits the previous day. The sellout crowd and pretty much everyone on the field, including McCovey, expected a pitching change. But Terry wanted McCovey.

"Houk asked me how I felt," Terry said. "'I feel all right.' How's your control? 'I think it's all right.' Elston agreed. It was hard at Candlestick to adjust. In that wind, one curveball breaks a foot, another two or three inches. It took you a while to adjust to the strike zone. If I put McCovey on, we would've had a force at any base, but my thing was, you're in a National League ballpark with a National League umpire (Stan Landes), and if it's a close call, I'm probably not going to get it. I didn't want to walk in the tying run.

"I looked back at the Giants winning the pennant after (Walt) Alston had Stan Williams walk a guy to load the bases, then Williams walked the next guy to let in a run. So Houk asked me if I wanted to pitch to McCovey or Cepeda. 'Let me go after McCovey. I'll throw low and away, then high and tight. If I get behind in the count, I'll put him on.' That was the plan."

At least one teammate second-guessed the decision.

"If I were managing," Richardson said, "I'd have put him on."

In fact, Houk himself didn't seem fully confident with his decision.

"Later on, I played three years for Houk," said Felipe Alou, referring to the early 1970s with the Yankees, "and I asked him, 'Ralph, how come you pitched to Willie McCovey?' He said, 'You know what, when Willie McCovey hit that line drive, I thought I soiled myself.' He told me he had nightmares many months after they won the World Series because he could have made a big mistake."

McCovey stepped in the box still thinking he'd get walked. He was a pull hitter and accustomed to defenses shifting him to the right side. Third baseman Clete Boyer moved in the hole between third and short. Shortstop Tony Kubek was behind second base and a few feet on the left side. After Terry's first pitch, a changeup that fooled McCovey, who pulled it into the seats along the right-field line, Richardson slightly repositioned himself, though not all the way in the hole.

"He pulled a foul ball, tremendously foul, so I moved toward the first-base line," Richardson said. "Early in the Series, he had hit one in the hole, a ground ball, and I had just flipped it over to first. I looked at the replay, and I could see the line. That's how far over there I was."

With his second pitch, Terry tried to throw a fastball up and in but got it out over the plate. McCovey took a mighty hack and would have registered an eye-popping exit velocity if they had such readings back then. In a flash, the ball was in the grasp of Richardson, who took a quick step to his left and used two hands to haul it in.

"One of the hardest balls I've ever seen hit," Richardson said. "The ball had a lot of topspin. I saw Mantle hit balls like that. I thought when he hit it, it was a sure hit to right field, but it came down. I caught it high, but my momentum carried my glove down, almost to the ground."

Twenty-four years later, McCovey was inducted into the Hall of Fame as part of the 1986 class and delivered this classic line: "People ask me how I'd like to be remembered. I tell them I'd like to be remembered as the guy who hit the line drive over Bobby Richardson's head."

McCovey recalled Richardson not dramatically shifting into the hole on the right side, saying, "He wasn't playing me to pull like most second basemen would do. Everybody had those exaggerated shifts against me. Other than Ted Williams, I'm the only one who they had those exaggerated shifts against. But he was playing toward the bag, almost like a right-handed hitter was up, really.

"I didn't think they were going to pitch to me. If I had known they were pitching to me, I could've hit that first pitch out of the ballpark, but I hit it foul. It was surprising. It was a strike, and I thought it was a mistake. I jumped at it. The second pitch was right there, and I used my reflexes to hit the line drive. If I had known they were pitching to me, I would've had a different approach."

Had Richardson been positioned a few feet, maybe a few inches, either way, Alou and Mays would have scored to give the Giants a 2–1 walk-off victory. San Francisco fans wouldn't have had to wait until 2010 for their first World Series parade.

I thought they'd walk Mac, but Ralph Terry was a good pitcher, man. When we finally played after the rainouts, we had 'em beat. We didn't complete what we wanted to complete. Everyone remembers that last play, but the key to that game was the Yankees' left fielder, Tom Tresh, making a play in the seventh before Mac's triple. He made a catch on me on a ball I hit down the line. A one-handed, backhanded catch. I knew I'd have a triple out of that. He made a good play on me.

McCovey died in October 2018, and Mays took it particularly hard. They were more than teammates. When he got to the majors in 1959, McCovey took Hank Aaron's number 44—both were from Mobile, Alabama—but it was Mays who was like a big brother. McCovey was seven years younger and often deferred to his locker neighbor. The Willies met when the Giants sent McCovey to New York for the first of so many leg operations that

McCovey had lost count. McCovey still was a minor-leaguer, a prized prospect with Double-A Dallas, and the Giants still were playing in New York. Mays put McCovey up at his place.

"Willie would take me to the pool hall," McCovey said. "He liked to shoot pool, he and Junior Gilliam. So I would go sit and watch. Everybody looked up to Willie. You know that. Why wouldn't you, as a young kid? He was everything in New York at the time. He was Mr. New York. You got a lot of attention when you went out with him. He was amazing. Nobody was as good as Mays. I don't think he did any workouts in the off-season, and the first day of spring training, you'd think it was midseason the way he played. Everyone else was huffing and puffing trying to get in shape, and it was like midseason for him."

McCovey spoke often about Mays being the most complete player he ever saw, and Mays was awed by McCovey's pure power but also notes that the 6-foot-4 first baseman could beat teams with more than his bat. Willie and Willie hit three-four in the lineup, the most feared twosome of the era, though cases could be made for Mickey Mantle–Roger Maris and Hank Aaron–Eddie Mathews.

Mac was quiet when he was around people he didn't know. He wasn't quiet around me. He never boasted. I did the boasting for him. We talked between ourselves. He'd come over, run things by me. He was a smart guy. If he needed something, I got it. I had him next to me.

McCovey was immensely popular in San Francisco. Cepeda was the Rookie of the Year in the Giants' inaugural season in San Francisco, 1958, and McCovey was the league's top rookie the following year and debuted by going 4-for-4 with two triples off future Hall of Famer Robin Roberts. McCovey hit 521 homers and, like Mays, made it to Cooperstown on the first ballot.

Mac wore pitchers out, but they didn't knock him down. He was too big. If you're gonna start a fight, Mac's not the guy you knock down. They knocked me down because I'm smaller. Mac didn't like the flair. When I

say flair, he didn't like stealing bases. He didn't like to run much. He just wanted to hit. Don't get me wrong. He could run now. He was a good first baseman, very good. That was the problem we had at the beginning. Where do we play Mac? Because we also had Cepeda. Where do we play Cepeda? There were other guys, too. We seemed to have about five first basemen.

Mac was our judge in Kangaroo Court. He'd be at the podium and fine guys. He had the last word. When a guy makes a mistake on the field, he'd be fined. Not like going 0-for-4, but like dropping a ball or getting thrown out on the bases—unless a coach told the guy to run, then we'd back up a little bit. Might be ten dollars. If you protest and lose, you may pay twenty dollars. He'd play Marvin Gaye's "What's Going On," like he's saying, "What the hell's goin' on out there?" Mac got the money. It'd go on through the end of the season, and we'd have a party.

While they were a perfect on-field complement and came from the same state, Mays' and McCovey's personalities couldn't have been any more different.

"I didn't fraternize a lot then," McCovey said. "When I showed up at the ballpark and went on the field, I had my game face on. Willie was just the opposite. He'd be around the cage laughing and giggling with all the visiting players. Not me. I didn't talk to any of them unless they came to me. I was a little standoffish.

"Willie kept the clubhouse loose. He had that grin. He was always up-beat, and everybody gravitated toward his locker. He'd always give stuff away. He'd go to McGregor and get loads of stuff to bring back. His garage was full of golf clubs and stuff. He'd give them to visiting players. He was that way. He always had clothes or equipment for people. Visiting players couldn't wait to get here. Unfortunately, he couldn't help me. I wasn't his size, and I was left-handed."

So, would Mays have scored in the ninth inning of Game 7 if he were the runner at first base and somebody else hit that ball to right field?

Former longtime Giants executive Art Santo Domingo, now an official scorekeeper for Giants and A's games, says yes and bases his answer on watching Mays score many times when he appeared destined to be out. For example: July 1965 at Connie Mack Stadium, where Mays tried to score from first base on a roller and throwing error by Phillies third baseman Dick Allen. Catcher Pat Corrales did what he was supposed to do back then, as did Mays. Corrales blocked the plate with his body, and Mays used his body to initiate a violent collision. Both exited the game, Corrales with a gash in his neck and Mays with a sore hip.

Umpire Augie Donatelli initially ruled Mays was out, but the impact made Corrales drop the ball, and Donatelli signaled safe.

"Willie was going to score whenever he came home," Santo Domingo said. "You just weren't going to stop him from scoring. Matty was a little guy and didn't have Willie's speed. He wasn't going to crash into the catcher. Willie crashed into Corrales, which isn't allowed today. Back then, the catcher would stand right in line with the plate, and you couldn't get to the plate unless you hit him."

Let's go to an on-field source. Mr. Richardson?

"When Willie told me he would've scored on the ball he hit and 'we would've beat y'all,' I said, 'You're probably right,'" Richardson said. "Yeah, he probably would have scored. As it turned out, my throw home took a big bounce. Accurate throw, but a high hop. I can just see him sliding under it."

The 1962 World Series was full of examples of how winning and losing can come down to a matter of inches. It wasn't something Mays let haunt him.

I don't believe in that. If you're gonna hit the ball, it's either a base hit or somebody's gonna catch it. You can't ask, "What would've happened if it was a few inches this way or that way?" It's done. You can't get it back. You can analyze it all you want, but it's not changing anything. Maybe I'm different that way, but you gotta move on, man.

12.

NEVER GIVE UP

The Story of a 16-Inning Classic

"Sometimes you're asked to do more than you expect. Take it on.
Keep going. Keep being strong."

—*Willie Mays*

WARREN SPAHN WON more games than any other pitcher since the 1930s
and more than any other left-handed pitcher who ever lived, 363 in all. He
was a 20-game winner a whopping 13 times, once when he was forty-two
years old.

He took a backseat to no one.

Unless we count Willie Mays.

**Spahnie was around the plate all the time. He threw a lot of breaking
balls and screwballs, and I felt I could hit that. He was a nice man. We
played together one year, and he was a good friend. He'd always ask, "Can
I do something for you, Willie?" I'd say, "No, just get out there on the
mound." That was usually enough.**

Mays had a special connection with Spahn, who pitched the first 20 of his
21 seasons with the Boston/Milwaukee Braves. Fans of the 1960s can cite

classic duels between Mays and Don Drysdale. And Mays and Bob Gibson. But nobody faced Mays more than Spahn, and nobody gave up home runs to Mays more than Spahn.

Two, in fact, were among the most memorable hits in the Say Hey Kid's career.

As a twenty-year-old rookie in 1951, Mays began 0-for-12, and not until he faced Spahn for the first time on May 28 did he get his first hit, a home run over the left-field roof at the Polo Grounds.

The other came July 2, 1963, in a game that never will be duplicated and featured a forty-two-year-old Spahn against a twenty-five-year-old Juan Marichal, two future Hall of Famers known for high leg kicks and high inning counts.

Spahn and Marichal each registered more complete games than wins, and please digest that for a moment. *More complete games than wins.* It's unfathomable in today's era. The most games any pitcher completed in 2019 was three. If a pitcher finishes five innings, he gets a pat on the rump from his manager and high fives from his teammates.

But in the days of Spahn and Marichal, complete games weren't just the goal, they were the expectation.

So when they converged on that cold and windy night at Candlestick Park, a redundancy if ever there was one, both anticipated they'd go the distance. And they did. Each pitched scoreless ball through nine innings. And 10 innings. And 11 innings. And 12 innings. And 13 innings. And 14 innings. And 15 innings.

It was 0–0 through 15 without a single pitching change. Pinch-hitting for pitchers was not an option. Neither starter was prepared to back down. Marichal took the mound for the 16th and retired three of four batters, including the great Hank Aaron for the second out.

Marichal got the final out with his 227th pitch, a ridiculous figure that some of today's pitchers would need three starts to reach. As he came off the field and headed toward the Giants' dugout adjacent to the first-base line, Marichal made sure to wait for Mays jogging in from center field.

In the midnight hour, with far less than the original crowd of 15,921 still in the house, Mays was due to bat second in the bottom of the 16th.

That was funny, man. I was running across the field, stepping on first base like I always do. I usually stepped on first or third depending on where our dugout was. Marichal cuts me off and taps me on the shoulder. "Chico, I'm tired. I'm tired. You gotta get me outta here." He didn't want to come out. I tried to make him relax. I said, "Hold on a minute. I'll take care of you. Let me see what I could do."

I didn't know I'd hit a damn home run. I wasn't trying to. I hit a home run, and Marichal's the first guy out there to greet me.

Marichal recalls it well.

"I didn't want to come out, and I understand Spahn didn't want to come out, either," Marichal said. "Alvin wanted to take me out in the ninth inning. I didn't let him. Alvin was getting mad, and I told Willie, 'I'm not pitching any longer.' Willie said, 'Don't worry, I'm going to win the game for you,' and he did. I was so happy. Willie was the best. I was so proud to play with him."

Spahn hung a screwball to Mays with his 201st pitch, and Mays hung Spahn with the loss, one of the most heartbreaking of his career. Spahn was midway into his final 20-win season, and his 23–7 record and 2.60 ERA demonstrated his dominance even at an advanced age. He won 75 games in his forties, and his 77 complete games in his forties rank second all time to Cy Young's 119. But it took him a while to get over the loss in San Francisco.

"That one haunted him. He had nightmares about that pitch," said Greg Spahn, Warren's son who was fourteen in 1963 and in attendance that night. "He busted his ass for all that many innings, and he was so frustrated he hung that screwball to the best hitter in baseball. I left him alone and hung out next to his locker and didn't talk to him much until he was ready. He was pretty much devastated."

Marichal was elated. And thankful for the help he received from a

Juan Marichal was thrilled in 1963 when Willie Mays homered in the 16th inning to beat the Braves 1–0, ending a marathon pitcher's duel between Marichal and Warren Spahn. (Associated Press)

teammate. Actually, it wasn't Mays' first assist of the night. Way back in the fourth inning, the Braves threatened when Del Crandall hit a two-out sinking liner to center and Norm Larker took off from second. Mays charged the ball, gloved it on one hop, and unleashed a strike to the plate. Larker was out. Inning over.

Another close call came in the seventh. Spahn, an exceptional hitter for a pitcher (35 homers in his career), swatted a two-out double off the wall, the Braves' only extra-base hit, but was stranded. The game went on. And on. Marichal, seventeen days removed from no-hitting Houston, famously told manager Alvin Dark he wouldn't exit so long as the old man across the way kept pitching.

Alvin tried to take him out at least twice. "No, no, no. If that old guy can pitch, I can pitch." That's what he told Alvin. You couldn't take either of

those guys out. They were very similar. They threw a screwball, a first-pitch screwball. They had the kick in their windup. Marichal's might've been a little higher.

Felipe Alou was the Giants' cleanup hitter that night. More than a half century later, he can relate to what Mays did for Marichal. Alou recalls Aaron doing him a favor after he joined the Braves.

"I was playing center field, and Hank was in right," Alou said. "We were leading by two runs, and a guy hit a long fly to right-center, and I caught the ball. I thought that was the third out, and it wasn't. I started running with the ball in my hand, and two guys scored. Hank took the ball out of my hand and threw it back to the infield. That tied the game. It was kind of a knucklehead play.

"Next inning, I was the leadoff hitter. I hit a triple. The coach stopped me. I kept going, trying to redeem myself. They threw me out at the plate. Two mistakes now. Hank was picking up his bat and said, 'Felipe, don't worry about that. I'm going to do something about this.' He hit one out. We won the game.

"You play with great players like Hank and Willie, you realize they are at a higher level than you. I had more than 2,000 hits, more than 200 home runs. I played in the All-Star Game, the World Series. I consider myself a pretty good player, but there are other players that operate at an altitude that I don't know. I was not born to be there."

What does Aaron remember about the 16-inning game?

"It was very, very cold," he said. "Candlestick Park was not the easiest place to play baseball, at least not for me. But you had two of the all-time great pitchers in Warren Spahn and Juan Marichal, so it's a type of dynamic baseball game that a lot of people don't know existed, really. You're talking about having an opportunity to go to a baseball game and watch two of the all-time greats."

More than that, actually. Seven future Hall of Famers played in the game. Mays, Aaron, Marichal, Spahn, Willie McCovey, Orlando Cepeda, and Eddie Mathews. In the end, just one took a celebratory journey around the bases.

Harvey Kuenn made the first out in the 16th, and Mays stepped up, swung at the first pitch and hit the ball down the line in left. Likewise, in the ninth, McCovey had pulled a towering drive that sailed over the right-field foul pole, a game-ending homer in the minds of McCovey, manager Alvin Dark, and other Giants. But umpire Chris Pelekoudas called it foul.

Fast-forward seven innings, and Mays didn't know on contact if his ball would stay fair.

The difference between Mac's and mine was, mine was lower. This was Candlestick, man. You never knew what the wind was going to do. It could knock the ball down or blow it foul. I hit it low. That's the only way you could get it out of there. To left field, I'm talking about. I curved it around the pole.

Alou remembers.

"That ball changed directions about ten times," he said. "It was like a snake before it finally broke through the wind. It was fair, but there was a fear it would get lost in a gust."

It was a Tuesday night series opener and Greg Spahn's first Candlestick experience. "I was amazed at how cold it was," he said. So was another Candlestick first-timer who was sitting behind the Braves' dugout off the third-base line, having arrived in summer clothes expecting a warm night.

"I'm telling you, talk about someone underdressed going to Candlestick Park, that was me," Bud Selig said. "I'll never forget that. I was sitting with John McHale, the Braves' general manager, and he went and got me a big Braves parka. You'd wear these in Green Bay in January for a Packer game, and that's what I was wearing. And this was July. If John McHale hadn't rescued me, I probably would have frozen to death that night. I wouldn't have made it to my thirtieth birthday."

The frigid conditions made it extremely tough on hitters, making it difficult to stay loose, grip a bat, and drive the ball, which played into Spahn's and Marichal's hands. Now, Aaron says of his friend Selig, "I wish he could've sent a parka to me down in the dugout. I would've loved it."

Selig, then twenty-nine, was the Braves' largest public stockholder. Three years later, the team moved from Milwaukee to Atlanta, and Selig led the drive to relocate the Seattle Pilots to Milwaukee in 1970. He became owner of the Brewers and later baseball's ninth commissioner. On that frosty night at Candlestick, nobody wanted the Braves to prevail more than Selig. Spahn and Aaron were his guys.

"I stayed the whole game," Selig said, "and Spahnie and Marichal went all 16 innings. Now think about that in today's world. What a historic night. Of course, Willie won the game in the 16th, which proved his greatness. Not that he had to prove anything to anybody."

It was one of Mays' 18 home runs off Spahn. Vern Law is second on Mays' hit list (14) followed by Drysdale (13) and Lew Burdette (12). Spahn once joked that if he had struck out Mays in that at-bat back in 1951, pitchers might have gotten rid of Mays forever.

Spahn's final season was 1965. He opened with the Mets, got released in July, and quickly signed with the Giants, with whom he won his final three games as Mays' teammate. Spahn died in 2003.

"Willie was really a Spahn family favorite," Warren's son, Greg Spahn, said. "He always used to come up to Dad and hug him and say, 'You old man, you put me in the Hall of Fame.'"

Mays mentioned it in his Hall of Fame speech, too, and playfully referred to Spahn as "that bald-headed guy over there." Other pitching duels lasted longer. Some combined for fewer hits. But none had the star power and celebrated brilliance as Marichal and Spahn. Or featured such an ending delivered by such an icon.

The pitchers had much in common, though one was a young, right-handed Dominican while the other was an old, left-handed Buffalonian. That season, Spahn led the majors in complete games, Marichal in innings pitched. Spahn was the winningest pitcher in the 1950s, Marichal in the 1960s. Both were stylish 6-foot, sub-200-pounders with exaggerated leg kicks. They were masters of control and deception with ample repertoires— Marichal's assorted arm angles and release points were legendary. Both relied on screwballs; in the case of Spahn, who developed his later in his career, they broke away from right-handers, though his final one on July 2, 1963, didn't exactly do that.

The home run was one of Mays' 22 in extra innings, a record. He's the only man to hit homers in every inning one through 16. Of course, no one can forget his first. For Mays, that was off Spahn.

In those days, you didn't know what was going on. They brought you up. They put you out there. You played.

Mays was far more accomplished by 1963, his 10th All-Star season. He was thirty-two, in his prime and strong enough to take mighty swings in the final moment of a four-hour, ten-minute marathon, which McCovey called the best game he ever played in—even though he thought he got robbed of a walk-off homer in the ninth.

I just kept playing. It didn't bother me. I never thought about the length of a game. If you start worrying about that, you can't play how you need to play. We were all tired, but you keep the strength.

13.

HAVE FUN ON THE JOB

The Story of All-Star Pride

"Keeping the right attitude in high times and low times makes a big difference. Any position you're in, stay upbeat, make the best of it, and enjoy it."

—*Willie Mays*

ONE OF THE beauties of All-Star Games during Willie Mays' career was the sense of pride and unity displayed by players from different teams joining together to take on the rival league, an opportunity to show their talents to wider audiences on a national stage.

Mays absolutely loved playing in All-Star Games and treated them as if they were the playoffs, not exhibitions. He went all out and played with boundless energy and joy.

That's what the All-Star Game is all about, isn't it? That's what I always thought. It was for the fans, and they wanted me to play nine innings every game, so that's what I did. Sometimes 10. I wanted to win. I thought winning was the key to the whole thing.

Mays signed with the Giants at a time of American League dominance. The league was in the midst of winning 15 of 19 World Series, mostly courtesy of the Yankees, and had won 12 of the first 16 All-Star Games.

Two years after Jackie Robinson broke the color barrier, the All-Star Game finally was integrated in 1949, and the National League—far quicker to add African-American and Latin players than the American League—altered the balance of power in the 1950s and 1960s, paralleling the careers of Mays, Hank Aaron, Roberto Clemente, and other minorities who joined forces.

Mays played in 24 All-Star Games, each one from 1954, his first year out of the Army, to 1973, his final season, and the National League's record in those games was 17–6–1. Nobody was more spectacular than Mays, whose 23 hits and 20 runs are All-Star records that aren't expected to be broken.

Warren Giles was the National League president through most of Willie's career and held clubhouse meetings before every All-Star Game to preach the importance of winning and encourage players to take pride in rallying against their American League foes. Mays accepted the challenge.

This is what they told me: "The American League is killing us, man." I said, "Uh-uh. I don't know about anybody else, but I'm going to play nine innings. We're going to change that." Then Hank and all the other guys came in. Frank Robinson, Clemente, and we started winning games. They felt the same way. I wanted to play every inning until the game was decided one way or another.

Aaron remembers the pregame speeches. His first All-Star Game was 1955, a year after Mays' All-Star debut: "I didn't start the game. I don't think Willie started. I don't think Stan Musial started, but I remember Stan Musial hitting a home run in the 12th inning. From that point on, we started winning ballgames, and we caught up with the American League, passed them, and were able to stand on our own. I think one reason for that, and let's face it, the American League was so far behind in trying to bring in

Stan Musial was one of the players Willie Mays adored while growing up. Later, Mays was Musial's teammate on many All-Star teams. (Ron Riesterer)

black ballplayers. The National League was always ahead of them in using black talent."

In those days, not every All-Star felt entitled to play. Making the team was privilege enough, and starters played much longer than they do nowadays. All-Star Games in 1961 and 1966 lasted 10 innings, and Mays started and played until the bitter end in both. In fact, consider the winning rally in the 1961 game at Candlestick Park: Aaron singled up the middle. Mays' double scored Aaron. Clemente singled home Mays.

That's quite a cast to be in the game in the 10th inning. Years later, All-Stars found themselves bowing out after two plate appearances, clearing out their lockers and leaving the ballpark well before the final pitch.

With the advent of free agency in the 1970s that led to rampant player movement between the leagues and interleague play in the 1990s that diminished the league-versus-league rivalry, All-Star Games lost some of their luster for the new generations of players.

The luster never was lost on Mays, who has more All-Star Games to his name than seasons played because of a four-year stretch in which games were played twice a year (from 1959 through 1962) to generate more revenue for the players' pension fund. Mays hit for the cycle in 1960—a single, double, and triple at Municipal Stadium in Kansas City and two days later a homer and two singles at Yankee Stadium.

The homer was off Yankees ace Whitey Ford, which was nothing new. Ford is a Hall of Famer, 236-game winner, and five-time World Series champion, but Mays was his Kryptonite. Mays collected hits in his first six All-Star at-bats facing Ford in 1955, 1956, 1959, and 1960. Two homers, a triple, and three singles.

I loved to hit off Whitey. I liked Whitey. He was a good pitcher. He won 20 games a couple of times. You just see the ball very well against certain pitchers. Sometimes you can't explain it.

An explanation wasn't required.

"I remember Whitey coming back after All-Star Games saying, 'I don't care what I throw, he hits it,'" Yankees second baseman Bobby Richardson said. "Willie was the show of seemingly every All-Star Game."

Ford finally got Mays out in the 1961 game hosted by the Giants, albeit not necessarily by following the rules. The day before the game, Ford and Yankees teammate Mickey Mantle played golf at San Francisco's Olympic Club, guests of Giants owner Horace Stoneham, and then went on a shopping binge and put it on Stoneham's bill.

That night, Ford and Mantle attended a party hosted by Stoneham at the St. Francis Hotel, the aftershock of which ensured a place in baseball lore.

"We play golf and then spend about $600 on sweaters and shirts and golf balls and charge it to Horace," Ford said. "We get to the party, and I tell Mickey, 'Let's give him $300 apiece.' We're about to do that, and Horace says to me, 'I tell you what, if you get in the game tomorrow and face Willie and get him out, we'll call it even. But if he gets a hit, you owe me $1,200.' I said, 'Sure, I'll bet you.'

"Well, we were rooming together, me and Mickey, and Mickey got only six hours sleep. We were drinking quite a bit. But the only thing Mickey thinks about is the bet with Stoneham. So in the first inning, I get the first two outs, and then Willie's up and hits two foul balls about 500 feet.

"I say to myself, 'This is not an official game. They're not watching me closely. Let's screw with the ball a little.' So I throw him a spitball, and it starts right at him. Willie about falls down. He thinks the ball is going to hit him, and the umpire says 'strike three.'

"The inning ends, and Willie walks by me and says, 'What the hell was that you threw?' Mickey's coming in from center field clapping, and Willie says, 'What's that crazy SOB clapping for?'

"I told Willie I'd tell him after the game. We ended up getting all the sweaters, hats, and golf balls, no charge."

Mays remembers the story and laughs about it. It was his final All-Star at-bat against Ford, making him 6-for-7. Throw in the 1962 World Series (4-for-9), and Mays was 10-for-16 against the Yankees' lefty, an astounding .625 batting average.

That's a true story. Whitey finally got me out, and Mickey's blabbing out there. Nobody told me why at the time. Finally, Elston Howard said, "You know why?" "No, what's wrong with that SOB?" He said, "They had a bet. They saved $1,200." Mr. Stoneham told them if they got me out one time, he'd pay for all the stuff at the Olympic Club. Whitey got me one time.

Mays impacted practically every All-Star Game he played. He started a record 18 of his 24 games, including 14 straight. He said he came to win, and he usually did.

Here's a closer look at the Say Hey Kid's All-Star adventures through the years:

1955 (County Stadium in Milwaukee): The National League trailed 5–0 before Mays ignited the greatest comeback in All-Star history. For starters, he leaped high at the fence in the seventh inning to steal a home run from Ted Williams, who famously once said, "They invented the All-Star Game for Willie Mays."

Leading off the bottom of the inning, Mays singled off Ford and scored his league's first run. His two-out single in the eighth, again off Ford, started a three-run rally that tied the game 5–5. With Mays on deck in the 12th, Stan Musial hit his walk-off homer.

1956 (Griffith Stadium in Washington): Mays crushed a pinch-hit homer off Ford in the fourth inning for a 3–0 lead, and the National League won 7–3. Furthermore, Mays recorded an assist that isn't seen in

Ted Williams said the All-Star Game was invented for Willie Mays, who robbed Williams of an All-Star home run in 1955. (Collection of Rick Swig)

the box score—he defused a possible Dodger conflict between Duke Snider, who had pinch-hit for Frank Robinson in the fifth inning, and National League manager Walter Alston, who managed Snider in Brooklyn.

I'm going out to center field, and Walt calls me over and says, "We've got a problem here." I say, "What's that?" He says, "You gotta play right field." "What the hell you talking about?" He says, "Man, if I take Duke out, I might lose him. He may not play for me. I need him, Willie. I need him."

"Okay, Walt. I'll go out there and play right field so we won't have no problems." Walt says, "Thank you very much, you saved me." So Duke goes to center, I go to right, and Stan moves to left. Here I am helping the Dodgers, of all teams. But Walt was a nice man, and I liked Duke.

1959 (Forbes Field in Pittsburgh): The American League scored three runs in the top of the eighth for a 4–3 lead, but in the home half of the inning, Aaron hit a run-scoring single, and Mays stepped up against . . . wait for it . . . Mr. Ford and hit a triple that bounced near the 436-foot marker in right-center to score Aaron for a 5–4 victory.

1960 (Municipal Stadium in Kansas City): The National League's lead-off hitter, Mays tripled to open the game and singled and doubled his next two at-bats. He flied to deep right in his final trip and exited in the sixth inning of a 5–0 game, replaced by Vada Pinson. The final was 5–3, National League.

Think about it. We had so many good players, so many good outfielders. Hank, Clemente, and I liked to play the whole game, but over the years we had Frank Robinson, Willie Stargell, Vada Pinson, Orlando (Cepeda), Felipe (Alou), Billy Williams, Lou Brock, Curt Flood, and also Stan and Duke.

The only game I took myself out was in Kansas City. I wanted Vada to play. He went in for me. Really nice man. That kid could run, boy. He'd hit a triple, and by the time the ball hit the ground, he was halfway to third base.

1960 (Yankee Stadium in New York): Again making an early splash, Mays opened the game with a single off Ford. He also homered off Ford. The final was 6–0.

1962 (D.C. Stadium in Washington): The American League threatened in the ninth with two runners on base, but Mays chased down a ball hit to deep right-center by Luis Aparicio, making a game-ending basket catch. National League, 3–1.

1963 (Cleveland Stadium): Mays singled, walked, scored twice, drove in two runs, and stole two bases in a 5–3 victory, the first of eight straight All-Star wins and 19 of 20 for the National League. He also took an extra-base hit from Joe Pepitone with a running basket catch in deep left-center and won the game's MVP award, which wasn't introduced until 1962, his 12th All-Star Game. He probably missed out on a few.

1964 (Shea Stadium in New York): The National League trailed 4–3 in the ninth, and Mays battled 6-foot-6 Dick Radatz for an 11-pitch walk and stole second to initiate the winning rally.

The guy I had trouble with was the kid from Boston, big ol' strong guy, Dick Radatz. He pitched the last couple of innings the year before and struck me out, and here I was about to face him again in '64, the last inning, we're down a run. But I couldn't find the ball. I couldn't find it to hit it.

As I'm walking to home plate, Walt Alston says, "When you get on, steal second." He didn't say *if* I got on, he said *when* I got on. "How am I going to get on, man?" He said, "Don't worry, you'll get on some kind of way." I went to home plate and tried to find the ball. I couldn't find it. The only thing I could think of was a walk. So I walked.

Cepeda's after me, and I give him the sign I'm stealing, and I steal second. Then he hits a little flare to right field. There's a throwing error, and I score. With two outs, they walk a guy, and then Johnny Callison comes up, hits a home run, we win. That was a fun day.

1965 (Metropolitan Stadium in Minnesota): In a 6–5 victory, Mays homered to open the game, walked twice, and scored twice, including the deciding run.

1966 (Busch Stadium in St. Louis): Mays singled and scored the first run in a 2–1 victory. The game featured 19 future Hall of Famers, which made filling out a lineup card challenging. Alston sought Mays' help.

Walt had a lot of good players but didn't have a leadoff hitter. He asked me to make out the lineup, so I said okay. I'll lead off because I could get on base somehow and steal. I hit Clemente next because he could go to right field and hit behind the runner. I put Hank third because he had power and could hit a fly ball and get a run in. I put Mac at cleanup, then told Walt, "After that, who cares?" He could fill in the rest of the guys.

1968 (Houston Astrodome): Mays won another MVP after scoring the game's only run. This was the Year of the Pitcher, after all. He singled off Luis Tiant to open the first inning, advanced to second on an error, took third on a wild pitch, and scored when McCovey bounced into a double play.

That left Mays, then thirty-seven, with an All-Star batting average of .348. He played five more All-Star Games but didn't get another hit, his career average settling at .307.

"Ted and Willie were the toughest batters I ever faced," Ford said. "But I had a little success against Ted."

To this day, no one has more All-Star hits, runs, steals, multiple-hit games, extra-base hits, total bases, or triples than Mays, who took pride in showcasing his multilayered talents and helping the National League win significantly more than it lost.

All-Star Games were important to me. I loved them. I was fortunate to play in a lot of them and play just about every inning. A few of us stayed in the game until it was decided. A lot of times, that was in the eighth or ninth inning. For me, if you're not in the game, it's hard to have a feeling for it. I was just honored to go and represent the National League and play to win. That was true for a lot of us.

14.

YOUR FOE CAN BE YOUR FRIEND

The Story of a Heated Rivalry

"Try to avoid conflict, racially and otherwise, by being reasonable,
being cool. I've heard it all. All the insults. Be bigger than that.
Keep it clean on the field and off."

—*Willie Mays*

JACKIE ROBINSON WAS traded to the Giants. Let that sink in for a moment.

The legendary and noble Robinson, the widely respected civil rights pioneer and American hero who broke baseball's color barrier and became the
heart and soul of the Brooklyn Dodgers, was dealt after the 1956 season.

For journeyman pitcher Dick Littlefield and $30,000.

Perhaps more stunning than the trade itself was the fact it involved,
of all teams, the Giants. Or as Maury Wills calls them to this day, the
"dreaded Giants." Robinson wound up retiring, nullifying the trade.

Robinson in a Giants uniform would have been as peculiar and inappropriate as Willie Mays in a Dodgers uniform.

**Man, I'd probably hit more home runs. They had a good ballpark over
there in Brooklyn. It was pretty small. Duke was hitting 40 home runs
every year. When they moved to Los Angeles, they played at the football**

stadium a few years, the L.A. Coliseum. I hit a couple home runs there. Wally Moon, man, he hit a lot of home runs there. Then, when they moved to Dodger Stadium, he couldn't get it over the fence as much. That was bigger. A lot of memories with the Dodgers. Good memories.

Unfortunately for the Dodgers, one of their scouts, Wid Matthews, failed to endorse Mays and filed a report that the teenaged center fielder on the Birmingham Black Barons couldn't hit a curve.

Shoot, I thought that was my best pitch. I could hit a breaking ball at seventeen. When I was in high school, not everyone threw hard. Most of the guys tried to throw a breaking ball, and I hit that. They slowed it up. It was easier to hit. They would've been better off throwing the fastball. I don't know what the hell the Dodgers' scout was talking about. He must've gotten out of there in a hurry. I hit a lot of home runs off breaking balls, a lot of them.

Nobody knows better than Tommy Lasorda, who has worked in the Dodgers' organization a mind-boggling seven decades. Long before his 21-year Hall of Fame managing career, Lasorda was a left-handed pitcher who appeared in 26 big-league games in the mid-1950s. After the 1954 season, he played winter ball for the Mayagüez Indians in Puerto Rico and had an unforgettable start against the Santurce Crabbers, who featured Mays in the wake of his first National League MVP award and the Giants' World Series championship.

"First time I saw Willie, he hit a home run off me," Lasorda said. "He had gone back to the States to get an award and came back and homered off me. I couldn't believe it. I said, 'Hey Willie, you think you're a great hitter, huh? You just showed you are.'"

The pitch Lasorda threw?

"I hung a curveball," he said. "As he was trotting around the bases, he said, 'You can get guys out in the minor leagues, but you can't get 'em out in the big leagues.'"

Mays hit the very pitch Wid Matthews said a younger Willie couldn't hit.

In Mays' years as a Giant, the Dodgers were the dominant team, winning six pennants (we're not counting 1952 and 1953, Willie's years in the Army) and four World Series: 1955, 1959, 1963, and 1965. Meantime, the Giants won three pennants and one World Series: 1954.

With the teams regularly fighting for National League supremacy, the rivalry remained hostile. They had a long history of bad blood, but Mays never was an instigator. More of a peacemaker, pulling bodies off the pile instead of piling on.

It never was more apparent than on August 22, 1965, when he single-handedly defused an infamous brawl that many thought could have carried into the stands and streets without his intervention. Mays tried to keep the peace after Juan Marichal used his bat to club Dodgers catcher John Roseboro over the head, leaving Roseboro drenched in blood and so incensed that he wanted to attack the Giants' ace.

In the heat of the moment, Mays grabbed Roseboro by the jersey and forcefully escorted him to the Dodgers' dugout, a single Giant surrounded by a sea of enemy blue. None of the Dodgers' players objected to Mays' actions, and many said afterward they gained further respect for him and credited him for preventing the melee from extending to the crowd of 42,807 at Candlestick Park.

This was at the time of the Watts riots near Roseboro's home in South Central Los Angeles and a civil war raging in Marichal's native Dominican Republic. Civil unrest issues hit home for both players, and this four-game series was particularly edgy, even by Giant-Dodger standards. So after Marichal brushed back a couple of Dodgers in the finale and Sandy Koufax refused to retaliate, Roseboro took matters into his own hands when Marichal came up to bat and threw a ball back to Koufax that clipped Marichal's ear, prompting an exchange of animated venom.

That's when Marichal bashed Roseboro with his bat, causing a two-inch gash above the catcher's left eye.

Right away, it was, "Shoot, I gotta get out there." Roseboro and I were pretty good friends. I always talked to players on other teams. A lot of my friends were on other teams. They all found me if they needed something.

Dusty (Baker), Frank (Robinson), Vada Pinson, Tommy Harper. I always tried to take care of them.

With Johnny, I just tried to do what I had to do when something like that happens. To me, when you see a fight like that, you gotta get the source. You gotta get him out of the way. Sometimes, other guys don't even know what they're fighting about. So I got Johnny to the bench, and blood was all the way down his jersey. I got a wet rag and started wiping. He wanted to get back on the field and fight.

I told him, "Johnny, your eye is out, man." Then he stopped. I knew I had him. But after a little while, he cussed me out and said, "You SOB, nothing wrong with me, let me go."

I said, "No, no, no, you don't want to go out there. Just relax a little bit." He said, "You SOB, why you bring me over here?" I said, "I didn't bring you over here, you came with me."

I said, "Johnny, please, you don't want to go out there all over again, somebody's going to get hurt." He looked at me and said, "You're right." Now I've got to go get Marichal off the field. "C'mon, Chico, let's go." That stopped everything.

I was trying to make sure everyone was okay. At that point, it's just a game. They say a riot might've broken out if Roseboro got to Marichal. We didn't need that.

The inning didn't resume until fourteen minutes after Marichal's bat attack left Roseboro with a wound requiring fourteen stitches. A shaken Koufax walked two batters, and Mays hit a three-run homer to decide a 4–3 Giants victory. The incident affected the pennant race because Marichal was suspended 10 games, fined $1,750, and missed two starts. The Dodgers won the pennant by finishing two games ahead of the Giants and went on to beat the Minnesota Twins in the World Series.

Over time, Marichal and Roseboro graciously moved on from the incident. Roseboro's public forgiveness helped Marichal get to the Hall of Fame on his third attempt, and Marichal was an honorary pallbearer and delivered a eulogy at Roseboro's 2002 funeral. "I was very sorry for what happened, but we made up after that," Marichal said. "I invited him to come to the Dominican to play in my golf classic, and he came and brought his wife and daughter. We became good friends."

If Mays hadn't intervened, there's no telling what that day's outcome and the long-range relationship between Roseboro and Marichal might have been.

Willie's involvement didn't end in the Dodgers' dugout. He recalls entering their clubhouse after the game, a rare gesture for any player, especially someone who hit the game-deciding home run.

I did that so there would be no problem. I went in the clubhouse and checked on both of them, Roseboro and Koufax. Koufax, he was in there getting his arm rubbed. I said, "What's wrong with your arm?" He said, "Why?" I said, "You threw me a slider." He never threw me a slider, never. Every time he threw me a slider, it was a home run. He said, "Ah, I was just trying to get the game over."

Orlando Cepeda wasn't surprised by Mays' diplomacy. Seven years earlier, when Cepeda was a rookie, Mays did him a huge favor and prevented a likely violent and bloody brawl. In a game in Pittsburgh, amid a string of brushbacks and plunkings, Giants pitcher Rubén Gómez drilled Bill Mazeroski, and Pirates pitcher Vernon Law retaliated by throwing high and tight to Gómez. When the umpire warned Law, Pirates manager Danny Murtaugh shot out of the dugout to intercede and found himself in a dustup with Gómez, Cepeda's countryman and mentor from Puerto Rico. That prompted Cepeda to grab a bat and storm toward Murtaugh.

Then came Mays, out of nowhere, with a flying tackle to bring down Cepeda. Damage was averted. Cepeda came to grips and retreated to the dugout.

"In those days, they threw at you a lot," Cepeda said. "Willie knocked me down and brought me back to the dugout. He said, 'Chico, easy.' He looked out for me. They used to hit him a lot, and he didn't say anything. Just went to first base. He knew how to behave."

More than a half century after the Marichal-Roseboro incident, former Dodgers shortstop Maury Wills vividly remembers Mays consoling Roseboro.

"John got hit over the head with a bat, and Willie was the only one who focused on him as far as I know," Wills said. "Roseboro was bleeding. Willie took him aside and directed him off the field. That wasn't surprising. No one could ever get angry at Willie Mays. He'd beat you up on the field and embarrass you, and yet you still loved him and admired him."

Now it can be told: Wills, the Dodgers' main catalyst and fiercest competitor in the '60s, had a soft spot for the Say Hey Kid.

"I fancied myself as the motivating force on the Dodgers, and he was the motivating force on the Giants," Wills said. "Willie and I, as captains of our respective teams, used to bring the lineups up to home plate when the umpires exchanged lineup cards. I was in the minors for eight and a half years, and now I'm at home plate with the great Willie Mays exchanging the lineups. We knew if we could stop Mays, we could beat the dreaded Giants. And I guess they felt if they stopped Wills, they could beat the Dodgers. That was flattering, little ol' me and the great Willie Mays.

"I didn't let them know I felt that way, though. I always wanted them to feel I was thinking of myself as being one of the greatest. That was my own way of getting ready for the game. He was always the greatest as far as that

Don Drysdale was an intimidating pitcher, but Willie Mays batted .330 with 13 home runs against the Dodgers' right-hander. (San Francisco Giants)

was concerned. It was always nice to visit him at the plate and call him only what his close friends knew him by, which was Buck. He coined a nickname for me, Pee Wee. That was flattering coming from Willie Mays. Anybody else call me Pee Wee, I would've taken offense because I thought I was a giant on the field. Excuse the expression."

At that time, dealing with Wills' baserunning was one thing for Mays and the Giants. Dealing with Koufax, the stylish left-hander who led the league in ERA five straight years, and Don Drysdale, the intimidating enforcer who struck fear into hitters, was another.

Mays had a tougher time with Koufax, hitting .278 with five home runs in 122 plate appearances. When he wasn't hitting the deck trying to avoid Drysdale's brushback pitches, Mays hit .330 with 13 homers in 243 plate appearances off the right-hander.

Seemed we never did play the Dodgers without facing those two guys. I'd be thinking about them four or five days beforehand, but I knew how they threw. Koufax, good curve, but you've got to anticipate fastball. Quiet guy. Good guy.

Drysdale will knock you down. Every game, every at-bat. He tried to keep me from aggressively going at the ball, and I knew that. I always told him after the season, "Why you scared of me, man? Why you knock me down all the time?" We were friends. We played golf together in the wintertime. People loved to see us go at it. He'd throw at me, I'd be on the ground, and Roseboro would get the ball back to him in a hurry. That's all right, you won't hit me, and the next pitch may be over the fence.

Lasorda laughed in disbelief when informed Drysdale drilled Mays just twice in his career. "Drysdale used to let him know he was out there on that mound," Lasorda said. "Willie would never complain. All he did was swing that bat at you. As he trotted around the bases, he said, 'Don't ever throw at me, you woke me up.'"

Manny Mota laughed for another reason—his favorite Mays story. Mota broke into the majors with the 1962 Giants but was traded midseason to Pittsburgh and played most of his career as a Dodger, retiring with the record for most pinch hits. On September 23, 1970, at Dodger Stadium, the Giants trailed 8–0 but frantically rallied to win 14–10 in 10 innings. Mays hit his 629th home run, but it didn't count because of a botched call by third-base umpire Ken Burkhart. Mays retired with 660 homers. It should be 661.

"I was in left field, and Willie hit a line drive over the fence," Mota said, "but he hit it so hard, the ball hit a seat and bounced back to me. Right away, I threw it to the infield. Only a single. I had my back to home plate and was blocking the umpire. Not too many people know that. I can still see Willie's face. He was trying to tell the umpire it was a home run. It's a funny story, but Willie made me a better player. I learned more from Willie in three months in '62 than I learned the next five years. He taught me how to play the game, respect the game, and play hard. No, he didn't teach me how to turn a home run into a single."

As passionate as the rivalry has been in California, all the way up to the dustups between Madison Bumgarner and Yasiel Puig and Bumgarner and Max Muncy, participants from the New York days say the rivalry was far more vicious on the East Coast. In California, it's a 380-mile drive from ballpark to ballpark. In New York, the rivalry was just a borough away. The uniqueness of the Polo Grounds, where both teams walked to their clubhouses through center field, often heightened the intensity.

"There was a door between the clubhouses," said Vin Scully, the renowned voice of the Dodgers from 1950 through 2016. "They nailed that door shut because there was such anger between the teams. Now, with the Giants in San Francisco and Dodgers in Los Angeles, there isn't the same friction there was in Ebbets Field and the Polo Grounds. I used to go to Giant-Dodger games saying a little prayer, 'Please don't let anyone get hurt.'"

Vin Scully and Willie Mays reminisced during the final weekend of the legendary broadcaster's career in 2016. Naturally, his final broadcasts were Giant-Dodger games. (John Shea)

The Giants and Dodgers, we'd always fight. Every time we played, it seemed. Not me. The teams themselves. The guys on the Dodgers didn't bother me.

They're all my friends. We'd hang out afterward. Junior Gilliam got to be my best friend when he got to the Dodgers. He played in the Negro Leagues in Baltimore and could play any position. When he came to the Dodgers, he took over for Jackie at second base, and Jackie moved to third and the outfield.

Junior was a great guy. Even though he knocked my front teeth out. I made a mistake and tried to dive into second on a steal. He caught the ball and hit me with a backhand right in my mouth. He didn't do it on purpose. He was late getting there, and he caught the ball and just put it down. I hit him with my mouth. He was just trying to get me out.

In Harlem, we shot a lot of pool together on Seventh Avenue right by Smalls Paradise around the corner from Campy's liquor store. Junior, Campy (Roy Campanella), (Don) Newcombe, Joe Black. The owners at the pool hall thought we should fight because we were Giants and Dodgers. They wanted everybody to fight so they could draw more people. We just had a good time, man. We didn't go there to fight.

Fighting was more of an on-field pastime, though one of the most intense altercations from the New York days wasn't a fight at all, as Mays recalls.

Ebbets Field, 1955. Sal Maglie knocked down Jackie, and it wasn't the first time, so Jackie wanted to get Maglie back. Jackie bunts to the right side and figures he could run over Maglie covering first. But Sal didn't cover. He delayed. Davey Williams, our second baseman, covered. Jackie hit Davey and broke his back. After that, the guys were saying we needed to get Jackie. Anybody running to third base, where Jackie was playing that day, get 'em back.

So Alvin Dark hits a double and keeps going. He took out Jackie. Alvin played football at LSU. He knew how to hit a guy. Everybody waited for Jackie to retaliate. He got up, picked up the ball, rubbed it in his hands like most guys do, and threw it back to the pitcher. Everybody in both dugouts waited to see what would happen. We were waiting for a fight, but you can't fight when no one's fighting. Nothing happened. Jackie did nothing.

Dark, near the end of his life, said his collision with Robinson led to a mutual respect they shared from then on.

"Davey Williams was my roommate," Dark said. "Jackie wanted to get Maglie. Well, he was mad enough—and I might've done the same thing—that he ran over Davey Williams. That started the downfall of Davey's career. He had a bad back from then on. We had a meeting under the grandstand between innings. I said, 'Somebody's got to get Jackie Robinson.'

"Lo and behold, I'm hitting next inning and hit a ball to left-center. I can't stop at second base. I just got through saying we've got to run into Jackie Robinson. Well, Jackie had the ball twenty feet before I got to third. I was out by a mile. So I left my feet, and I hit him. He went one way, his glove another, my hat another. Everything was spread out. He dropped the ball, and I got back on the bag. He went back to his position and said, 'I'll get you at second base,' and I said, 'I'll be there.'

"Now, Jackie and I turned out to be real good friends. We played in golf tournaments together, and I respected him so much because of what he went through, more than any other player I've seen in my life. Never did anything happen between us after that. He did everything he was supposed to do, and I did everything I was supposed to do. When I slid into a base he was covering, I slid in with a hook slide. Both of us had chances to really rip each other up if we wanted because of the positions we played, but after that, we never tried to hurt each other. It turned out where we both respected each other."

Mays respected both participants and didn't think it was unusual that he had kinships with many other Dodgers.

Nobody bothered Gil Hodges. He was a big, strong guy, a catcher before Campy took over. Gil Hodges, Pee Wee Reese, and Ralph Branca, they were there for Jackie. Those guys played on Jackie's barnstorming team.

Then there was Carl Furillo, the right fielder who had a beef with Durocher dating to Durocher's time managing in Brooklyn. Two years before Mays arrived as a rookie, Furillo was beaned at Ebbets Field by the Giants'

Sheldon Jones, presumably under orders from Durocher, and carried off on a stretcher.

Furillo was a tough ballplayer with a good arm. He didn't care what people thought. He was going to say what's on his mind. He and Leo didn't see eye to eye when Leo managed the Dodgers, and that carried over to when Leo managed the Giants. They went at each other pretty good.

I was in the Army in '53 when Furillo broke his hand in a fight at the Polo Grounds. They tell me he and Leo charged each other. They were on the ground, and guys were trying to break it up when someone stepped on Furillo's hand. He missed the rest of the season, but his average held up, and he won the batting crown.

Carl Erskine, a Dodgers pitcher from 1948 to 1959, witnessed too many brawls between the teams to count and said, "We had a lot of really bad exchanges with the Giants. There was a lot of bad blood because Durocher had been the Dodger manager. When you think about it, there were only eight teams in the league, and you played the other teams 22 times, 11 at home, 11 on the road, but with the Dodgers and Giants, all 22 games were in the same town. That fed the rivalry. Your manhood was on the line when you played the Giants. It didn't make a difference what the standings were. You were in the middle of a rivalry that lasted for decades."

Erskine couldn't cite a single scuffle that Mays ignited, saying, "Willie was their sparkplug, but he was never a loudmouth."

When Mays broke into the majors, Dodgers catcher Roy Campanella, who had played many years in the Negro Leagues, would razz him at the plate in an attempt to distract him. Campanella, forbidden to play in the majors when he was Mays' age, figured Willie needed to pay his dues. Over time, Campanella, who was ten years older, warmed to Mays. Even on the Dodgers, Mays had no enemies. That eventually went for pitcher Don Newcombe, who was five years older and became the first African American to win an MVP award, Cy Young Award, and Rookie of the Year award.

Don Newcombe, an MVP, Cy Young Award winner, and Rookie of the Year, played for the rival Dodgers, but Willie Mays was his friend. (William Jacobellis/Kidwiler Collection/Diamond Images)

"I've seen them all in my time, and Willie is the greatest all-around player of my lifetime," Newcombe said. "Nobody could do everything on the field the way Willie did. He was the best with the glove, his arm was fantastic. He hit with power and would go the other way if you needed a base hit. He knew the game as well as anybody. He never made a bad decision when it counted. He was the best base runner, too, right there with Jackie. I honestly don't believe anybody in the history of the game was as great as Willie."

Former Dodgers president Peter O'Malley, whose father, Walter, spearheaded the team's move west, calls Mays "likable and respected. Everybody liked him, on the Dodgers' team as well. I don't recall Willie being booed in any ballpark, including Dodger Stadium or Ebbets Field. Even though the rivalry was intense, I can't see Willie being booed. I don't think any individual player played a more prominent role in the rivalry."

The Robinson trade was fascinating, especially because it came at the height of the rivalry and involved the most storied Dodger in the organization's history. Despite common belief that he retired because he didn't want to be a Giant, he was quitting anyway and going to work as vice president and director of personnel at an East Coast chain called Chock Full o'Nuts. He was thirty-seven and feuding with owner Walter O'Malley, who had essentially gained control of the team from Branch Rickey and pushed for general manager Buzzie Bavasi to make the trade a year before the Giants, struggling to draw fans to the Polo Grounds, and Dodgers moved to California.

"If he went to the Giants, they might still be in New York," Bavasi said decades later. "He'd have meant that much to them. If Jackie played for the Giants, they would've had a great '57 and '58. Imagine Jackie and Willie Mays together. Plus, the Polo Grounds were exactly a half mile from the middle of Harlem."

Peter O'Malley disputes Bavasi's claim, insisting nothing was going to stop the teams' relocation, not even a Mays-Robinson merger. As for the friction between his father and Robinson, O'Malley said Rickey deserves all the credit for signing the infielder and that no one, including his father, could have lived up to Rickey and what he meant to Robinson. The younger O'Malley equated it to the Mays-Durocher relationship.

Jackie wasn't coming to the Giants. If he meant that much to the Dodgers, why would they trade him? It didn't make sense to me. I'd want Jackie on my payroll.

The feeling was mutual. Robinson and Campanella, after their barnstorming tour through the South, spoke with the Dodgers about scouting the teenaged Mays. Willie had become well known around Birmingham for helping the Black Barons reach the final Negro League World Series in 1948.

The Homestead Grays won the World Series, but Mays had the decisive ninth-inning single in Game 3 and threw out Hall of Famer Buck Leonard at third base. Leonard praised Mays' defense but said the kid had trouble hitting a curve.

Wid Matthews wasn't alone.

What if the Dodgers had signed Mays?

"That would be the greatest thing to happen for us, having a guy like that play for the Dodgers," Lasorda said. "We had some great players, too, but Willie's got to be on everybody's All-Star team. He was a quiet, hardworking youngster out of Alabama. The whole world was in front of him, and he conquered it."

Mays is perfectly fine that he didn't spend his career in Dodger blue.

Like I said, I had good friends on the Dodgers. Good friends on all the teams. It's much easier that way. I had no regrets. Regrets? For what? The only time I had a regret is when I got traded back to the Mets, but it worked out. Mr. (Horace) Stoneham said he had no money, and Mrs. (Joan) Payson wanted me there so she could take care of me after I retired.

15.

YOU CAN GO HOME AGAIN

The Story of a Return to New York

"If you leave a place, there's a chance someday you could go back, so keep it positive just in case."

—*Willie Mays*

WHEN THE GIANTS and Dodgers moved to California after the 1957 season, New York, the epicenter of baseball's Golden Era and home of 23 of the first 53 World Series championships, was left without a National League team for the first time since the 1800s.

Nobody was more devastated than Joan Whitney Payson, who vehemently fought the relocation as a minority owner of the Giants and was quick to sell her 10 percent share of the team, which featured her favorite player, Willie Mays, once it was destined for San Francisco.

A tireless attempt ensued to bring another big-league team to the city— to the extent attorney William Shea proposed a third league, the Continental League—and New Yorkers were rewarded through the 1962 National League expansion with the New York Mets.

Payson led the ownership group that ran the Mets, who were uniformed in orange and blue to represent the colors of the departed teams. She oversaw Casey Stengel's inaugural club that lost a stunning 120 games and the

World Series–winning Miracle Mets of 1969, but through it all, she missed Mays dearly and dreamed of him playing again on her team.

Early in the second month of the 1972 season, with Mays in the twilight of his career and Giants owner Horace Stoneham financially strapped, Payson—baseball's first female owner who didn't inherit a team—acquired Mays for pitcher Charlie Williams and cash.

They traded me when we were in Montreal, and Mrs. Payson calls me in the clubhouse. She says, "I finally got you. You're coming to New York." The next call is from my wife, Mae, who had a beautiful suite waiting for me at the hotel in New York. It was like I was home. Like I never left.

I thanked Mr. Stoneham for making it possible. Mrs. Payson, she did everything for me, took care of me, anything I wanted. She was a really, really, really nice lady. When I retired, I was going to come back to San Francisco, and she said, "No, no, no. You've got to stay here. This is your home now."

She says, "Write your own contract." Well, no one writes his own contract. So she gives me a contract, and I write, "I, Willie Mays, will do what I want when I want." No way was anyone going to sign that. She says, "That's what you want?" She signed it. I'll never forget that.

Mays' time playing in Queens was brief but extraordinary for not only Payson but fans of New York baseball who had been without the Say Hey Kid for fourteen-plus seasons as he resumed his Hall of Fame trail on another coast.

When Mays slipped on his new Mets uniform with his familiar number 24 (Jim Beauchamp agreed to swap 24 for 5), he openly was welcomed by his new teammates, including pitcher Jerry Koosman and first baseman Ed Kranepool, who turned into two of his closest friends on the team.

"It was like a godsend for us," Koosman said. "You couldn't have asked for anything better for our ballclub than Willie Mays. Willie probably had the greatest instincts of anyone I've ever seen, and he was still a threat when he came to the Mets. It pumped up the whole club when we got Willie.

Toward the end of Willie Mays' career, the cash-strapped Giants traded him back to New York. His new team: the Mets. (New York Mets)

He was a great leader in the clubhouse, and you couldn't have asked for a better teammate. He was leery about coming to the Mets, but we made him feel at home. It was just a great pleasure, the highlight of my career, to play with Willie Mays."

Kranepool grew up in the Bronx a Yankees fan but went to the Polo Grounds plenty of times to watch a young Mays, then played against him, then with him.

"We all loved seeing Willie come into the clubhouse," Kranepool said. "The excitement and electricity he generated in the stadium, it was something you couldn't replace. Willie had so much to offer, and he was willing to give it to all the players who needed help."

Payson inherited Mays' $165,000 salary, paid him the same in 1973, and tacked on a ten-year, $50,000-a-year personal services contract, security that Stoneham couldn't provide.

New Yorkers never stopped loving Mays, but those expecting to see the same Willie from the Polo Grounds era were disappointed. Not to mention unrealistic. Mays had turned forty-one a few days before the trade, an age most players reach well into retirement.

Mays was just one year removed from hitting 18 home runs, leading the league in on-base percentage, posting his best OPS (on-base percentage plus slugging percentage) in five years, and helping the Giants win the National League West. But he didn't have the pop, speed, or arm from his glory days. He no longer was an everyday player, but he still was capable of big moments.

His first, in fact, was a home run in his first game as a Met—against the Giants, by the way. On May 14, leading off and playing first base, Mays crushed a Don Carrithers fifth-inning pitch over the left-field wall at Shea Stadium, his first homer of the season and 647th of his career. It broke a 4–4 tie, proved the difference in a 5–4 victory, and predictably prompted a thunderous ovation from 35,505 fans who welcomed back an old friend.

It was a great feeling but a little odd because these were my teammates for so many years. It took me twenty minutes to get around the bases. Every guy I went by talked to me for five minutes. What's so unique about it, if you ever see the film, the umpires did nothing. Didn't say a word. They just stood there and said do what you gotta do.

The Mets had a terrific pitching staff with Tom Seaver, Jon Matlack, and Koosman, as good as any starting threesome in the league, and the best closer in the game in Tug McGraw. The offense was punchless, however, and Mays was an asset despite playing just 69 games in his first Mets season. He hit .267 with eight home runs and led the team in on-base percentage and OPS.

I told the guys I didn't come here to try to create a problem. I came here to help you guys win, that's it. I played about half the games my two years in New York. It was very difficult to sit on the bench when the guys were losing. I wanted to go out and play, be an example for the guys, and make sure they knew how to play. I think we played very well that first year.

It was clear that 1973, Mays' most physically draining season, would be his swan song. He had swollen knees throughout the season—let's not forget this was the era that introduced artificial turf, initially as hard as concrete and a menace to many a player. He hurt his shoulder in early May and was shelved for a month, the first disabled list appearance of his career. He ran into a metal railing in pursuit of a foul popup while playing first base September 9 in Montreal and cracked two ribs.

Aside from the knee injuries that limited his running and the shoulder injury that limited his throwing, the latest injury limited his swinging. He didn't play another regular-season game and finished with a .211 average. In 66 games, he hit six homers, including his last one, number 660, off Cincinnati's Don Gullett on August 17 in New York, a Mays special to right-center.

Clearly, Mays' body didn't allow him to display his five-tool supremacy of old. One example came soon after he was reinstated from the disabled list in a June 11 game in San Francisco. A ball was hit into the power alley in left-center, and both Mays and left fielder George Theodore gave chase.

"It was hard for him to throw. He kind of had to sling the ball, but his reflexes were incredible," Theodore remembered. "The ball's hit between us in the gap, and I rush over to get it, but Willie beats me there because his reflexes are so good, and he flips the ball to me underhanded at the fence. I'm about eight feet from him and expecting him to throw the ball in, but he's thinking ahead and flipping to me, which shows his sense of the game, like no other. I fumble it and then throw it in. They give me the error on the play and eventually changed it to Willie's error, but I was never more honored to get an error than right there."

On September 20, Mays announced at a news conference that he'd retire after the season, and the Mets won seven of their final nine. In the final week, he was honored at Shea Stadium. Willie Mays Night attracted 43,805 fans and featured an emotional ceremony in which dignitaries such as Joe DiMaggio, Stan Musial, Monte Irvin, Bobby Thomson, and heavyweight champ Joe Frazier paid their respects. Mays was showered with gifts and praise and spoke to the crowd for several moments, thanking his fans, acknowledging the perseverance and drive of his teammates, and

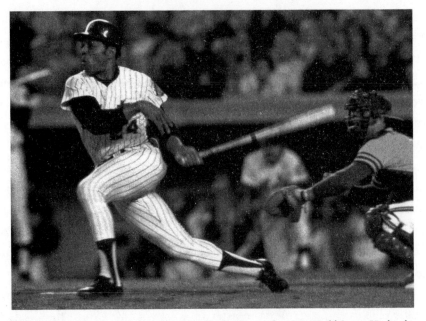

In Willie Mays' final big-league season, he played for the Mets in the 1973 World Series. His last hit was off Rollie Fingers. (New York Mets)

closing with, "Willie, say good-bye to America." It was impossible not to be teary-eyed, and that went for Willie, too.

"When Willie told me, 'Koos, I'm getting tired, I think I'm gonna quit,' I said, 'Willie, you better not quit. As old as you are, you're still the best ballplayer on our club,'" Koosman said. "I begged him not to quit. He said, 'Koos, I'm tired.'"

The Mets were in the cellar on August 30 and rallied to overtake five teams and win the division on the final day. McGraw's catchphrase, "Ya Gotta Believe," was a rally cry for a group coming together at the right time.

We had a good team in '73. We had a good staff, man. The pitching was better than the hitting. Seaver, Matlack, Koosman. McGraw out of the bullpen. We brought in George Stone, a tall lefty who had a good year. We had good guys. We enjoyed each other.

I wasn't able to do much because of injuries. When I hurt my side in Montreal, chasing that ball near the dugout, I could still play first base but couldn't swing the bat. I was going to be there for everyone. For me, I was finishing up. It was time.

The Mets faced the Reds in the National League Championship Series, and Mays didn't play the first four games of the best-of-five series. In all, he missed 22 games following the mishap in Montreal. After a one-month break, Mays finally returned to the field October 10 in the NLCS finale and legged out a pinch infield single during a decisive four-run rally that decided the 7–2 Mets clincher.

Perhaps Mays' biggest contribution in the series was helping to prevent a riot in the aftermath of the legendary Pete Rose–Bud Harrelson fight in Game 3. Rose slid hard into the Mets' scrappy shortstop in a failed attempt to break up a double play, and Harrelson found himself in an altercation with the eventual hits king.

Order was restored, but Mets fans were outraged. When Rose took his position in left field, he was the target of insults and debris. Cincinnati manager Sparky Anderson pulled his team off the field, and league president Chub Feeney, who was the Giants' general manager during much of Mays' time in San Francisco, threatened to forfeit the game to the Reds if the crowd couldn't be controlled. That's when Mays and a contingent of Mets, including manager Yogi Berra, walked to the outfield and persuaded fans to cool it.

The game resumed, and the Mets won to take a 2–1 edge in the series.

I was in the dugout, and Yogi says, "Willie, you gotta come out with me. They won't shut up for me." So I go out there. They settled down. It was just a little scuffle. Those guys, Harrelson and Pete Rose, ironed it out and became teammates in Philadelphia.

At the time, though, it was an ugly scene. Not as ugly as the Juan Marichal–John Roseboro incident in 1965, which Mays helped curtail with his peacemaking efforts, dragging Roseboro off the field when the Dodgers' catcher wanted retaliation for Marichal clubbing him over the head with a bat. Witnesses swore Mays singlehandedly prevented a riot in the Candle-stick Park crowd.

This time, at Shea Stadium, he also helped make sure the scene didn't worsen.

"They threw whiskey bottles and everything else at me," Rose said. "I had a Jack Daniel's bottle land two feet from me thrown from the third deck. Of course, New York fans . . . the bottle was empty. They made sure to drink it before they threw it at me. Willie went out to left field to tell them to quit throwing all that garbage at me. He was like that. He played hard and played to win. He didn't want fans throwing objects at players. He understood competition. He understood what was going on between me and Bud and the Mets. Willie was the peacemaker. If you're trying to do something like he was trying to do, he's the right guy to come out there. Everybody respected Willie. He just wanted to have a good game and for everybody to abide by the rules. That's the way he was."

Mets players weren't surprised by Mays' gesture. Even in the short time he was in New York, he was known to avoid confrontations rather than intensify them.

"Willie was beloved by the fans and went on the field and calmed them down," Kranepool said. "They paid attention to him. Yeah, we almost had a riot. But that was Willie. He didn't start fights. If he wanted to fight, he had many opportunities to fight. Look how many times he was knocked down on purpose in his career. Today, pitchers can't pitch inside. Well, with Willie, they always tried to knock him down. They thought they were intimidating him. He just went about his business. He was very profes-sional on the baseball field. He had a flare, but he didn't embarrass people like some of the guys today. He didn't need to."

The 1973 World Series pitted the Mets and Oakland A's, and Mays got the biggest ovation in introductions before Game 1 at the Oakland Coli-seum, across the San Francisco Bay from Candlestick Park. Bay Area fans passionately expressed their love for the visiting Mays even though the A's were on the verge of a dynasty. The series lasted seven games, and Mays started just once, the opener, in place of injured Rusty Staub, who hurt his shoulder in the NLCS. It was Mays' final big-league start. In center field and hitting third, at forty-two the oldest position player in World Series history, 22 years after his first World Series appearance, he went 1-for-4 in a 2–1 loss.

Staub returned to the lineup for Game 2, one of the most memorable (and forgettable) games Mays ever played. Memorable, because he got the game-winning hit in the 12th inning of a 10–7 Mets win, a single off future Hall of Famer Rollie Fingers. Forgettable, because images from that game depicted a stumbling Mays in a negative light, as a past-his-prime player who stayed in the game too long, an example cited by cynics suggesting icons shouldn't wait long beyond their prime to retire.

Circumstances either overlooked at the time or forgotten over the years tell another side of the story.

"You know what? The reason they say that is because he wasn't a superstar in the end," Kranepool said. "You can't be. As great a player as he was, his skills had diminished. You saw flashes of the greatness, but you knew what he could do and what he couldn't do. If he was on the field as the real Willie Mays, you wouldn't take him out of center field. We knew that. He knew what his limitations were. When he played first base, he would toss his glove to me in the seventh inning and say, 'Ed, go out for defense.' I don't blame him for staying around. It's tough to give up what he had. There are a lot of reasons you play. Recognition, camaraderie. He loved being at the ballpark. He loved that whole spectrum of playing the game. He knew he was going to retire. He announced it early. He didn't wait around. Nothing wrong with that. Everyone's an individual."

Rickey Henderson scoffs at people who say Willie played too long. Rickey played in the majors until he was forty-four and then played independent ball until he was forty-six. The running joke was that he might miss his Hall of Fame induction because he had a game.

"You weren't playing that long just because you were trying to achieve something. You were playing because you loved it, you enjoyed it," Henderson said. "That's why Willie played. He had been the greatest, the most successful player he could be. After all that's said and done, it's how much you enjoy the game. That's what made you tick, what made you live through it. That's your life, and you want to do it as long as you can. My time in independent ball, those were some of the most precious times in my career."

Phil Niekro, who knuckleballed his way to the Hall of Fame, pitched until he was forty-eight and said, "I didn't believe in the age factor. There's always going to be someone who's the youngest, someone who's the oldest. They're going to put the best players on the field. If you could do the job, you could do the job. You pitch against Willie Mays, you don't think about age. I don't care if he's fifty-two years old, you better have your stuff together to get him out."

Mays entered Game 2 in the top of the ninth as a pinch-runner for Staub and stayed in the game on defense for the bottom of the inning. With the Mets leading 6–4, there was some confusion as Mays warmed up in right field, thinking he was taking Staub's spot. Just before the inning began, Mays got word from the bench to switch with center fielder Don Hahn.

At that point, the lights went on at the Coliseum, which prompted A's manager Dick Williams to complain to umpire Augie Donatelli. Because the lights were off in the top of the inning, they shouldn't have been turned on until the inning was completed. So the lights went off. But the sun was a major problem. It was particularly bad on this day, several players from both sides struggling to track fly balls and popups.

Because the series opener began at 1 p.m. and lasted two hours and twenty-six minutes, it ended long before the sun would have become an issue. But Game 2 began at 1:30 p.m. and lasted four hours and thirteen minutes, to that point the longest World Series game in history. As a result, the later innings were played in twilight with the sun setting behind the home-plate side of the bowl at the Coliseum. When Mays entered the game, batters were in the shade while pitchers were in the sunlight. Sure enough, the first batter on Mays' watch hit the ball in the air to shallow center.

Their first baseman, Deron Johnson, came in off the bench and hit it to me. I couldn't find the damn ball. It got past me. I never played over there in Oakland. I played on all kinds of fields in different elements. I just missed the ball.

Mays drifted several steps to his right but lost the ball in the sun and tried to make a shoestring catch at the last moment and fell, the ball skipping by him. He gave no excuse, and Johnson was credited with a double. The A's rallied for two runs to tie the game 6–6 and force extra innings.

"The sun was so bad that day," said Kranepool, coming to Mays' defense. "Nobody could see the ball. Look, Willie could play the outfield at any age. Maybe he couldn't run as fast as he used to, but he still had the instincts. The sun was difficult for everyone. If Willie can't catch it, nobody can."

Reggie Jackson played center field that day for the A's and said, "It was a brutal sun in center field. I made a great catch off Jerry Grote, but the sun was bad. Willie Mays didn't screw that ball up. It was the sun. In October, there's not a worse place."

More controversy ensued in the 10th. The Mets thought they took the lead when Harrelson tagged on Felix Millan's fly to left. Joe Rudi's one-hop throw was slightly up the third-base line, and catcher Ray Fosse attempted a swipe tag. Donatelli, who positioned himself behind the plate—on his belly, of all places—ruled Harrelson out. The Mets vehemently argued, led by Mays, the on-deck hitter who dropped to his knees near the batter's box so he could make his case with Donatelli eye to eye. Berra and others stormed out of the dugout. Harrelson was livid, believing he sidestepped Fosse's tag as he tried to score without a slide. Replays seemed to side with Harrelson.

The lasting image of Mays, captured in photographs—on his knees, both arms in the air, helmet fallen from his head in the heat of the moment, arguing in vain—made it appear as if he himself had blundered. In fact, Mays was pleading for a teammate. He actually had a better view of the play than Donatelli.

"Willie didn't argue for the hell of it," Koosman said. "He was on his knees begging with the umpire because he really missed the call. If Willie's going to argue like that, he's right. You could see from the dugout he was safe, and Willie was right there to see it."

Donatelli wasn't the only witness to believe Harrelson was out.

"I did tag him. I grazed his uniform," Fosse said nearly a half-century later. "He didn't feel it, but I grazed him as he was trying to avoid the tag.

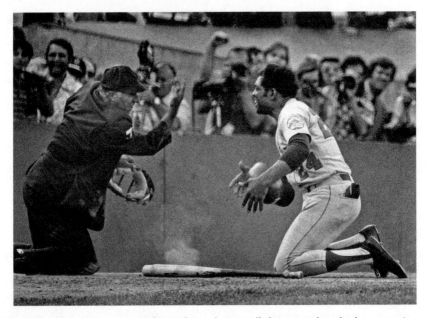

Willie Mays pleads for teammate Bud Harrelson, who was called out on a close play by umpire Augie Donatelli in Game 2 of the 1973 World Series. Mays singled home the winning run in the 12th inning. (Ron Riesterer)

Willie had his hands in the air like I didn't get him, but I got him. Nowadays, there'd be a thousand angles for replay, and it would've shown I got him."

The Mets would disagree wholeheartedly. In retrospect, Fosse made another point about Mays.

"The reason Willie was so close to the play, he was telling Harrelson to slide, and I thought he was going to slide," said Fosse, who drew a comparison with another memorable play at the plate from the A's-Yankees 2001 Division Series. "If somebody did that for Jeremy Giambi, the Derek Jeter flip play never would've happened. Jeremy didn't know what to do, and nobody was there to tell him. Willie was there doing that. He was a pro and knew the game. Then Harrelson was called out, and Willie erupts and throws his arms up. That's the picture you see."

On to the 12th inning. Tie game, two outs, runners at first and third. And here comes Mays, who still could outfox his foes. He took the first pitch and immediately complained that he couldn't see because of the Coliseum backdrop, loud enough for Fosse to hear. In fact, it was a decoy. Fosse called for a fastball, thinking Fingers would simply blow it by Mays. But Willie was prepared. He had no problem seeing Fingers' pitch and bounced it over the mound into center field for an RBI single to give New York a 7–6 lead.

The Mets rallied for four runs, thanks largely to second baseman Mike Andrews, who made errors on consecutive plays and was forced onto the disabled list after the game by A's owner Charlie Finley, who cited a fake injury. Teammates were furious, and Commissioner Bowie Kuhn reinstated Andrews and fined Finley. Dick Williams, saying he could no longer work for Finley, resigned after the World Series.

"Yeah, it happened. He said it," Fosse said of Mays. "We were in the twilight. That time of year, that time of day, you're in the shadows. It was brutal. Willie said later, 'I set 'em up, I told 'em I couldn't see, I deked 'em.' But it's not like the pitcher's not going to throw a fastball. I don't care if he can see or not see. You know it's gonna be a fastball. But maybe it helped him, thinking if we thought he couldn't see, he'd be looking fastball.

"The irony of it all, if Willie doesn't get that hit and extend the inning, Andrews doesn't make those two errors, and it's a whole different story."

Mays lost one more ball in the sun in the bottom of the 12th, enabling Jackson to leg out a triple. Reggie scored, but the Mets won 10–7. Despite the issues with the injuries, the long layoff, the sun, and the mix-up with the positions, Mays walked away from Game 2 with the game-winning hit, grateful he could still deliver in a big moment.

I was happy we finally won the game. It was a long day but an important win going back to New York. People were saying I should've retired before then. I wanted to play as long as I kept contributing. It was a tough year physically. I wasn't used to being hurt. So much of my career, I was used to playing every day.

But I still enjoyed the game. I loved the guys. I tried to help the guys, and it was fun to see them win. There were times I was ready to quit. Mrs. Payson wouldn't let me. She said the guys wanted me around.

In retrospect, Fingers is thrilled that he surrendered Mays' last hit.

"He was my first autograph," Fingers said. "First year of Dodger Stadium, my dad takes me to a Giant-Dodger game. He asks where I want to sit. I say, 'Center-field bleachers. Willie Mays is right there.' After the game, I go to where the players come out. You can't get close to anybody, and I'm standing sixty, seventy feet back from where everyone comes out. I see Koufax, Drysdale, Maury Wills. And then off to my left, a door opens. It kind of catches my eye. I look over, it's Willie Mays. He's sneaking out.

"So I'm chasing Willie between the cars at Dodger Stadium. I get to the car where he's at, and I say, 'Mr. Mays, can you sign an autograph?' He signs. Next time I see him, it's the '73 World Series. I was on the mound for Willie's last hit, his last RBI, and his last strikeout. I don't see him again until I'm inducted into the Hall of Fame, and I go up to him and say, 'It's a good thing you signed my autograph or I would've drilled your ass.' He laughed.

"I'd have never hit Willie, though."

Two African-American stars on the 1973 A's who grew up admiring Mays found themselves across the field from their boyhood idol. In the days before interleague play and free agency, players rarely got the chance to see their peers in the other league. This was a cool opportunity for Reggie Jackson and Vida Blue.

"He was my guy," Jackson said. "I had a paper route growing up in Pennsylvania and had to deliver the papers before I went to school. The paper would have just Willie's first two at-bats from the West Coast, and if he had a good day, I had a good day at school. If he had a bad day, I had a bad day at school. I followed him my whole career. When I got to Arizona State, I learned how to run like Willie. I got to meet him at my first spring training. He came over and said, 'Somebody said I was your guy,' and he shook my hand and said, 'I heard you got a lot of power. Keep going. Do your thing. I'll be watching you.' I was always a fan, always loved him."

Blue, who grew up in Mansfield, Louisiana, said, "We all wanted to be Willie Mays. He was my favorite player. I played center field in high school until they brought me in to pitch because I threw so hard. Willie was the epitome of what a young African American wanted to be. Sports isn't the only way out, but it's a way out. I don't know how old Willie is, but he'll always be twenty years old in my mind."

The World Series moved to New York for Game 3, and Mays grounded out as a pinch-hitter, the final at-bat of his career. To this day, he wishes he got one more.

In the ninth inning of Game 7, the Mets trailed 5–2 with two outs and two aboard. Fingers was replaced by lefty Darold Knowles, who was setting a record as the first pitcher to appear in all seven World Series games. According to Knowles' career splits, he was much more effective against lefties, but Berra sent Wayne Garrett, a left-handed batter, to the plate. Garrett popped out, and the A's celebrated their second of three straight World Series championships.

Mays wanted that last at-bat.

I was ready to hit. I kick myself. I could've gone to Yogi and said, "I gotta pinch-hit, man." I think he would've said, "Okay, go ahead and pinch-hit." I think that's what he would've said because we had that type of relationship. But I said no, that's not how to do it. I never did that. That's not the right way to do that.

After the game, I didn't change my clothes. Don Hahn asked for my glove, and I gave it to him. Then I got in my car and went on home.

Mays wasn't the only one who wondered if he should be hitting in that situation.

"Obviously, you would put Willie up," Kranepool said. "Wayne is a good guy, but it was lefty against lefty, and Willie still had enough in him to have one at-bat. Willie wanted to win. He was a team player. We were all upset with the outcome of the '73 Series. We should've won that series. Blame the people at the top, whoever made those decisions. There were decisions made that I thought were wrong. I think everybody did. You can't go back."

A more controversial decision by Berra was starting Seaver on short rest in Game 6 rather than holding him back and letting him pitch Game 7 with the usual four days between starts. Seaver wasn't quite his overpowering self and took the loss—Catfish Hunter outpitched him, and the A's won 2–1—and Matlack, also starting on short rest in Game 7, failed to finish three innings and gave up home runs to Bert Campaneris and Jackson.

The alternative was to have George Stone, who flashed a 12–3 record and 2.80 ERA in his best career season, start the sixth game and Seaver the seventh.

"He should've never pitched the sixth game," Kranepool said of Seaver. "No reason for it. Absolutely none. We were up 3–2. We don't have to win the sixth. What would be the purpose of pitching him on short rest? There were a lot of decisions that were questioned, and that's the difference between Gil Hodges, who was our manager in '69 when we won, and Yogi in '73 when we lost. He's a nice guy, but he wasn't as good a manager."

Mays tried to focus on the big picture. He still does.

I think we should've won the Series. We let the thing get away. But I was proud of the guys. We weren't supposed to be there. We had a lot of injuries. The guys rallied together at the end, and we got to the final game of the World Series. Overall, we did very well.

Mrs. Payson wanted me to manage. I said, "No ma'am." I didn't need none of that. I was happy just retiring.

16.

STRIVE FOR EXCELLENCE

The Story of Hank Aaron and 1,415 Home Runs

"You can reach new heights when you put your heart and mind into it."
—*Willie Mays*

WERE WILLIE MAYS and Hank Aaron rivals?

Were they jealous of each other? Did they spend time strategizing how to outdo one another? Did they resent sharing the spotlight? Did they compete for records, dollars, and fame? Did their elite talent and intense drive make each the other's nemesis?

A better question: Does it really matter?

What matters is that the world, not just the baseball world, is fortunate Mays and Aaron came together when they did, where they did, and how they did. Beyond the home runs, RBIs, and brilliant all-around performances that they provided their teams and fans, they brought a new level of magnetism and dignity to the game while exciting a new generation of fans, opening the door for other minorities to follow, and doing it all in the face of discrimination.

We barnstormed together. We played on All-Star teams together. We did autograph shows together. We had good times together, man. Rivalry?

Hank Aaron, like Willie Mays, was born and raised in Alabama, played in the Negro Leagues, broke into the majors at age twenty, and went on to a Hall of Fame career. (National Baseball Hall of Fame and Museum)

What the hell is that? There was no rivalry. We didn't play that way. We always laughed at that kind of stuff. They had to talk some way about us, I guess. We've had a respect for each other. Hank was always my friend.

Mays and Aaron were raised in the Jim Crow South in Alabama, Mays from the Birmingham area, Aaron from 230 miles south in Mobile. Both played in the Negro Leagues, Willie for the Birmingham Black Barons and Hank for the Indianapolis Clowns. Both broke into the major leagues as twenty-year-olds and overcame hardships and racism to become baseball legends and American heroes, Mays playing on the coasts in New York and San Francisco, Aaron in Milwaukee and Atlanta.

Three years older, Mays was a rookie in 1951, and when he returned from the Army in 1954, Aaron was a rookie, transitioning from the infield to the outfield. They were number three hitters and the heart and soul on every team they played. Both appeared in 24 All-Star Games, and they combined for 1,415 home runs.

Both were traded and played the final two years of their careers in their original city but on different teams—Mays as a Met, Aaron a Brewer—and both have worked for their original franchises for several decades—Mays as a Giant, Aaron a Brave.

In 2019, Willie celebrated his eighty-eighth birthday, Hank his eighty-fifth.

"No question about it, it was certainly a mutual respect," Aaron said forty-five years after he broke Babe Ruth's all-time home run record. "I respected Willie's all-around ability to play the game of baseball and to play it with ease and to play it the way that he knew how to play it. A lot of people said, 'Well, he's hotdogging.' That was not the case. Willie played it the way that he knew how. I marveled at some of the things he did and did not try to copy things he did. I played my own style because I couldn't do things he was doing his way and be successful at it."

Their playing styles were noticeably different and, to an extent, mirrored their personalities. Both played with grace and extraordinary knowledge, but Mays was flamboyant and breathtaking while Aaron was unpretentious and steady. Mays made basket catches and hit, ran, and slid with flair, his cap flying off as he darted around the diamond. Aaron got the big hits and made the big plays but without flash. He was country to Mays' city, blue-collar to Mays' white-collar, Hammerin' Hank to Mays' Say Hey Kid.

Which in retrospect is gloriously perfect and universally embraceable.

Hank's a good guy, a quiet guy. He wanted to just go out and play every day. They used to tell me, "Hey, Willie, there's a kid playing second base who's coming up, he could hit the hell out of the ball." "Who's that?" I wanted to meet him. I didn't know who he was until I came out of the service and started watching him, and the first thing you notice, he could hit.

After the 1955 season, Aaron's second in the majors, he played on a historically talented barnstorming team known as the Willie Mays All-Stars that made good money touring across the South to the West, an offshoot of barnstorming teams in previous winters spearheaded by Jackie Robinson and Roy Campanella and inherited by Mays. Willie and Hank consider it the finest team ever assembled. There were four Hall of Famers in the outfield alone, which also included Larry Doby and Monte Irvin. Campanella was behind the plate, Ernie Banks, Gene Baker, Junior Gilliam, and George Crowe were on the infield, and Don Newcombe (who helped assemble the team), Connie Johnson, Sam Jones, Joe Black, and Brooks Lawrence were on the mound. The team played 28 exhibitions and won them all.

A legendary barnstorming team, which toured the country after the 1955 season, featured Willie Mays, third from left in the front row, and Hank Aaron, fifth from left in the back row. (Collection of Rick Swig)

"Hey, when you've got that kind of talent on a ballclub, you don't expect to lose many games," Aaron said. "It was the best team I ever played on. With Doby, Willie, Monte, and myself, I guess we flipped a coin and said, 'Who's going to play the outfield tonight?' Most people who came out to the ballgames were black. They came out to see Willie and myself play."

Mays and Aaron teamed in All-Star Games from 1955 to 1973, taking great pride in overseeing National League dominance at a time when the American League was much slower to integrate. Mays started a record 18 All-Star Games, one more than Aaron. In one 14-game stretch when Mays and Aaron were teammates, the National League was 12–1–1 with eight straight wins.

"I felt so at ease in the company of Willie at all the All-Star Games, and we did some great things together," Aaron said. "We would get there a day before. Today, guys go with the idea of playing in the Home Run Derby or something else. We got there and went to the hotel. We sat and talked a long time about baseball, just baseball, which really helped me more than anything in the world, sitting and talking to Willie about baseball. He may not have thought it, but he gave me some insight on what I needed to do to make myself a better ballplayer."

There was plenty to discuss, considering what they could share about pitchers, ballparks, and conditions they faced as pioneers who would pave the way for minorities for generations to come.

If he went in a slump, if he was 0-for-15, I'd say, "What's going on? Here, take this bat." Same thing with me. If I'm 0-for-15, he'd do the same for me. If we did card shows together and I was making more than Hank, I'd tell the promoter, "Hey, you gotta give this guy the same you're giving me."

The Mays-Aaron dynamic was closely monitored not only by fans but by teammates and opposing players. The comparison questions constantly were asked, and people still ask today.

"Willie was spectacular, colorful, all out," said Felipe Alou, who played six seasons with Mays and six with Aaron. "I'm not saying Hank wasn't all out. Hank was all out. He had a good arm and, like Willie, could steal bases. But Hank was like a machine. A machine is the same every day, every day doing damage with the bat. Willie did it with color."

Hall of Fame manager Joe Torre grew up in Brooklyn loving the Giants and especially Mays, then spent half of his 18-year playing career with Aaron's Braves. His perspective comes as a former catcher watching the differences between Mays and Aaron at the plate.

"Henry was a little patient. Willie wanted to hit right now," Torre said. "I wouldn't give a sign when Willie was up. I wanted him to wait. He'd say, 'I know what you're doing.' He was fidgety. Even when he sat still, he wanted to be moving. One time I asked him a question. As he was answering, he hit the ball out of the ballpark. I said, 'Okay, I guess that doesn't work.'"

Torre added, "Willie got more attention in New York than Hank got in Milwaukee, and that was part of it. There's only one New York. I don't think Hank minded being under the radar. He'd get the ball and hit the cutoff man. Willie would throw it on the fly to the catcher. It was more attention-getting. Not that he did it for that reason. Hank and Willie were different people with the same ability."

Hank and I had a different way of hitting. He was a left-center hitter, but with his strong wrists, he could flick the ball to right-center or left-center. He's strong, man. I didn't hit that way. I had to use my whole body to hit. I was all over the ballpark. Leo (Durocher) made sure I didn't pull everything and got me to start hitting to all fields.

Right-handed power hitters without monstrous bodies—Aaron was 6-feet, 180 pounds, and Mays was 5-11, 180—they put up comparable numbers. Mays had a .302 batting average (to Aaron's .305), .384 on-base percentage (to Aaron's .374), and .557 slugging percentage (to Aaron's .555).

Mays had an edge in stolen bases (338 to Aaron's 240) and triples (140 to Aaron's 98) while Aaron had an edge in doubles (624 to Mays' 523) and, of course, home runs (755 to Mays' 660).

Mays was the second member of the 600 homers club behind Ruth and remained No. 2 until 1972, the year Aaron passed him. Mays retired after the 1973 season, and Aaron played through 1976.

I didn't talk much to Hank about the home runs. I was way ahead for a while, and then I was right there with him. I just said, "Keep your head up. Don't let anyone hurt you. Keep going." He was going through so much. I thought he handled it all very well. He kept going.

Their home runs were hit at a similar clip—Mays one per 16.5 at-bats, Aaron one per 16.4—but Aaron had nearly 1,500 more plate appearances, largely because while each played over a 23-year span, Mays missed most of 1952 and all of 1953 in the military.

Much could be debated about the advantages and disadvantages of the home ballparks, but the bottom line is that Aaron hit his 715th homer to pass Ruth on April 8, 1974, and hit 40 more, his final 22 in the American League as a designated hitter. Through it all, he showed integrity, class, and courage in the face of bigots who didn't want a black man to break the most prestigious record in sports, owned by a white man.

"I never considered this as anything other than having the ability to play the game as Willie did and as I did," Aaron said. "When I started playing ball, I was not up to trying to challenge anyone's record, whether it was Babe Ruth's or anyone else's. I was just trying to do the best I could possibly do. Hey, I could've ended my career with 500 home runs, even 200, really. The greatest thrill I had in baseball was when my career was over with, when I was voted into the Hall of Fame. I thought that was the greatest thing that ever happened to me as an individual."

Breaking Ruth's record should have been one of the greatest moments in Aaron's life, but it was one of the most painful. Instead of feeling joy, he felt despair. While his Hall of Fame induction validated his entire career, the home run record led to abuse in the form of death threats and hate mail filled with racist venom.

Aaron kept the letters and published some in his important 1991 book, *I Had a Hammer,* written with Lonnie Wheeler. Meantime, Mays received his share of hate mail and responded his own way.

I didn't think about those damn people. Whoever wrote those letters, come and see me, show me who you are. I didn't pay it no attention. I just threw it all away. I didn't keep all that stuff. There might be somebody who didn't like me. I didn't give a damn. We had all that going back to the Negro Leagues. We did what we had to do.

Another powerful Aaron book was published in 2010, *The Last Hero: A Life of Henry Aaron,* by Howard Bryant, who penned a thorough biography of the homers champ and his noble journey through life. The book portrayed a tense Aaron-Mays relationship, and Bryant submitted that Mays had difficulty accepting that Aaron was catching up in the home run race, especially because Mays, three years older, led Aaron most of his career. Also, while Aaron deeply admired Mays and craved his approval, he didn't feel totally appreciated.

The book cited a reporter who claimed he was doing a TV interview with Aaron in his fourth season, 1957, and Mays was in the background ragging him and suggesting he was naive for not getting paid for the appearance. In 2019, both Aaron and Mays said they didn't recall such an episode, and Mays pointed out that players have a penchant for teasing each other and quickly letting go.

Aaron said he believes the perception of Ted Williams and Joe DiMaggio, white superstars in the American League, was different than the perception of him and Mays. "They just said they were great ballplayers. 'They didn't like each other'—I never heard that," Aaron said. "But each time they mentioned my name and Willie's name, there always was a competitiveness to it. Hey, I had enough problem worrying about trying to hit Bob Gibson's fastball and Sandy Koufax's curveball than I did worrying about what people said. It made me feel horrible that people would even think about that because Willie played the game the way he knew how to play it, and yours truly played the game the way I knew how to play it. And I don't have one scar mark on me for saying I didn't like the way that it was going on."

Broadcaster Bob Costas has interviewed Mays and Aaron several times, including together in a July 2008 HBO shoot, and Costas said if there had been tension between the men in the past, there wasn't any longer. Filmed at New York University a day after the Yankee Stadium All-Star Game, the show was scheduled for fifteen minutes and lasted nearly an hour.

"My impression is that they more than reconciled," Costas said. "They came to appreciate one another. I saw some real affection and enjoyment in each other's company as they sat there. Hank was good in talking about his experiences, but when Willie started off on some story that made the audience laugh, Hank became a very willing audience. Hank just got out of the way and let Willie roll. You saw the smiles and the laughter from Hank. He definitely appreciated it."

Dusty Baker has close ties to both men. He played in Atlanta with Aaron, his mentor, and was on deck when Aaron broke Ruth's record. Baker also managed 10 years in San Francisco, where he hung out with Mays. In retrospect, Baker concludes that the two icons were good for each other.

"I don't know how close they were as players, but they respected each other big-time, and they've probably gotten closer since," Baker said. "Hey, there was tension between Muhammad Ali and Joe Frazier, but they helped make each other a lot of money and made each other better. You can't tell me Hank and Willie didn't have their eye on each other. They were the best. These guys motivated all of us. They put the African-American players on the map of the elite with Ted Williams, Mickey Mantle, and Duke Snider. They even bypassed them."

Aaron's record lasted 33 years until Mays' godson, Barry Bonds, hit his 756th homer in 2007. During Bonds' chase, he was investigated by a federal grand jury in the BALCO steroid scandal, putting Aaron and Mays in an uneasy predicament, constantly getting asked questions about the legitimacy of the record. Both strived to take the high road. Aaron didn't attend the record-breaking game but taped a congratulatory message that appeared on the scoreboard, and Mays supported his godson by appearing on the field for a quick in-game ceremony.

"Well, records are made to be broken. They're not made to be standing still," Aaron said. "I broke it. And, eventually, somebody will break the record that Barry has. I try to make people understand that I don't have any larceny in my heart."

The age-old question "Who is better?" is asked in every sport, every industry, every business. Baseball fans love comparing players from different eras or ranking players who man the same positions—Willie, Mickey, or the Duke?—but in the case of Mays and Aaron, perhaps we should take Felipe Alou's word for it and move on, because no one would have a more qualified voice: "Hank Aaron was a better hitter. But the best player all around? Willie Mays."

In the golden days of baseball, there were no finer players or example-setters. Jackie Robinson opened the door, and Mays and Aaron busted through to take superstardom to a new level. They had similar backgrounds and converged in the same league, often on the same field, sometimes as teammates. Legends, both. As Joe Torre said, "We make superstars of people after a year. To watch them year in and year out, they gave people what they expected to see. Living up to yourself is not easy to do."

Mays and Aaron provided a lifetime of memories for countless fans and made dreams possible for countless generations. They're continuing to make a difference by living exemplary lives and giving back through Mays' Say Hey Foundation and Aaron's Chasing the Dream Foundation, both offering assistance and opportunities to underprivileged youth. Which each once was.

Hall of Famer Willie McCovey, who was raised in Mobile, idolized Aaron, and wore his number (44) as Mays' longtime teammate, played down talk of a rivalry but understood how the perception could exist, saying, "Sportswriters tried to cause friction between guys. They tried to make me and (Orlando) Cepeda enemies. They tried to make me and Mays enemies. I don't know why, but they did."

Joe Morgan, a Hall of Famer who grew up in Oakland and saw Mays play at Seals Stadium and is a close friend to both, said, "I was around Willie and Hank a long time. There was never a rivalry between them. There was a rivalry the media tried to create, Willie against Hank. They were the studs, man. They were the guys. Both of them earned their spots and reputations in history, especially in the black community. They were great for any community they lived in."

Yes, their personalities are different, but that's the beauty of their uniqueness as ballplayers and legends. As contemporaries, they brought out the best in one another, and their popularity and prominence continued to soar in retirement. They'll forever be known for their abilities, toughness, and perseverance, pioneers who made baseball and society better.

Rivalry? They've endured so much. Overcome so much. Contributed so much. Accomplished so much. It's offensive to even ask.

We go way back together. If Hank needed something, he'd call me. If I needed something, I'd call him. People talk about the home runs, and I say, "What's wrong with 660?" Or joke with them, "660 wasn't enough?" I'm happy with it. We went through a lot, Hank and I, and understand what we've been through, and that's why you have that respect between us.

17.

RESPECT EVERYONE LIKE
YOUR TEAMMATE

The Story of the Absurdity of Racism

"Make a difference by teaching kids how to respect people of all
backgrounds and races. Set an example so they can set an example."

—*Willie Mays*

WILLIE MAYS COULD have quit. He could have returned to his Alabama
roots. He could have re-signed with the Birmingham Black Barons. Or
accepted odd jobs around his home in Fairfield. It sounds far-fetched now,
but there was a time in Mays' early years that he second-guessed his baseball dream.

It was 1950, his first year in the Giants' farm system.

**I was in Trenton by myself. Not just the first African American on the
team but the first African American in that whole league. Three months
by myself. Stayed in the room by myself. Ate by myself. There were times
I said to myself, "Is this worth it, getting into sports this way?"**

Is it worth it? Thankfully, yes.

Talks with his father, lessons from his Negro League teammates, and assurances from the Trenton players helped the nineteen-year-old maintain his drive to overcome racist environments and succeed as a ballplayer and man.

Willie stayed with it. He played out the season and was in the big leagues the following spring. He went on to play 22 years in the majors and live an honorable life. He worked hard, stayed clean, and was true to himself amid a string of hardships. From hearing abuse at his first professional stop to getting rejected in his pursuit to buy a house in supposedly a liberal city to playing for a manager perceived as narrow-minded, he dealt with bigotry in his own way. He united people from different walks of life with his passion and persona and fought discrimination on his terms. He had a knack for making people forget about race. He tried to break down prejudicial barriers by demonstrating character and leadership. It was a conscious choice, and he stood by his convictions.

In the Negro Leagues, Mays learned to fit in, watch his back, and conduct himself with dignity and grace. It was how he saw his older teammates live and survive, and it had a lasting effect. Most of all, Willie led by example, perhaps the most powerful way to lead, but he wasn't afraid to take someone aside and guide him down the right path.

My dad was the guy who called me all the time. "Junior, don't say too much now because I know how you are when you start saying the wrong things. The next day, you're fighting." We'd talk all the time. I didn't raise no hell about nothing, but I didn't back up, either. I never backed up. I always went forward. The Birmingham guys prepared me to do that.

I was a guy that, "Hey, I'm going this way, and I'm not going to turn. If you're in my way, you might knock me down, but I'm going to get up, and I'm going to go as far as I can see." I'm not going to start it, but I'm not going to run away, either.

Mays influenced people in different ways. Joe Morgan, the exceptional second baseman on Cincinnati's Big Red Machine of the 1970s, said Mays was a major inspiration in his life, not only as a kid from Oakland watching his idol play across the bay in San Francisco but as a young big-leaguer who was taken under the Say Hey Kid's wing.

"He did a lot of things behind the scenes with the African-American guys," Morgan said. "He told us what our role is, what we're supposed to do. In one of our conversations, he told me it's up to me to leave the game better than the way I found it. I always remembered that. I tried to pass that along to other young players. With all those numbers you put up, what are you accomplishing? If you left the game better than you found it, you accomplished something. Jackie's quote, 'A life is not important except in the impact it has on other lives,' well, there's no doubt Willie was special to the black community and black players who played in that era, but he did it in a different way."

Mays adored Jackie Robinson. When Robinson signed with the Dodgers and reported to their farm team in Montreal, Willie's father told him reaching the major leagues was realistic. Mays looked to Robinson as a role model and perfect choice by Branch Rickey to break baseball's color line. Just four years after Robinson's 1947 Brooklyn debut, Mays arrived in the majors and always highly respected the man who opened the door for him and so many other African Americans.

While considered a genius on the field and astute with how he handled race relations, peacekeeping, and uniting people, Mays now says he wasn't cut out to be like Robinson.

Jackie was there by himself and carried himself very well, I thought. Branch Rickey gave him two years not to say anything. Pee Wee (Reese) and them spoke for him for two years. Mr. Rickey said after two years he can voice his opinion any kind of way he wanted. He did that very well.

Jackie was a very smart man. I'm talking books, life, everything. Jackie came in when I was in high school. From UCLA. I don't think I was smart enough at the time to do what Jackie did. I'm talking about when he came to the Dodgers. I don't think I was smart enough to go through that all by myself, to be in the limelight like Jackie was when he went to Montreal, then to the Dodgers.

That's my opinion. I might've been because I was by myself in many avenues. I grew into it. I grew into a lot of stuff. You talk about different things, I can educate you about what it is, how it is, why it is. But at that particular time, Jackie was the one, and I thought he did very well for us.

Robinson was a Dodger from 1947 through 1956, overlapping just five seasons of Mays' career. After Robinson retired, Mays played another 17 seasons. Robinson continued to advance the cause of African Americans with his tireless work in business, politics, academia, and, of course, baseball. He became heavily involved in the civil rights movement and with the NAACP and teamed with good friend Martin Luther King, Jr., to fight against prejudice and social injustice, often at King's side. Robinson was at the Lincoln Memorial in 1963 for King's "I Have a Dream" speech and joined the March on Washington.

More than once in retirement, Robinson publicly suggested Mays could have done more for civil rights. In his 1964 book, *Baseball Has Done It*, Robinson was critical of Mays and Dodgers shortstop Maury Wills for two reasons, not agreeing to be interviewed for the book's oral history of baseball and integration and not doing enough for the black cause: "I hope Willie hasn't forgotten his shotgun house in Birmingham's slums, wind whistling through its clapboards, as he sits in his $85,000 mansion in San Francisco's fashionable Forest Hill. Or the concentration camp atmosphere of the Shacktown of his boyhood. We would like to have heard how he reacted to his liberation in baseball and to his elevation to nationwide fame. And about his relations with his managers, coaches, fellow players and his many loyal friends, black and white."

The words were hurtful to Mays and stung him but didn't lessen his admiration for Robinson, who was twelve years older and acknowledged in the book that Mays "didn't exactly refuse to speak. He said he didn't know what to say." At the time, articulating his thoughts on race wasn't as comfortable for Mays as expressing them with his actions and deeds. "Willie is the hero of a Negro success story," Robinson wrote. "What has he learned from life? We'd like to know. I hope that he will think about the Negro inside Willie Mays' uniform, and tell us one day."

Nearly six decades after the book was published, Mays remains inspired by Robinson and thankful for making it possible to follow in his footsteps, having spent a lifetime trying to do the right thing not just for African Americans but all Americans.

Jackie got recognition at the time, which we all appreciated because those were very difficult times, *very* difficult times. Jackie did a lot of things for the race. I did what I did. I didn't always go out and talk in the public. Sometimes I'd do it behind the scenes. Behind the dugout. Away from the ballpark. I didn't tell everyone what I did.

Maury Wills can vouch.

"I loved Jackie Robinson," said Wills, who became a Dodger three years after Robinson's final season. "I got to know him and barnstorm with him. I admired him then, and I admire him now. But I don't think it's fair to label Willie in any way like that. Willie was liked by all people, all races, different walks of life. It was just the person he was. He wasn't the type of person who'd go out and march or shout. But he was right in the middle of it when he needed to be. He got in between Juan Marichal and John Roseboro and broke up that brawl, being the peacemaker. We always admired Willie Mays. No, I don't have anything negative or any ill feelings about Willie Mays, even if he spiked me a few times."

Hall of Famer Reggie Jackson, fifteen years younger than Mays, said Willie got across his message on race relations by demonstrating and setting a tone. Jackson said it was a perfect complement to the words of others.

"He was tremendous for civil rights, a tremendous representative of all minorities," Jackson said. "He was an absolute gentleman and was one of the greatest ever. It's not who some people are. Some people need to do it with actions. Willie did it with actions. He managed himself and handled himself with class on the field and off the field. Some people are able to

Reggie Jackson, right, said Willie Mays was "tremendous for civil rights, a tremendous representative of all minorities." (Ron Riesterer)

speak about it, able to give a narrative that is impactful. Willie wasn't the guy to speak about it. The way he handled himself was exemplary, and I'll always think that. The way he and others paved the road for us, today's players don't get that, and that's no slap at them."

Many legendary players, black and white, participated in the oral history of Robinson's book, including Hank Aaron, Ernie Banks, Larry Doby, Monte Irvin, Don Newcombe, Roy Campanella, Elston Howard, Frank Robinson, Bill White, Carl Erskine, and Alvin Dark. Aaron became vocal on race issues, especially after his playing days, and has indicated he would have liked for Mays to do the same, though in retrospect, Aaron says he respects Mays for handling racial matters the way he did.

"I understood that very well," Aaron said. "You can't be everybody, and you can't do every thing. Sometimes I kick myself in the rear end for not being as good as Dr. King was. So you do the very best that you can. I'm sure Willie did about as well as he probably could do by playing baseball and doing the things that he could do and things that he was involved in."

Back in 1950 when Mays wondered in Trenton if it was worth it, the answer was abundantly clear. Absolutely. He didn't dare quit. He persevered. He went on to bring people together and defuse conflicts with a firm hand, magnetic personality, and radiant enthusiasm for baseball and life that helped him overcome prejudices and put people of all colors and backgrounds at ease and accepting of one another.

I did what I had to do. I did as much as I could. A lot of people didn't know what I did at the time because I didn't raise no hand. I just did what I had to do for that particular person at the time. I didn't tell anyone to follow my lead. You follow your own lead. I'll help you get to where you want to go, but you've got to do it yourself.

In the mid-1950s, in Hot Springs, Arkansas, a ten-year-old boy was thrilled when his family bought a black-and-white television. The images of Willie Mays racing across the screen were inspirational and never forgotten, and the boy fell in love with the player and followed him throughout his career. The kid became significant in the civil rights movement and later a U.S. president who befriended Mays. They became golf partners and supported each other's foundations.

Now, Bill Clinton reveres what his childhood idol did for all races.

"Because of the way he played and the way he conducted himself, Willie Mays made it absurd to be a racist," Clinton said. "There are very few paths when words can be used to change people's minds. Once in a while, somebody does that. But indelible images can do that. Every time he took the field and played his heart out, every time he played with joy and cheered his teammates when they did well, without regard to race, he was making a statement. People may not take that seriously now, but anybody who lived through what Jackie Robinson and then Willie Mays and all the early black players faced knows that.

"The most powerful thing he did was just prove Branch Rickey right. That's what Willie Mays did every day. Here was this incredibly gifted and intensely admirable human being who's overcome a ton of obstacles and is great at what he does. That helped a lot in the early days. The great thing about baseball was, they had a lot of day-to-day fans who would watch all these games, and you got to see a person for a long time. It's very hard to fake it for a whole season, to pretend you're something you're not.

"Willie Mays, just by being Willie Mays and playing his heart out and by being happy doing it, made a real contribution to melting the iceberg of at least more overt forms of racism. It's certainly not going away, and

*President Bill Clinton, with Bobby Bonds, left, was ten years old when he began idolizing Willie Mays.
(Daniel Murphy)*

we learned the hard way it can be quickly brought back. But it has always got to be more than words to change. People have to see things to know."

The year Robinson published his book, the Giants were divided as a team thanks in large part to their manager, Alvin Dark, who was despised by some of the team's minorities because of how he treated them, how he disrespected them, how he didn't understand the beauty and reality of cultural diversity. He didn't want Latin American teammates speaking Spanish with one another, which was a distasteful edict at a time when Latinos were beginning to flow into major-league clubhouses, especially in San Francisco. It was particularly revolting for the three Alou brothers. Imagine growing up together in the Dominican Republic, earning the right to play together on the same big-league team—and then being told to speak only English, including in private company. Even by early 1960s standards, Dark's treatment of minorities was appalling.

It got so bad in 1964 that at one point the Latin players were ready to walk out and protest Dark's bigotry. It would have made national head-lines and ripped apart the team more than it already was. They didn't. They continued to play ball. The reason? Mays stepped in. Instead of join-ing them, he redirected them.

Listen, I had been there, by myself. I knew what it was like, what they were feeling. I heard a lot of the things Jackie heard. I didn't want that team to break up. We were in the World Series two years earlier, and I was going to solidify everybody, not let them go in different directions.

The racial tension hit a boiling point in July when Dark, in his fourth season managing the Giants, was quoted in the New York tabloid *Newsday* as saying, "We have trouble because we have so many Negro and Spanish-speaking ballplayers on this team. They are just not able to perform up to the white ballplayers when it comes to mental alertness. You can't make most Negro and Spanish players have the pride in their team that you can get from white players."

Today, someone uttering those words wouldn't last two seconds in the manager's seat. In 1964, Dark survived, at least temporarily. Because of Mays, who considered Dark a friend. They were teammates in New York, and it was Dark who appointed Mays team captain, the first African-American captain in major-league history, a deeply significant and mean-ingful title for Mays.

Dark said the quotes, appearing in a column written by Stan Isaacs, were not his and maintained that stance until the day he died in 2014, insisting he was misquoted. Isaacs stood by his story. In 1964, Robinson publicly supported Dark, his onetime nemesis amid one of the most intense eras of the Giant-Dodger rivalry, and called him unbiased. Mays remained in Dark's corner throughout the turmoil that was heightened by the Isaacs column, if only because he was more about unifying than dividing.

Particularly offended by the words and actions of Dark were Felipe Alou and Orlando Cepeda, who were stars on the team though they played in Mays' shadow, as nearly everybody did over the years. Alou was traded before the 1964 season to the Milwaukee Braves. Cepeda remained a Giant until 1966 and claimed years later that Dark cost the Giants multiple pennants because of his racist practices while running baseball's most diverse team. In the wake of the Isaacs column, when Cepeda and others were prepared to boycott Dark and sit out, Mays met with the Latin players at the team hotel in Pittsburgh and talked them out of rejecting Dark by saying, "Don't let the rednecks make a hero out of him."

Yeah, I did say that. I knew Alvin better than anyone else on the team knew Alvin, from our playing days in New York, from our backgrounds in the South, me from Alabama and Alvin from Louisiana. Orlando was from Puerto Rico, and I wanted to make sure he understood what was involved with walking out. I told him, "You're not playing for Alvin, you're playing for the team." Alvin wasn't signing the checks. Mr. (Horace) Stoneham was signing the checks. They wanted me to join them. Orlando asked me, "Are you going to play?" I said, "I'm going to play. If I have to fill two positions, I'm going to play." We're trying to get to a World Series here. We calmed it down and got everybody focused on baseball.

Dark was fired after the season. From afar, Alou paid close attention to the continued friction with his former team. After all, his two younger brothers, Matty and Jesus, still were Giants. In the Isaacs column, Dark called out Cepeda and Jesus, the youngest of the ballplaying Alous, for "dumb" base-running mistakes. Felipe read the column and, as he says now, "believed it. I mean, it was hard to believe when I saw it. But the problem is, he did say so many things in front of me. Here's a guy who said he didn't want me talking Spanish. If the quote was we as black players don't have the brains to play baseball or whatever, we have to believe it even if he didn't say it. Because we know he said so many other things."

Alou and Mays, while sharing a common goal, were different with their approaches to fighting racism.

"Alvin Dark came in to manage us without ever managing one inning in the past," Alou said, "and he brought with him some of his Louisiana racism. He was hard especially with Latinos. He had a meeting in spring training and said he didn't want us speaking our language while we were in uniform or in the clubhouse. As soon as we came to the parking lot, we could not talk anymore in Spanish. We were good baseball players, good people, black and white. Willie Mays told us to be careful. Willie came with the team from New York, and none of us did. We were a good, young core of players who came up together in San Francisco, Cepeda and (Willie) Mc-Covey, myself and others, and Willie perceived we didn't know the experiences he had dealing with racism. That's what he wanted us to understand, be careful. You see, Willie was a pacifist. He wanted to fix a problem without a fight. There are men like that. My brother (Jesus) was like that. I was not like that. I was rebellious. I'm still rebellious. That's why I was traded."

The game's racist tendencies at the time went far beyond Dark's injustices. When the Giants called up José Pagán and McCovey in July 1959, setting the stage for two terrific months that were all McCovey needed to win the Rookie of the Year award, two other players needed to be removed from the roster: Felipe Alou and Andre Rodgers. Two players of color called up, two players of color sent down. The quota was maintained, in Alou's mind. Except he refused to report to the Triple-A team in Phoenix, partly because he knew he deserved to remain in the majors and partly because he didn't want his pregnant wife living in the desert heat. The couple went home to the Dominican Republic, where Alou quickly got word that the Giants wanted him back, in the big leagues. So he returned.

"I told the GM I was going to go home, and I went home," Alou said. "I'm not afraid to say what I mean. I know Willie said those things about always being careful, and I used to be careful and keep my mouth shut if it was okay to keep it shut. He was that kind of guy. Well, he is that kind of guy. I just didn't always keep my mouth shut."

The resentment initiated by Dark stuck with many Giants players for years, and he found it difficult to distance himself from the racist tag, though he kept trying until his death at ninety-two. In his final interview, for the purpose of this book, Dark said the comments in the Isaacs column weren't his and, at the very least, were taken out of context.

"I never said anything like that," Dark said. "I've never been disrespectful like that. I never at any time in my career did not respect every black guy I ever played with. The only thing in the game of baseball is ability. It didn't matter what color you were, and it didn't make a difference who you were. When you try to defend yourself on that particular thing, you're in trouble. No one could defend me because no one was in that office except Stan Isaacs. When I read that article, I thought, 'What in the world was he doing?' He was just a liar, that's what he was. How many black ballplayers or black people will say, 'Oh, now wait a minute, that can't all be false, what Dark was talking about. He must've said something along those lines,' but I didn't say anything along those lines."

Dark spent years seeking to make amends and later in life apologized to Alou, Cepeda, and others.

"Yes, he did apologize. He apologized with tears," Alou said. "We got to be really, really close friends. Alvin apologized for everything. I was managing the Expos then, and he apologized to me in Phoenix, where we had an old-timers' game, the only old-timers' game I ever played. It was before spring training, and we had players from the '62 Dodgers and '62 Giants. He apologized at the hotel, and our wives were with us. They became friends. He became such a sweet person, incredible. He apologized to any black player that he could find. He came up to me, Cepeda, Matty Alou, all the blacks. We all accepted his apology. We could really, really see a sincere person. He felt terrible. He regretted it. I believe then he was a true believer of religion. I think he realized when he died, he didn't want that in his heart."

"Looking back," Cepeda added, "he made some mistakes, and he said, 'I want to apologize to you and Felipe and José Pagán.' It takes a man to do that. He found out Latin players come from a different culture. He said he wanted me to forgive him. I said, 'Alvin, that's in the past. I know you want the best for me.' We had a nice visit every time we saw each other. Sometimes we make mistakes. We're human beings. We grew up in different environments. Times change. We all change."

Did Dark apologize to Mays?

No. Listen, Alvin and I played together in '51 in New York when I came to the Giants. He was a mentor, he taught me about playing in the big

leagues, about what was going on in the game from day to day. He used to give me signs when he was at shortstop and I was in center field. I didn't know all those hitters. Behind his back, he alerted me as to what pitch was coming, he and (second baseman) Eddie Stanky. I kept my eye on them, and the other two outfielders would focus on me to see what was coming. So Alvin and I were close before he came out to San Francisco. I didn't need an apology. I understood Alvin.

That was a different time, a different place, a different culture. When the Giants fled west from New York, Mays was prepared to settle in a city known for its diversity, tolerance, and willingness to welcome all people from all backgrounds. By then, he was a full-fledged superstar, a tremendously gifted and popular twenty-six-year-old who had won over the media capital of the baseball world by helping the Giants win a World Series championship, earning an MVP award, and playing the game with a brilliance and panache that broke down barriers and drew people to him as a role model and symbol of strength, consciousness, and courage. Furthermore, he served in the Army and honorably fulfilled his duty as an American, missing one full season and most of another.

While former Giants manager Alvin Dark angered several minority players, Willie Mays, who was Dark's teammate in New York, acted to prevent a mutiny. (San Francisco Giants)

Yet, when Willie tried to buy a house in a prominent San Francisco neighborhood, where he wanted to fit in and get acclimated to his new baseball home with the new season approaching, he was rejected because of the color of his skin.

It was November 1957, and the house was on scenic Miraloma Drive adjoining the prestigious St. Francis Wood neighborhood. Mays and his then-wife, Marghuerite, had agreed to pay the full asking price, $37,500, and owner Walter A. Gnesdiloff at first was willing to sell to them. But neighbors complained about living next to black people, and real estate brokers and local builders argued the Mayses' inclusion in the neighborhood would depress property values. So the owner, a builder himself, turned down Mays. Yes, progressive and sophisticated San Francisco was happy to be introduced to Major League Baseball so long as none of the team's black players lived next door.

That's the house I wanted, 175 Miraloma. I didn't want another house. It was three bedrooms, two stories, a big two-car garage, views of the ocean, just what I wanted. I thought it'd be no trouble. You're not looking for trouble when buying a house. I thought I could live where I wanted. I wasn't trying to make the newspapers. I didn't want it to be a big deal. It's your private life, but they didn't want to sell it to me. It was disappointing, but you don't give up. They said they could find another house for us. No. This was the house.

Many sides got involved including the mayor, George Christopher, and other city officials along with an influential civil rights advocate named Edward Howden, who was the director of the local Council for Civic Unity. Christopher helped bring the Giants to his city, and yet his city was refusing not only the team's star player but the best overall player in the game. Howden was a valuable mediator and made his presence felt with the owner of the house and Christopher and was among those warning the owner of the public relations nightmare that would ensue if it got out that the Mayses were being turned away based on their skin color. Howden also tried to convince the owner that selling to Mays wouldn't harm housing prices.

Still, the owner didn't budge, and all hell broke loose. The *San Francisco Chronicle* screamed this headline on November 14: "Willie Mays Is Refused S.F. House—Negro." The front-page story stated Mays "ran into the color barrier here yesterday. He and his wife were turned down in their attempt to buy a home—because they are Negroes." A builder in the area, Martin Gaehwiler, was quoted as saying, "I happen to have quite a few pieces of property in that area, and I stand to lose a lot if colored people move in."

Ultimately, the owner buckled to the negative publicity, backpedaled on his racially motivated decision to refuse Mays, and sold him the house. "Mr. Mays," he said in a phone call as local media chronicled every word, "I want to tell you my decision personally. I am very happy to have you buy my home." Nevertheless, the story created a stir locally and nationally as other media outlets picked up on the *Chronicle* article and, in some cases, portrayed San Francisco as anything but an accepting municipality. It was an embarrassment on many fronts, including to the city, and slammed home evidence that even in San Francisco, racism and housing discrimination were rampant. If Willie Mays could be victimized, anyone could. The difference was, an African-American individual or family lacking fame or stature wouldn't have been a focus of the mayor and media and would have gotten little attention when denied trying to buy a home in the area because of their race.

In retrospect, Willie helped integrate the neighborhood, and San Francisco was forced to reevaluate race relations in the city. Not that the incident by any means led to racial peace, but it was a loud statement against the resistance to integration. The NAACP took notice and, through chapter president John Adams, Jr., said, "What happened in Mays' case is dramatically enacted daily by hapless Negro families whose lack of prominence does not command the attention of the press and official San Francisco. Segregated islands of residency are springing up all over this city due to practices and policies of real estate groups."

The incident emphasized the need for a law covering private housing, and the NAACP sought legislation to make racial housing discrimination in California illegal, which eventually was passed and made law. The Mayses moved out after two years but not before they again were victimized, this time in June 1959 by someone who threw a bottle containing a racist note through the front window.

Through it all, Mays never raised his voice, put up a fuss, or made threats. He was calm through the ordeal but persistent and determined to push for what was right because he knew if he didn't back down, he'd open the door for the next black family to buy in the neighborhood. He had experience with intolerant people, including in his first season in the Giants' farm system when he paved the way for minorities as the only black in his league. Here he was again, away from the diamond but still trying to unify, teach, and lead by example by fighting for what's right.

It was unfortunate how everything went down. I was able to buy the house. It worked out for me, and I wanted to make it easier for the next folks who came along and wanted to buy a house. And to make it easier for the sellers to feel comfortable about selling to minorities. It helps when everyone is more educated on how it works, how it shouldn't matter what a person's skin color is when he wants to live in a certain area, how diversity is a good thing in America.

Mays' experiences with racism when he broke into pro ball were more extreme than the experiences his young Giants teammates endured when reaching the majors in the late 1950s, but Cepeda's, Alou's, and McCovey's experiences were no less dreadful. Mays was among the players who laid the groundwork for the new generation, and what he saw as a teenaged ballplayer made him thick-skinned and tolerant. When he needed to get involved or take a stance, he did.

"I never saw him go out and embarrass anyone," Morgan said. "Willie didn't drink. He didn't smoke. So you never saw things happen at a club because he wasn't going to be there. How Willie carried himself in center field and how he carried himself on the way home, that's what I would tell a kid to look at. A lot of people did a lot of things. I'm not going to condemn them. You do what you do. But Willie made a good impact on the rest of us. He was a role model.

"Remember, Hank didn't speak out either at first. The only guys who spoke out as players in my mind were Frank Robinson and Roberto Clemente. Hank didn't do it. You've got to think back. I've become very good friends with Hank. He felt I could do more. Yes, he spoke out against the injustices. But when Willie and Hank were coming up, there were quotas as far as black-skinned players and Latin players. And here we are in 2019, and there's one African-American manager out of thirty, so you tell me how much has changed. With Willie and Hank and all those guys, they all had an effect."

Jackson said Mays "handled himself the way he needed to, with dignity. It's the way he carried himself on and off the field. He didn't complain or bitch about everything. He went out and played ball every day until he fell on the ground."

Bob Kendrick, president of the Negro Leagues Museum in Kansas City, said while some people's words brought people together during the civil rights era, Mays' actions on the field had a similar result.

"We're not all monolithic," Kendrick said. "We're not all called to do the same thing. Willie went about his business in a way that made him an absolute unifier. Simply by the way he conducted himself and the way he played the game. Willie Mays was never booed even in the opposing team's ballpark. That's the reverence people have for him. Willie was affable and likable, and I think that's a reason he carries hero status in the minds of so many. The images of him playing stickball with those kids in New York City had a role in bringing people together, too. We all have our own cross to bear, and the way we bear the cross may be a little different person to person, but it could be just as impactful, and in many ways, Mays was vitally impactful."

In 2019, Sharon Robinson was asked about the relationship between her father and Mays in light of events from decades earlier and said, "My father had deep respect for Willie Mays." She mentioned several examples in which her dad was complimentary, including at an NAACP dinner when addressing Mays' problems buying a house, and added, "My father held, and my family continues to hold, Willie Mays in the highest esteem."

Jackie Robinson's background was far different from Mays'. Robinson was well schooled in integrated Southern California including at UCLA, where he met his future wife, Rachel Isum, and excelled in four sports with great family support. Mays didn't have a traditional two-parent upbringing and came from an area in which college was but a dream.

"I don't think you can underestimate the impact of Jackie Robinson going to UCLA, marrying Rachel, and living the way he did to develop his political consciousness," Bill Clinton said. "I don't think Willie would've ever felt comfortable trying to do that, because of the way he came up. I understand why Jackie felt that way because it was lonely for him a lot of times, and a lot of people on more than one occasion hadn't given up their prejudices. It was, 'You should just shut up and play baseball.' Like (Laura Ingraham) said of LeBron James, 'Just shut up and dribble.' Jackie Robinson had a better education and cultural preparation for being more politically active. I never felt Willie let the cause down. I think Willie led by the power of example, and that was effective.

"I always thought when I was in politics, one of my most important jobs was to give people something to look forward to when they woke up in the morning. The thing that causes the most frustrations in people's lives is not so much poverty as stagnation. It's feeling like every tomorrow will be like yesterday, and there's not a damn thing you can do about it. Willie Mays gave people so much joy without having to say the words. African Americans all over the country can look at him and say, 'Boy, his tomorrows are different than his yesterdays, and I can move, we can move.' Even today, there are a whole lot of studies that show what drives people nuts is feeling stuck. Willie Mays was a walking embodiment of being unstuck. It was, 'Look at the talents God gave me. Look at what I did with them. Look what I've been able to do. Look at the life I've been able to build.'"

While Mays appreciates and is humbled by the praise, he's quick to credit others who led the way for him.

I hear how I inspired people, and I'm glad I can be a positive influence in people's lives, especially children, but I have to say I've been fortunate to have so much support from others throughout the years who stood by me and looked out for me.

When I got to the Giants, I had Monte Irvin and Hank Thompson and Ray Noble, who was from Cuba. That was a big help. At the time, they limited teams to four black players. You could have four but no more than four. I didn't know Jackie well until I got to the Giants, but he was a great inspiration long before we crossed paths. I can't thank him enough, and that goes for so many people who opened doors for me. I'd like to think I helped open doors for others.

18.

FOLLOW YOUR DREAMS

The Story of a Kinship with Barack Obama

"Anything's possible, man. Don't believe otherwise."

—*Willie Mays*

WILLIE MAYS NEVER was more joyful and proud than on the night Barack Obama won the 2008 presidential election.

And never more scared.

I couldn't believe it. I was watching Barack's victory speech in Chicago, and my biggest fear was, he's going to get shot. I was so scared. I closed the door and locked it. I sat there for hours. I was thinking, "I hope they get him off the stage right now."

Think about it, all we've gone through. Imagine being this kid from Westfield, Alabama, how the hell could I have thought there would be a black president in the White House? When I was a kid, we didn't even have blacks in the big leagues.

Mays has developed a strong bond with the forty-fourth president, who often drops Willie's name in speeches by calling him a pioneer who laid the groundwork for an African American to become president, declaring the sacrifices made by Mays and others led to the Obama White House.

Their relationship dates to Obama's 2006 visit to San Francisco during his *The Audacity of Hope* book tour, two years before the election—Mays got a signed book, and Obama got a signed ball. Mays was in awe of the Illinois senator, though it often appeared Obama was more in awe of him.

Mays was at the White House for all three of the Giants' celebratory visits after they won World Series championships in 2010, 2012, and 2014, and it was a great thrill for the president to introduce the legendary athlete who's thirty years his elder. At the visit following the team's first championship, Obama mentioned all the dignitaries in attendance, including the San Francisco mayor, California lieutenant governor, several members of Congress, and the secretary of defense, but his energy level escalated when he introduced a "very special guest, the Say Hey Kid is in the house," which drew the biggest applause of the day.

I met this young man when he was a senator. He just seemed to understand and said, "We're going to do all we can to make this country right." I thought he made a difference, myself. He represented all the people. Not just some of the people. That's why he got elected.

Election night, I was scared for him. For us. Then I saw the crowd, the people who were rejoicing and crying. I saw Oprah, who was in the front. I felt relief and happiness. I cried most of the night and stayed up until seven or eight in the morning. I knew he was all right. I knew we were all right.

Mays has met the last nine presidents, some before they were in office, some after, some in passing, some with whom he built close relationships. Democrats or Republicans, it doesn't matter to Mays as long as their hearts are in the right place. He's pictured with presidents in several photos on walls in his home. He hung out with Richard Nixon at the Candlestick Park opener, played golf with Gerald Ford and Bill Clinton, crossed paths with Jimmy Carter at the dedication of the Clinton Presidential Library, knew Ronald Reagan the actor before Ronald Reagan the president, talked baseball with the Bushes, and met Donald Trump at a long-ago boxing match, where Trump wanted to shake his hand.

And, of course, Obama. While Mays was confident an African-American president one day would occupy the White House, he wasn't sure it would happen in his lifetime. That is, until he met the young senator from Illinois. They were introduced by Jeff Bleich, Mays' attorney, who would become ambassador to Australia under Obama.

After the election, a note was sent to Obama:

Dear Mr. President,
Move on in.
Your friend,
Willie Mays

In the summer of 2009, Obama threw the ceremonial first pitch at the All-Star Game in St. Louis and brought Mays along for the ride. On Air Force One. Mays' presence on the plane created quite a buzz. The White House press secretary, Robert Gibbs, said he hadn't recalled such onboard excitement among the media. "Very rarely when I'm on Air Force One am I the second most important guy on there," Obama said. "Everybody was just passing me by. 'Can I get you something, Mr. Mays?' What's going on?"

Obama also noted, "As cool as Air Force One is, it is much, much cooler when Willie Mays is with you on the plane."

On the trip, which Bleich had a hand in arranging—"Willie would never ask for a favor. He just mentioned casually that he'd never been on Air Force One"—Mays gave Obama advice for the first pitch at Busch Stadium: "follow through." (Obama wound up following through, but the ball floated short of the plate and was caught by a reaching Albert Pujols.) On the plane, the men shared a serious moment when Mays thanked Obama and told him how proud he was of his service and achievements. Mays shared thoughts of growing up in Alabama, his emotional election night experience, and how he had dreamed of a black person becoming president. Obama, who often recognizes Mays for his trailblazing, philanthropy, and military service, said to Willie, "Let me tell you, you helped us

President Barack Obama gave Willie Mays a lift on Air Force One to the 2009 All-Star Game in St. Louis. (Official White House Photo by Pete Souza)

get there. If it hadn't been for folks like you and Jackie, I'm not sure that I'd ever get elected to the White House. The spirit you played the game, how you carried yourself, all of that really makes a difference. It changed people's attitudes, absolutely. So you played a part in it, and now here we are on Air Force One. That's all right."

To which Mays said, "Oh my God, is it."

They smiled and embraced, realizing the significance of the moment, how much their lives had impacted a country and the countless people they had inspired. Together on the majestic Boeing 747-200B, which represents the power of the presidency yet transcends any administration, a historic moment was shared by the Commander in Chief and the Say Hey Kid.

You can't imagine coming where I'm from to be a guest in the White House, let alone fly with the president. But I must say, when Barack got elected, one of the things I thought of was, "I'd love to ride on Air Force One." Not that I thought it'd happen. Then it did, and I couldn't believe it.

It wasn't about riding Air Force One, it was the thought of someone from my race inviting me aboard. It was a dream come true to know that all the tough things I went through, they were worth it.

By the way, what does one do aboard Air Force One?

Oh my God. I was so elated. I brought jerseys and balls, everything I could think of to take care of everyone on the plane. They asked me, "What do you want to eat?" I wasn't in the mood to eat but said, "Just give me a hamburger." They said, "You could have anything you can think of." Well, I guess no one eats a damn hamburger on Air Force One. But they found me a hamburger. No ice cream, though.

The press guy asked me to go back and talk to the reporters. I said of Barack, "He's the president." They said, "No, they want to talk to you." So I went back with them and talked baseball.

In 2015, midway through Obama's second term, he paid Mays the ultimate tribute when giving him the Presidential Medal of Freedom, the highest honor for an American civilian. Willie returned to the White House to join sixteen other honorees, a distinguished group including filmmaker Steven Spielberg, singer and actress Barbra Streisand, musician James Taylor, composer Stephen Sondheim, violinist Itzhak Perlman, and NASA mathematician Katherine G. Johnson, an African American whose calculations were instrumental in America's first manned space missions and the Apollo 11 moon landing. Also honored posthumously were baseball great Yogi Berra and Shirley Chisholm, the first African-American congresswoman.

The honor is presented to those who "made especially meritorious contributions to the security or national interests of the United States, to world peace, or to cultural or other significant public or private endeavors." During a ceremony in the East Room, when he heard his name, Mays stood up and removed his familiar Giants cap, and Obama draped the medal around his neck.

"We don't have time to list all of Willie Mays' statistics—660 home runs, .302 lifetime batting average. The list goes on and on," Obama said.

Willie Mays earned countless accolades, but none compared with the Presidential Medal of Freedom he received from Barack Obama in 2015. (Official White House Photo by Pete Souza)

"I won't describe that miracle grab at the Polo Grounds, either, because Willie says that wasn't even his best catch. I will say this: We had never seen an all-around, five-tool player quite like Willie before, and we haven't seen one since. He could throw and he could field, hit for contact and for power. And, of course, he was so fast he could barely keep a hat on his head. On top of that, Willie also served our country, and his quiet example while excelling on one of America's biggest stages helped carry forward the banner of civil rights.

"A few years ago, Willie rode with me on Air Force One. I told him then what I'll tell all of you now. It's because of giants like Willie that someone like me could even think about running for president."

Mays gleefully recalls not only the honor bestowed but the company gathered.

I was sitting next to Katherine Johnson, and until she checked her numbers, John Glenn wasn't going to go up in space. It was an honor to be

alongside her that day. Growing up, you never think you'd receive anything like this. I was so proud to be there, especially to receive it from
Barack.

The day Mays turned eighty-five, a San Francisco cable car was dedicated
to him—car number 24, naturally—and Obama offered a video message
to wish him happy birthday.

"When the Giants moved west, Willie Mays said he'd walk barefooted
to San Francisco just to get into the lineup," Obama said. "Once he got
here, he hit many of his 660 homers against the winds of Candlestick
Park. He collected more than 3,000 hits, many times running farther than
his cap. So when they say the San Francisco cable car was the first national historic landmark that moves, they forgot to count Willie on the
base paths.

"Willie rounding second or running down a pop fly, that is baseball.
A cable car rolling down these hills, that's San Francisco. Both of them
could be fearsome sights for whoever got in their way. Trolley dodgers on
the street and L.A. Dodgers on the diamond. Today, with Willie's own
number 24 cable car, two American icons come together to create a new
landmark.

"But Willie, your city loves you because you are as complete a person
as you were a player. A mentor, a community leader, an Army veteran, an
ambassador for the game and someone with that special ability to put a
smile on a kid's face. When Willie would visit sick children in Bay Area
hospitals, he refused to hand out baseballs he'd already signed. He wanted
the kids to watch him write his name so they'd know the autograph was
real. That's who Willie is: the genuine article. I've gotten to spend some
time with Willie in the White House and on Air Force One, two places
I'd never be if people like Willie hadn't pushed us towards a more inclusive
America. His legacy is that giant."

Joining Mays at the White House were many friends and associates:
Jeff Bleich, Malcolm Heinicke, Dan Sanchez, David Rapaport, Phillip Saddler, Rene Anderson, Lee Mendelson, Jack Morrissey, and Harry "Ace" Bell,
along with Larry and Pam Baer.

President Barack Obama chatted with Willie Mays and manager Bruce Bochy during the Giants' White House visit in the wake of their 2010 World Series championship. (Official White House Photo by Pete Souza)

I wanted a lot of friends to share it with me, and one was Ace Bell, my second baseman in Trenton, where I started in pro ball with the Giants. I hadn't seen him since 1950. We had hooked up, and I thought it would be special for him.

I was sad that Yogi couldn't be there. He was honored but had passed a year earlier. We played in New York at the same time, and Yogi was my manager with the Mets. It would have been special for Yogi. He was absolutely deserving.

Baseball accolades have piled up for Mays. MVPs. Gold Gloves. All-Star selections. Batting title. Rookie of the Year. Player of the Decade. Hall of Fame. Statue in San Francisco, statue in Birmingham.

The Presidential Medal of Freedom was different.

I've gotten a lot of awards, but not any that compared with this. It was such a great honor. Barack was good to me, man. I've been fortunate to go to the White House so many times, I know the security folks. That's humbling. Now, I can't tell you all that went on. That wouldn't be fair to the government. That's classified.

When Mays reflects on his race-related struggles of the 1950s and 1960s, from hearing fans' taunts to experiencing housing discrimination to the many other prejudices he endured, he can gain solace when realizing the country came far enough in his lifetime for the American people to elect an African-American president.

Twice.

I think the message was pretty clear. Times were changing, and we were living in a more accepting place. We know the country's not at the point it could be, but Barack's presidency brought us to places we had never been, and I'm thankful for that.

19.

BENEFIT FROM VERSATILITY

The Story of a Five-Tool Player

"It's good to be well-rounded and balanced with how you live. It's the same in baseball."

—*Willie Mays*

BRANCH RICKEY, A renowned pioneer of baseball's modern era, loved players who could do it all. In his 1965 book, *The American Diamond,* an enlightening look at the game he transformed, published in the final year of his life, Rickey attempted to distinguish all-around players from those who didn't measure up with all the tools.

Hitting. Hitting for power. Fielding. Throwing. Running.

The five essentials that, when all are executed at an elite level, define a complete player. Rickey cited just two players at the time who exhibited all five tools at exceptional levels. Both were center fielders. Mickey Mantle and Willie Mays.

Mays hit .302 in his 22-year career, and 660 of his 3,283 hits were home runs. He added 338 stolen bases, making him one of the greatest all-around offensive threats in history.

So, naturally, if Mays were to break down his five tools, he'd be most proud of . . .

FIELDING

Oh, defense. Yeah. Defense was my thing. We always had a lot of guys who could hit. I had to know all about our pitcher and their hitters. If you asked me how to play a guy, I had to know it. You might go on a streak at the plate and have some down days. But defense, you have to bring it every day.

I set myself like a wide receiver, ready to move forward or backward. I could get quicker to the ball that way. You see guys now standing straight up, their hands hanging down. Uh-uh. I used to get down low so I could pounce any way. Ball's in the air, I felt I could catch anything. Base hit, I'm coming at it. Running hard. Like a shortstop. I don't want to be too cautious coming up on the ball. I'm preventing that runner from taking the extra base.

Roberto Clemente, he was my teammate in Puerto Rico in the '54 winter league, the year before he broke in with the Pirates. He was just a kid. He used to wait for the ball to come to him. He came in and then he stopped, squatting with both legs down and both knees together. No, no, no. I told our manager, Herman Franks, we've got to change that. He's got to throw the ball quicker. He was playing it too safe. He was afraid the ball would get by him. So we came out every morning to work with him and make sure he could do it. We taught him to charge the ball, get it to the infield quicker. You do that by running up on the ball, swooping it with your glove, and getting it in. It makes a big difference. You don't throw the runner out every time, but you put in his mind that you could. Suddenly, he's not thinking about taking the next base. We also moved Clemente from left field to right field because he was too good, a good player with a good arm.

I charge no matter what. I didn't care who it is. Could be Maury Wills. Could be someone who can't run. The guys in the dugout are watching me. When the ball goes out to center field, they see you. If you slow up, they're thinking they can take the extra base. But when they see me charging, they feel they have to slow down a little bit. They see what you're doing out there. I didn't do that with just the fast guys.

Willie Mays extended his reach by putting his fingers, rather than his entire hand, into his glove, allowing him to get to balls that otherwise could not be caught. (San Francisco Giants)

I always tried to prevent runners going first to third, and it's one of the reasons I played shallow. I took away more hits that way. Not many balls are hit over your head anyway. I'll give 'em one to catch ten. Richie Ashburn was a tremendous hitter but not a home run hitter. He hit line drives. So I played him behind second base and took a lot of hits away. He'd cuss me out because of it, but that's how I had to play him. Maury hit a ball over my head for a triple, but how many times did I take hits from him by playing in?

To get some of these balls, I wanted the biggest glove possible, and it seemed longer because I pulled my palm out a little bit. A 12-inch glove is now 14 inches. I did that for twenty-seven years. I made the Vic Wertz catch with a Rawlings but mostly used MacGregors.

I put my finger out of the glove to control it better. Most guys back then didn't do that. I went through a lot of gloves because every time somebody borrowed one, I'd never see it again. The company would send a box with ten or so. Guys would come over and say, "Gee, my glove's not ready yet. Let me borrow one." Oh, man. I never saw it again. I gave some away to kids, too. Eventually, I had to tell people I'm down to one or two.

When the gloves came, they already had oil on them, so I could take one out of the box and go out and play with it. The guys knew it. I didn't care if they used them. They liked the gloves, and MacGregor wanted them out there. To get the glove how I liked it, I dipped it in water in spring training, then put two balls in it and wrapped it up with two sanitary socks. Do it again the next day. By the third day, it was right where I wanted it.

Later in my career, I started playing first base, sometimes in the second game of a doubleheader, but kept using my outfielder's glove. The umpires asked about it. They said, "Willie, you're supposed to have a first baseman's glove." I said, "I ain't got one." We just laughed.

THROWING

Cutoff man? When the ball goes to center field, you don't see anybody come out there. I'd say, "You're wasting your time, guys." Look at the film of the World Series catch. You didn't see Alvin Dark, the shortstop, come out. "Stay on the infield, guys." I mean, I want the guy to line me up if a runner's going to third. If I could throw him out, let it go, man. But if he does cut it, I want him to get the trailer, the guy who hit the ball who might be thinking second base. We get him, now there are two down rather than one. We got a lot of outs that way. We were always looking to deke the runner. We could still line up everyone to cut the ball—the shortstop lining up for a throw to third, the pitcher backing up third—but we didn't always play by the book. The guy who hit the ball, he's the guy we're going after a lot of times, not just the lead runner who's going first to third. If it looks like we're going after that lead runner, we can still get the guy trailing him at second. I want that guy.

We used to have fun teasing each other, runners and myself. Especially the fast guys. Richie Ashburn could run. He got a lot of singles and always tried to go first to third. I told Billy Bruton, a center fielder with the Braves in the '50s, "You better get back on that base." When we played the Dodgers, we had to watch out for Maury and Willie Davis. I'd tell Willie, "You know, you can't outrun the damn ball." Maury, too. Maury ran everywhere all the time. He'd hurt you. I'd be coming around the bases saying, "Man, don't run on me." I tried to put it in his head.

One game in L.A., I almost threw for the cycle. Almost threw a guy out at every base. It was 1966. I threw Don Drysdale out at first when I caught a ball and doubled him off. I threw Willie Davis out trying to go first to third when Ron Fairly hit a ball up the middle. I threw Maury out at home. He tried to score when Junior Gilliam doubled. I had another guy at second, but Tito (Fuentes) dropped the ball. He felt bad about it, but I told him don't worry, that's baseball. You don't get on a guy like that. I joke about it now.

Throwing out somebody at first is hard to do, but in those days, a guy would round the bag, turn around and put his cap in his back pocket. By the time they did all that, I had the ball coming. All I wanted for (Willie) McCovey to do was stand there. The ball was right there. I threw Drysdale out a few times at first base. We might not even have a play for five or six games, then all of a sudden, a runner forgets. Mac's standing there,

Willie Mays had one of baseball's strongest arms. That famous World Series catch? He said the key part of the play was his throw. (National Baseball Hall of Fame and Museum)

and the ball is on the way. I told our infielders, "Just be at your base. You never know when I could throw to you."

I remember my rookie year in New York, they gave me four balls to take home to practice my grip so I'd make sure to have my fingers over the seams. It became natural for me. Easy. Hold it another way, it's going to sail. You don't want it to sail. I got to the point where I'd catch the ball in my glove, and by the time I was ready to throw, I had my fingers lined up. It's not something you can worry about in a game. You worry about it, the runner's already gone.

Playing quarterback in high school, I could throw a football a long way, 50, 60, 70 yards, no problem. Throwing a baseball is different. Football, you spread your hand out to throw it. Basketball, you spread your fingers. They say I have big hands, but I never had a problem throwing a baseball. After I hit four home runs in the Milwaukee game, they asked me to take a picture with four baseballs in my hand. No problem.

RUNNING

When I hit, I'd hit running. I'd be almost to first base before an infielder could throw the ball. If the ball dropped in the outfield, I had a better chance for a double instead of a single, triple instead of a double. Extra bases were important to me. I'm not talking home runs.

It's why you'd see me running while looking over my shoulder. I didn't feel it slowed me down. I wanted to know for myself where the ball was. I liked to pride myself on not needing a base coach. If I could see the ball myself without relying on a coach, I'd have a better feel to make decisions on my own. So I kept my eye on the ball. It's not conventional. But they let me do that. If the outfielder was slow to the ball or lobbed it or bobbled it, I was gone. If I waited for the coach to tell me what to do, I lost time. I scored a lot of runs doing that.

If you see film of me sliding, it's always feet first. But when I was younger, I sometimes went headfirst, sometimes at first base. If I hit a

ball to the second baseman and he threw it up the line, I'd go headfirst
to avoid the swipe tag. But there was a chance I'd slide into the guy's
leg. One time, I almost got knocked out at third by Eddie Mathews. I'm
coming in headfirst, he's bending down for the throw, and I hit my head
into his knee. The Giants stopped me. They said just run through the
base at first. No more headfirst slides.

I led the league in steals four straight years but stole bases only when
we needed a run. My thing every year was to drive in a hundred and
score a hundred. Yeah, I could've stolen a lot more. Forty a year. But who
would've hit the home runs? It was about winning. If we led by five runs,
I didn't run like we're leading by one run. That doesn't mean I held back.
Like I said, the most important thing was scoring runs, and I tried to
do it any way I could. Even from first base, when a guy hits a single, I'm
looking to score.

You're always watching the other team and taking advantage of
mistakes. If I'm at first and a guy hits the ball to left field, you make 'em

*When Willie Mays ran the bases, he relied more on his instincts and field awareness than he did on base
coaches. (San Francisco Giants)*

think you're holding at second. I remember Wes Covington, left fielder in Philadelphia. Sometimes he'd throw it high. Other guys did, too. Throw the ball in the air rather than on a line, you're at third base. Same thing when a guy lobs the ball to second. You're home.

HITTING

When you're a rookie in 1951, you can't go in the clubhouse and say, "I need ten bats." I just used what they had. I don't even know what the hell I used. This is 1951 we're talking about. Whatever bat was there, I'd pick it up. If it feels good, that's what I'd use. Eventually, I was able to order my own bats. I used an Adirondack for the four home runs in Milwaukee. The bat I used the most was the Louisville Slugger S2. It was 34, 35 inches, 33½, 34 ounces. Wide grain so it wouldn't break.

The company would fix me up with dozens of bats, but I wouldn't use those until the next year because I wanted the wood hard. It gets harder the more you let it sit. I'll use a bat for a few months. Then I'd go in, clean it up, give it to a kid, and start using another bat. I don't think I broke more than one or two bats a year. Well, when I was young, I broke a bat over my knee. I struck out with the bases loaded. I put my leg up and just snapped the bat in two. I said, "You dumb SOB, you're going to break your damn leg." I never did it again.

In the on-deck circle, I'd swing a heavier bat, sometimes two bats. Take practice swings with a heavy bat, now your game bat becomes lighter. You swing quicker. By the time I get to the plate, I have to have a good idea what I'm going to do. I've seen the pitcher warm up, I know his best pitch, I know what's working for him. Batting gloves? I didn't like batting gloves. I couldn't feel the bat, couldn't control it.

The key to hitting was my eyes, seeing the rotation of the ball, the location of the ball. You have little time to adjust. But when you can pick up how the ball is rotating, the seams on the ball, you can adjust easier. You knew whether to pull the ball or go to the opposite field. I was able

Willie Mays swung a big bat and hit to all fields. He said hitting home runs "wasn't just strength. It was control." (Osvaldo Salas/Collection of Rick Swig)

to hit to all fields. I learned to get a lot of hits to right and right-center. You can't pull everything or you're in trouble. Leo (Durocher) got on me for that. It got to the point where the pitcher puts it out over the plate, I felt comfortable taking it the other way.

My left hand is my hitting hand. Sometimes my right hand comes off the bat, so I need the left hand to be the key hand. As for my stance, I don't have just one. You couldn't do the same thing every pitch, at least I couldn't. It's whatever got me in an aggressive swing, but I usually hit the ball. I struck out 100 times just one year, and I wasn't one of those guys who was a different hitter in different counts. How are you gonna do that? Protect with two strikes? If you're that scared, you shouldn't be going to the plate.

I needed to feel confident no matter what the situation. If they came over the plate, fastball, breaking ball, changeup, it didn't make no difference to me. I just hit it hard. I learned that a long time ago. If you're going to hit it, hit it hard. I was aggressive all over.

HITTING FOR POWER

Every now and then, I'd go up and try to hit a home run. Not often, though. It's not always that simple. The key for me to hitting home runs is putting a good swing on the ball, as basic as it sounds. If you hit it hard, it may go out. But I know when I hit the four home runs in Milwaukee, the hardest ball I hit didn't go out. The others, I hit in the air.

It's kind of difficult to go up to the plate and determine what you'll do. "I'm gonna do this, I'm gonna do that. I'm gonna hit a home run because I feel strong today." That wasn't my thing. For me, hitting home runs wasn't just strength. It was control. You gotta have a combination. You've got to be strong to hit it, but if you go up there and say I'm going to hit this ball over the fence, you might be too strong and overswing.

I felt I had some power as far back as high school. My father was a leadoff man. He was a runner, a bunter. I didn't inherit power. I inherited strength. I didn't lift weights like these guys today. I played sports all the time, though. Football, basketball, baseball. I've been asked how I got in shape. I never got out of shape.

I didn't hit the ball as far as Mac or Mickey or Frank Howard, the boy playing right field for the Dodgers. We called him Hondo. Big man, about 6-7, 6-8. Anybody hit a ball further than him? He got traded to Washington and hit balls all over the ballpark. The All-Star Game in Washington, in '69, Mac hit two home runs, and Hondo hit one just about out of the stadium. That's how I remember him.

When I was coming up, Joe DiMaggio was the best fielder, Stan Musial the best hitter, Ted Williams the best home run hitter. Who could beat Ted in home runs? He missed a lot of years in the military and still hit 521 home runs when he finished baseball, same number as Mac. I tried to do everything, combine all that stuff.

I never felt home runs were my strength. I didn't worry about hitting home runs. I'd hit 'em if I put a good swing on the ball, but I'll say it again, defense was my thing. I'm a believer that you gotta play good defense, and that's what I did. I liked defense more than I liked offense.

20.

EMBRACE THE MENTAL GAME

The Story of the Sixth Tool

"Keep your body in shape and also your mind. Believe in yourself, think straight, and carry it out."

—*Willie Mays*

WILLIE MAYS TRIED to envision what would happen before it happened. As with most of his exploits on the diamond, he often succeeded.

I visualized the whole game. Like I'm sitting here right now. I'd do it today for tomorrow's game. I'm not waiting until I get home. Let's say we're going to play Houston tomorrow. I would work on that right now. Then when we get to tomorrow, it's a breeze. You know what's going on with the twenty-five players on their roster, the nine on the field. I want to know what you can do and how you do it. Can you bunt? Can you hit? Can you hit for power? Can you run? When the guys ask me, "Willie, what's this guy all about?," now I've got something to tell them.

When the pitcher's warming up before the game, after batting practice, I'm in the dugout. I'm out there by myself. They don't pay me no mind when I'm in the dugout. Sometimes I'm out there ten, fifteen minutes watching the pitcher, and I'll have the clubbie bring my bats and shoes out.

I didn't focus on just the other guys. During the game, I'd go all over the field visualizing our guys. My mind ran through my eight teammates before the ball's pitched. Right field, left field, the infielders, the catcher. What can they do and not do? I needed to know. What's the pitcher going to throw? How's he going to throw it? Who'll need a cutoff man? In left field, whether it was (Willie) McCovey or (Orlando) Cepeda, I'd be prepared to get to the gap and catch anything they don't. In right field, we had Felipe Alou and Bobby (Bonds), both good outfielders, and they could catch anything, but I was still there to make sure everything was okay. You can't say later, "I wish I was there." If you can't do these things, you can't play center field. You're the captain out there. Wherever the ball goes, you've got to be there.

One time, Felipe lost a ball in the sun, a ball Duke Snider hit in L.A. So now, he's already saying he can't see the ball, and I don't go in front of him. I go behind him. He signals that he can't see it, but he can't find me because I'm behind him. The ball's easy to catch, and he says, "Thank you, thank you." I've already caught the ball, and it's already to the infield.

Mays was more than a five-tool player. Hitting, hitting for power, running, fielding, and throwing all were detailed on the scorecard, often glowingly, but he had a sixth tool that didn't show up in the box score and couldn't be quantified on a spreadsheet: thinking. He not only relied on his splendid physical traits, he also trusted his mental game to give him a greater advantage not only to outplay opponents but outthink them.

There are ample examples of the Say Hey Kid venturing out of the baseball box, letting his mind more than his legs carry the day.

Hitting in front of Mac, I wanted to make sure he hit and didn't get walked. I'd hit a ball in the gap, and it might've been a double. I'd do a pop-up slide between first and second and go back. I'd stay at first until Mac hits. I didn't want to take the bat out of his hands.

One day in San Diego, they throw two balls back to the screen, but I don't move. Mac strikes out. The next batter, I steal second. Our manager, Clyde King, asks, "Why don't you go to second?" He doesn't like that. I tell him I want to let Mac hit. Well, Mac goes 3-for-4, homers off the scoreboard, and knocks in six runs. The only time they get him is that time they struck him out.

After the game, I look for Clyde to tell him, "Did you see what he did?" But I can't find him. I think he got the point.

Joey Amalfitano broke into the big leagues with the 1954 Giants, the year Mays won his first MVP award. By the rules of the day, Amalfitano was classified as a bonus baby because his signing bonus exceeded a threshold and forced him to spend his first two pro seasons in the majors even though he wasn't ready. He spent far more time spectating than playing, so he studied how Leo Durocher managed and Willie Mays performed. Amalfitano hardly played in 1954 and 1955 and spent the next four years in the minors before genuinely earning a big-league roster spot. He didn't get his first hit until late in his second season, on August 7, 1955. In fact, he got his second hit the same day, too, in a tightly contested game at Cincinnati's Crosley Field.

With uncanny recall, Amalfitano cited three examples of Mays demonstrating a sixth tool, including that memorable day at Crosley Field.

Example 1: "We're coming into the ninth inning, the score's tied 5–5, and I'm leading off. Willie comes to me and tells me the pitcher, a guy named Gerry Staley, is going to start me off with a sinking fastball and that if it's a strike, he'll come back and throw a curve on the second pitch. So I go up there and take the first pitch, a sinking fastball for a strike. Sure enough, the next pitch is a curve, and I swing. The ball hits my bat, and it's a double. I'm at second, and Whitey Lockman bunts me to third. Now Mays comes up and hits a fly ball for a sacrifice fly, and we went ahead 6–5 and won the game. Amazing. Willie told me the script in advance, and that's how it turned out."

Example 2: "It's 1955, and we're in St. Louis, the first Busch Stadium, with the short right-field fence that Stan Musial used to tattoo. Anyway, I get dressed really early. I'm wearing a T-shirt and a pair of baseball shorts, just hanging out in the dugout. Then all of sudden, I see the Cardinals come out. Harry the Hat Walker is managing after Eddie Stanky was relieved of his duties. Here they were at second base, practicing to pick off runners. I'm watching what they're doing and thinking their intention is to pick off Willie. So when Willie comes to the ballpark, I tell him, 'Hey, I was out there early, they're working on a pickoff play at second, probably to get you.' Now what does Willie do? He gets on second. In fact, I'm thinking they wanted him to get to second so they could execute this play. Anyway, the stage is set. The shortstop bluffs him back, and the second baseman comes from behind, and they throw to second. By that time, Willie's three quarters way to third. He's wide open after his first step. Gets to third, doesn't even have to slide. He turns around and points his finger back at those middle infielders. Classic. Just classic."

Example 3: "One very cold night at Candlestick, we're playing the Dodgers, and they've got Larry Sherry on the mound throwing 90-plus. He throws a fastball inside to Willie, and the ball hits the bat five or six inches from his top hand, just shatters the bat. With that high-pitched voice, Willie yells, 'aaaaah.' Remember, it's a cold night, and your hands are hurting when a bat shatters like that. So he grabs a new bat and blows on his hands to warm 'em up. Sherry comes back with another fastball, in on the hands . . . over the fence. Willie hits a home run. You talk about Denzel Washington. Willie baited him. Great acting. It was beautiful."

A few other examples of how Mays' unique baserunning changed the complexion of games:

On April 25, 1960, Mays scored from first on a McCovey single to right off Bob Gibson, who was summoned in the seventh inning to put out a fire. Cardinals catcher Chris Cannizzaro thought Mays missed the plate and argued with Frank Secory, even bumping the umpire three times to earn an ejection and two-week suspension. The Giants won 9–8.

On May 30, 1960, Mays did it again in the nightcap of a doubleheader against the Cubs on another McCovey single to right, this time scoring the walk-off run in the ninth. Right fielder Bob Will threw to second to keep McCovey at first, and Mays never hesitated.

Willie Mays was the epitome of a five-tool player, but his sixth tool—the mental game—also set him apart. (Collection of Rick Swig)

On May 5, 1961, five days after hitting four homers in Milwaukee, Mays scored from first on Orlando Cepeda's two-out single to left in Philadelphia. Bobby Smith was playing deep and threw to shortstop Rubén Amaro, who relayed to second to hold Cepeda to a single. Meantime, Mays ran through a stop sign at third and scored the deciding run in a 4–2 victory.

On August 28, 1967, Mays did something new, scoring from second on a wild pitch. Dodgers pitcher Don Sutton had drilled Mays, who didn't take it lightly. So when the thirty-six-year-old was on second and Sutton threw a pitch past catcher John Roseboro, Mays sprinted all the way home, popped up and stared down Sutton, a clear message to the pitcher to refrain from throwing up and in.

On August 29, 1967, one day later, Dodgers right fielder Ron Fairly's lazy throw to the infield prompted Mays to dash from first to home on a Jack Hiatt single. Fairly assumed the play was over. Mays never stopped running.

On May 3, 1970, three days before his thirty-ninth birthday, Mays showed age didn't diminish his creativity against the Phillies by scoring from first on a bunt. McCovey faced an exaggerated shift to the right side with the left side wide open. So he put down a bunt that rolled all the way down the third-base line and into left field. Several moments passed before left fielder Tony Taylor retrieved the ball, and Mays easily scored.

That's what I mean by visualizing. You're knowing ahead of time what to do in all situations and making sure to be in the right place when you need to be. That way, nothing surprises you. You have a better feeling about what's expected not just for what you'll do but for what your teammates and the guys on the other team will do. I just wanted to make sure I did all I could to make it better for everyone else.

The sixth tool separates players who reach a high level from those with equal talent who don't. It can involve makeup, maturity, moxie, and the ability and desire to take an advanced mental approach to all facets of the game over a season's long grind.

Psychologists were taboo in baseball when Mays played, so players were left to figure out mental approaches and cope with anguishes and anxieties on their own. Not until the 1980s, when the A's hired Harvey Dorfman as a mental performance coach, did things slowly begin to turn. In 1991, Braves pitcher John Smoltz confessed he was seeing a sports psychologist, Jack Llewellyn, a shocking development at the time. Over the years, dealing with psychological issues in baseball became less of a sign of weakness for a player, and Dorfman's books inspired countless players to better handle the mental game. In a sport in which failures can outweigh successes, teams learned to embrace the importance of the sixth tool and began supplementing their coaching staffs with mental skills coaches.

One is Bob Tewksbury, who has coached mental skills with the Red Sox, Giants, and Cubs. Aside from earning a master's degree in sports psychology and counseling at Boston University, he pitched thirteen big-league seasons and was an All-Star for the 1992 Cardinals.

"There's definitely a sixth tool of mental toughness," Tewksbury said. "You go back to Willie's time, that wasn't as identifiable of a quality. It was the five tools. Now it's quantified a little better, and you can categorize it as a skill. Some players have that gift of mental toughness. Some don't. You can quantify it by the improvements a player makes in the way he deals with failure. How does he make adjustments with regard to events that are out of his control? Like a line drive that somebody catches, perhaps a bad call by the umpire, things like that.

"For many players, these events can compile at-bat to at-bat. Mental toughness can make an average player good. I don't know if it can make a good player great; maybe good-plus. From my experiences, the great players are able to separate at-bat to at-bat. Some players don't have that quality. Great players minimize their failures and maximize their successes. For example, if the average player is 0-for-2, he may go to the plate saying, 'I hope I get a hit' while the great player says, 'I'm due for a hit.' That's the separator. It's not like power and speed and arm strength. It's a gradual process you see over time. That's why people might not value or understand it as much because you don't see the results immediately.

"Willie and these great players, like (Wayne) Gretzky and (Michael) Jordan, they have the mental capacities to endure and succeed over time. They slow down the moment. They embrace the moment. They're focused on the task, not the outcome. Big moments aren't big to them. Their success is consistent over time. Willie played hard and worked hard but had all these characteristics. He wasn't a one-year wonder or five-year wonder. It's a decade-plus of success, and you can't do it without a special mental capacity."

The sixth tool, when it comes to Mays, is explained in different ways. But make no mistake. Hard work, dedication, and a desire to reach his potential and help teammates for the purpose of team success all were part of the equation, too.

"If I could describe it, Willie had whatever 'it' is," Amalfitano said. "He had the five tools that we all know about, but he also had 'it.' I don't know what the definition of 'it' is, but 'it' separated him from a lot of people, and he had 'it,' and he had 'it' at a very young age. Defensively, he always stood in the right place and followed the ball all the way into his glove. At the plate, he could remember everything. I always thought you don't coach him. He coaches you. I'm serious. I really feel that way. He had great aptitude retention. This guy, I don't know, he was just special. That's part of 'it.' Do other guys have 'it'? I haven't seen it."

Mays' instincts extended beyond his playing days. Fast-forward to the 1989 World Series between the Giants and A's, which was interrupted by an earthquake. When the Series resumed at Candlestick Park, Tony

Phillips hit a foul ball to the first row of seats off the first-base line, where Willie and the commissioner, Fay Vincent, were sitting.

"Here's the thing about Willie Mays that just dazzled me," Vincent said. "Will Clark came over and fell in my lap when catching the ball. What Willie did showed why he's in the Hall of Fame and the rest of us are not. He anticipated Clark's cleats would come down on us and reached out and grabbed his cleats and saved people from being gashed. He was anticipating what would be next. I didn't see Clark coming. I looked up at the ball, which shows you how smart I am."

Mays was comfortable enough with himself and teammates to share his insights and provide leadership, and those who chose to listen usually benefited. For instance, he met with certain starting pitchers, in particular Juan Marichal and Gaylord Perry, shortly before games in what Marichal called their "three-minute meeting," to determine in advance how the defense would approach every hitter. Mays wanted to know how the pitcher was feeling about his repertoire that day and would position himself and the rest of the defense accordingly.

If it was Marichal or Perry, I would ask, "How you feeling with your breaking ball?" "How you feeling with your fastball?" "What you going to do with each pitch?" They tell me, and I'll have the defense ready. I've got to make sure all the guys on the team are in the right position. Gaylord didn't talk to the guys before games, but he talked to me, so I had to make sure everybody was in line.

Marichal and Perry were Hall of Famers who combined for 557 wins and 547 complete games.

"Before the game, we had three-minute meetings, the catcher and Willie and the pitcher, Gaylord or myself," Marichal said. "Willie let you know how to pitch each individual you had to face. That really helped, playing with somebody who knew the hitter so well. He'd say pitch inside, outside, low, high, whatever. When you have a player who knows so much about the game and opposing players, that really helps. He knew everybody. We listened to him." Perry added, "It was great to see great defense. That's what I needed. When Willie was there and going over the teams, everybody paid attention."

Mays involved nonpitchers, too. Everyone had to be on board if his team was going to profit from the input, so he not only positioned the two other outfielders, but he situated the infielders as well. One of his favorites was Hal Lanier, a versatile infielder who played 10 years in the majors, eight as Mays' teammate.

"He would position me, tell me where to play," Lanier said. "He didn't have a book. It all came from his mind. I would look back at him, and he'd motion left or right or up the middle. He'd put up two hands, straight away. My first years, I played second base. He did the same thing when I moved over to shortstop. He helped me a great deal. He was such a big factor when I came up, defensive-wise especially. He just took me by his hand. I followed him around all the time and watched how he played. What a pleasure to play with a man of his caliber. He really took care of me. He was like my second dad."

Mays briefly played with Lanier's father, Max, in 1952, a season cut short for Mays because of military service. Hal remembered when he was nine years old and Willie brought him and other teammates' children out to center field to play catch. When Hal broke in with the 1964 Giants, Mays greeted him by nicknaming him "Maxie," an homage to Lanier's dad.

"Willie shared a lot with me from the standpoint of running the infield," Lanier said, "trying to get me to be that particular guy where the manager didn't have to come out and talk to the pitcher. Players accepted it. Nowadays, you have so many different coaches. We didn't have that. Willie was a coach to us. In fact, he was his own coach. One thing Willie did, he had a big picture at his locker of him swinging a bat, and it was taken when he was hitting really well. That was his hitting coach right there. He would look at that picture and see where his hands were, how far he was from the plate. I looked over, and I thought, 'Wow, that's amazing.'"

Another Mays favorite was Chris Speier, a rookie in 1971 who replaced Lanier at shortstop and credits Lanier for being his defensive mentor. Speier credits Mays on another level and appreciated his presence while it lasted.

It was Willie's last full season in San Francisco, and the Giants won a division title, their last playoff appearance for the next 16 years.

"Willie had the ability to see the whole game in its entirety. We all realized we were a step behind him," Speier said. "On the bases, he'd direct the runner behind him, wave to let him know what to do. He knew he'd get there, but he wanted the other guy to get there, too. He remembered everything about every single pitcher, every at-bat. His memory was phenomenal with how he knew pitchers. At the plate, he'd look like a fool on a slider to set the pitcher up and have him come back with the same pitch. They'd miss a little bit, and he'd hit the dog doo out of it. The thing about Willie, if you went to him, he'd do anything for you, but you had to make that first step. I learned that early on and started going to him religiously."

Along with tutoring others, Mays found ways to educate himself.

If I went 0-for-4, I'd come home and watch film from 1954. My wife, Mae, would have it all set up along with a plate of food for me. She knew if I came home after going 0-for-4, I'd want to see that film to see what was going on. I might've been moving my leg too far up front or too far back. I had to know. It was just for me. I'd watch it and then put it back. I didn't go 0-for-4 too much.

Because the sixth tool is not as easily quantifiable as the other five, it's not as universally acknowledged when evaluating players, but grit and guile, along with character and chemistry, all are part of a player's portfolio that figures into the finished product.

When Mays reflects on modern-day players, especially outfielders, he's intrigued by those able to display the most tools.

What about the sixth? Can he think?

When the subject turns to Mike Trout, the best all-around player in the modern game, the question needn't be asked. Mays and everyone else know it's a resounding yes, but it wasn't always so. At least not until a former Angels teammate took Trout under his wing.

"I really didn't know any of that until I got to the big leagues," Trout said. "Torii Hunter was big, influencing my mentality, just visualizing the play when it happens. If you visualize a play before it happens and you tell yourself what to do with the ball, I think everything else comes naturally. When the situation presents itself, you're not thinking about it right then. You've already told yourself what you're going to do."

Words dear to Mays.

Now listen, to say I was a coach when I played, I didn't embarrass the guys saying that. I just did it. I wouldn't say anything critical unless we were just by ourselves. They've got to eat, too, just like everybody else. They've got a job. You respect that. But you want to help them grow, and that's why I did it, to help them think a little more about how to do things. It's a big part of the game.

21.

IT'S NOT ALL ABOUT THE NUMBERS

The Story of Life Beyond 660

"In baseball, the ultimate is winning. Stats are a big part of the game. You try to put up numbers. But I played to help my team win, not to put up numbers."

—*Willie Mays*

THE PERSONIFICATION OF power and speed, Willie Mays likes to joke about never joining the 40-40 club. Oh, he hit 40 home runs, plenty of times, and he stole 40 bases. But never in the same season.

If you told me it was important, I would've done it.

Numbers don't define Mays, they just help epitomize him. The .302 batting average. The 3,283 hits. The 660 home runs. The 1,903 RBIs. The 338 stolen bases. The 7,095 outfield putouts. The 156.4 WAR. They don't tell Mays' entire story, but they're certainly an indication of his overall might on the diamond.

You talk about batting average, home runs, stolen bases. I could've done more every year—40-40, all that kind of stuff. Winning was the key. If you think about it, when you win, guys are going in the clubhouse, they're laughing and eating and having a good time. That, to me, is what feels good, what it's all about. But if you lose, even if you hit a couple of home runs, you go in the clubhouse, get a plate of food and don't talk. Nothing fun about that.

Mays retired in 1973, exactly thirty years before the 2003 publication of *Moneyball,* Michael Lewis' influential book that helped change the way baseball is played and how players are acquired and valued. Advanced statistics and analytics are used by all teams at various levels, from drafting and developing players to deciding where to place them on defense and in lineups. For the most part, Mays batted third. In the analytic age of baseball, he might be better served batting second, getting to the plate quicker and getting more plate appearances, roughly 18 over a full season. When Mays played, the second hitter was known to handle the bat, bunt, hit-and-run, basically sacrifice himself to move runners over with Mays on deck. But data shows a higher probability to score a run with a runner on first and no outs than a runner on second and one out, which is a reason second hitters are told to swing away; that is, unless they can draw a walk. The best hitters, preferably those with power, speed, and a high on-base percentage—Mays to a T—would bat second. With zero thought of bunting.

In 1954, the year we won the World Series, Leo (Durocher) told me I've got to stop hitting home runs. At first, I didn't understand why. I had 31 at the All-Star break. Why was he telling me that? Stop hitting home runs? I hit just 10 more that year, but I finished with a .345 average, knocked in 110, and scored 119. We won the pennant and World Series, and I won the MVP award and hit 41 homers but could have hit 50, maybe 60.

If I hit more homers in my career, I wouldn't have done other things as well to go with the homers. Leo's point was that he wanted me to get on base, get rallies going, things that would get everyone involved as a team. That's what he was talking about. Home runs are nice. But if you don't win, what does it matter? What good is it to hit four home runs in a game if you lose?

Valuing Mays by today's advanced statistics would shed new light on the Say Hey Kid, but he'd still top the charts no matter what the metric, offensively or defensively. The new information would provide a far more precise and telling description of Mays' skill set, and he'd likely be sitting atop an even loftier pedestal. For example, if today's data were available and utilized in Willie's playing days, he'd undoubtedly have far more than two Most Valuable Player awards. Eleven times, he ranked among the top three in the majors in Wins Above Replacement (WAR)—an all-encompassing statistic that measures players' overall contributions, not just on the offensive side, and allows for better comparisons of players in different generations—and only Babe Ruth did that more, 12 times.

When fully analyzing Mays' advanced numbers against the field, a case could be made that he was worthy of winning anywhere between eight and 11 MVP awards.

"He could have won a lot more," said national analytics writer Eno Sarris, who has worked for FanGraphs and The Athletic. "I think we lacked the ability to put numbers to well-roundedness back then. His game was ahead of his time. In some ways, he's kind of like the Mike Trout of his generation."

Decades later, Trout is the closest player to Mays, a sabermetrician's dream who is valued for his across-the-board skills, a perennial MVP candidate who can hit, hit for power, run, field, and throw, all at a high level, the five tools that set Mays apart from other all-time greats and put Trout on a path to the Hall of Fame and generational prominence.

Trout relishes baseball history. He grew up in Millville, New Jersey, and loved the Phillies. His father, Jeff, took his kids to Yankee Stadium, where young Mike took a liking to Derek Jeter and appreciated the rich baseball tradition in the Bronx. Eventually, Trout drew comparisons to another Yankees legend, Mickey Mantle, which certainly is fair when examining all the tools, especially Mantle's brute strength as a hitter. Only Mays is linked to Trout on this front: They're the only players with three seasons of 30 home runs and 20 stolen bases by their age twenty-seven season.

"As a center fielder, the way he played, you want to be like Willie," Trout said. "He catches everything, a five-tool player. I think every outfielder, every kid, they want to make that catch, that catch he made in the World Series. You see it everywhere. You've got to appreciate the five tools. You've got to appreciate the effort, day in and day out, night in and night out. On both sides of the ball. At a tremendous level, the way he did it. It's tough to be great at everything, and he was one of those guys: great at everything.

"I like to tell myself, pre-pitch, what to do if a certain situation comes up. You put it in your mind. You tell yourself, 'This is what I want to do with it.' That's been helping me defensively throughout my career so far. I think Willie's catch, it kind of puts in your mind, before each play happens, you can catch everything."

Willie Mays collected his 3,000th hit off Montreal's Mike Wegener at Candlestick Park in 1970. His manager that year was Charlie Fox. (San Francisco Giants)

Mays is on the same wavelength as Trout. Asked which stat was most important to him—homers, RBIs, runs, etc.—Mays took it in another direction.

Catching the ball was important. I'm talking about the hard plays.

There haven't been many harder plays than Mays' catch in Game 1 of the 1954 World Series at the cavernous Polo Grounds, where he tracked down Vic Wertz's tremendous drive.

Mays was every bit as successful at run prevention, which is controlled by the pitcher and his defense, as run production. He was proud of his fielding and throwing tools, but in Trout's mind, two other Mays tools stand out.

"Obviously, the power was great, and I look at his speed," Trout said. "If you have speed, it helps your all-around game."

Mays pondered.

Yeah, okay, power and speed. I used speed, but only when I had to use it. He understands. Mike Trout plays every day. I played every day. He's a five-tool player, and he has great instincts in the outfield. But you use your speed when you need to. For instance, if I hit a single, I wanted to be on second. It's not just about stealing a base. It's about being aware. If a guy hesitates in the outfield or slightly bobbles the ball, I'm at second. (Former Angels manager) Mike Scioscia told me about (Trout) long ago, so I knew about him when he came up. He's a big ol' guy, and he's good because he's consistent. He does it every year.

At the pace he's playing, Trout one day will join the legends. He has the tools. Now it's about longevity. Through 1,000 games, he was on a course few have taken, hitting .308 with 483 extra-base hits and 178 steals. By comparison, Mays hit .316 in his first 1,000 games with 484 extra-base hits and 169 steals. Alex Rodriguez (.311, 510, and 152) is the only other player since 1900 with at least a .300 average, 450 extra-base hits, and 150 steals in 1,000 games.

WAR deciphers how many more wins a player is worth than a replacement-level player. A 10-WAR season is historic and has been reached just 10 times in the 2000s, three by Trout and three by Barry Bonds. By comparison, Mays had six 10-WAR seasons. In fact, he had a 10-WAR average over a seven-year stretch, 1960 through 1966, and led his league in WAR a mind-blowing 10 times and the majors seven times.

Mays' career WAR according to FanGraphs is third all time at 149.9, behind only Ruth and Bonds. It's 156.4 according to Baseball Reference, which includes pitchers Walter Johnson and Cy Young in the mix. Trout's 72.5 WAR through the 2019 season ranked 87th on the all-time list, and all but eleven players ahead of him were in the Hall of Fame.

"It is surreal," Trout said. "You get compared to the all-time greats, you appreciate it, but once you really see what they've accomplished throughout their careers, it's unbelievable. It makes you feel like you're doing something right, and it makes you feel good about yourself. They paved the way for us. To be in the same sentence, it's an honor."

Trout puts up stats that make him an MVP contender every year. Much like Mays decades earlier. In fact, while Mays was the MVP in 1954 and 1965, he could have racked up . . . well, where shall we start?

How about 1962? The Giants won the pennant, and Mays led the league with 49 home runs and collected a career-high 141 RBIs while hitting .304 with a .384 on-base percentage and .615 slugging percentage. But he finished second in the MVP voting to Dodgers leadoff man Maury Wills, who made history by stealing 104 bases and capturing the imagination of the baseball world and MVP voters who sided with the novelty of triple-digit steals. Mays was instrumental in leading the Giants down the stretch, hitting .337 with nine homers and 28 RBIs in the final month and .455 with two homers in the best-of-three series required to break a 162-game tie with the Dodgers. Furthermore, he hit .361 with runners in scoring position and an alarming .441 with runners in scoring position and two outs. Wills' record base stealing helped him score 130 runs, the exact number of times Mays crossed the plate. Mays had 43 more homers and 93 more RBIs and posted a majors-high 10.5 WAR to Wills' 6.0.

Of course, today's advanced stats weren't available to voters in 1962. Or any other year Mays easily could have won the MVP.

When I first heard about WAR, I didn't know what the hell they were talking about, but I understand it combines everything. Fielding, hitting, baserunning. It's all things together, and they never had that kind of stat when I played. I like math, but whether you hit 30 home runs or 50 home runs, whether you make a play or steal a base or drive in a run, it's all about doing something that'll help you win. That's the reason you play, the reason for this stat, breaking you down by wins.

You can do one thing well or several things well. The more you do, the more you win. I could've spent all my time piling up home runs or stolen bases or batting averages, all that kind of stuff, but you're more valuable helping your team in a whole bunch of different ways.

Mays won his first MVP in 1954 and thought his 1955 season was better. He had 10 more homers, a league-leading 51. It was one of five seasons he had an on-base plus slugging percentage (OPS) above 1.000. Catcher Roy Campanella, whose Dodgers won the pennant, was the 1955 MVP with a 5.2 WAR compared with Mays' 9.1.

Solid cases could be made for Mays winning MVP awards in 1954 (the year he won his first), 1955 (Campanella's year), 1957 (Hank Aaron), 1958 (Ernie Banks), 1960 (Dick Groat), 1961 (Frank Robinson), 1962 (Wills), 1963 (Koufax—like most hitters, Mays wasn't a big fan of pitchers winning MVP awards), 1964 (Ken Boyer), 1965 (Mays), and 1966 (Roberto Clemente).

Groat was the Pirates' shortstop who led the league in hitting in 1960 but had just two homers. Pittsburgh easily won the pennant, and voters preferred someone from the league champions even though they chose Banks the previous two years when the Cubs had losing records. Groat's WAR was 6.2. Mays' was 9.5.

So, yes, Mays might have been snubbed more than once. Voting isn't science. It's a subjective method of determining a league's most valuable player, and any number of peripheral factors can be considered, such as where a player's team finishes, how he treats the media, and the concept that voting for the same guys every year is boring. A consistently high level of play is the goal, but it could lead voters to search for a trendy alternative. Ask Mike Trout. In the outfielder's first full eight seasons, he won three MVPs, finished second four times, and fourth once. He's the first player in history with seven top-two finishes in an eight-year span. Imagine if the Angels had been a regular postseason participant. Imagine if the Giants had won more pennants under Mays.

"Mays was terribly neglected in the MVP voting, and it's not difficult to see why," said Rob Neyer, a statistical-savvy baseball author who has worked for ESPN.com, SB Nation, and STATS, Inc. "The numbers we have, the numbers people used in the past, don't quite go all the way toward measuring how great he was. Mays was probably the best player in the league six, seven, or eight times and just wasn't going to win because the Giants weren't winning the league. But it's not difficult to make the case that Mays is even better than his WAR, which is phenomenal. WAR is a good baseline, but the data isn't comprehensive with players of the past. We don't have the granular data for outfielders that we have now. Same thing for baserunning. Certainly no player today compares with him except maybe Mike Trout."

Trout led all major-leaguers in WAR in 2012, 2013, and 2016, was second in 2018 and third in 2014, 2015, and 2019. Like Mays, he could (some say should) have more MVPs. The most glaring oversight, in the minds of advanced analytic advocates, was the 2012 MVP race in which Tigers first baseman Miguel Cabrera topped Trout after winning the first Triple Crown since Carl Yastrzemski in 1967. Trout was the superior base runner and defender at a premium position and had a far better WAR (10.4 to 7.1).

"WAR is pretty good for this exercise because it credits for longevity and adjusts for your peers and the type of ball played in your time," Sarris said. "It's easy now to sort the WAR leaderboards for center fielders and say, 'Yeah, Mays is easily the best center fielder of all time.' The fact Mays is third in all-time overall WAR behind Babe Ruth and Barry Bonds, that's Mount Rushmore for me. Mays was the precursor to Trout. But if you look at individual categories, there are players with more home runs, more stolen bases, and better batting averages than Mays. It's like when Trout lost the MVP to Cabrera. In many ways, Trout's contributions were superior, but winning the Triple Crown happens so rarely, and that fits in with Mays losing to Wills, who stole all those bases in '62."

A difference is that Cabrera's Tigers reached the postseason, and Wills' Dodgers did not, though only league winners went to the postseason in 1962. Yes, WAR is an imperfect stat. The websites Baseball Reference, FanGraphs, and Baseball Prospectus calculate it slightly differently, after all, but it serves a purpose for helping to quantify players' value and compare them from different eras.

"It's pretty unique," Trout said of WAR. "There's much more attention to it. Over the years, it's been brought up a bunch. Nowadays, you hear about it every day. I couldn't tell you how they factor it, but if I prepare myself each day and do good things on the field, the number should go up. People are seeing what it really is. Back then, they really didn't have that."

Back then, as in when Mays played. When advanced stats weren't at everyone's fingertips.

I had my own advanced stats. I learned hitters' tendencies and memorized their strengths and weaknesses, which put me in the right position to succeed and allowed me to place teammates in the right position to do well, too.

Beyond the advanced stats, baseball uses advanced technology to analyze a player's movements and talent level through a scientific approach. Among other things, Statcast measures the speed of a ball when it's hit (exit velocity), the direction and height of the ball when it's hit (launch angle), and the movement of the ball when it's thrown (spin rate). It also tracks routes and the speed of base runners and defenders and provides criteria for players who excel at an elite level with the five tools. It's fair to suggest Mays—and Trout—would get top grades across the board. Here's the cutoff in each category for big-leaguers to rank in the top 10 percent, based on their season-long averages in 2019 and gauged by Statcast:

Hitting: hard-hit percentage of balls with exit velocity at least 95 mph ≥ 46

Hitting for power: home run distance ≥ 411 feet

Running: sprint speed ≥ 29 feet per second

Fielding: outs above average ≥ 8

Throwing: throws ≥ 90 mph

Long before they were readily available and evaluated online, baseball stats could be found in sports sections of newspapers, in *The Sporting News* (a weekly once considered baseball's bible), in *The Official Encyclopedia of Baseball* (which began publishing in 1951, Mays' rookie year), and on the backs of baseball cards, mostly with the simplest of data: games, at-bats, runs, hits, doubles, triples, homers, RBIs, average. Sometimes far less. Radio was king, and TV was in its infancy. Fans attending games heavily relied on the eye test to judge talent, form opinions, and determine their favorite players. In that regard, no one was more pleasing to the eye than the flamboyant Mays, but it wouldn't take much to examine the most basic of stats to conclude he was one of a kind. Trout has the advantage of advanced metrics and technology that captures data few could have imagined. Still, Trout, like Mays, breaks baseball down to its simplest, see-ball, hit-ball form, trying to keep stats out of his mind when he's hitting, throwing, and running.

"I don't think about putting up numbers," Trout said. "I go out there and prepare myself for the situation that presents itself and put myself in the best situation at the plate or on defense while trying to get better every day. I think if you worry about numbers and individual stats, that's when you put pressure on yourself and you start thinking about it, and that's when you start to fail."

Like I said, I didn't play for that kind of stuff. Let other guys hit home runs as long as we win. I kept all that to myself. If you start bragging, it's not the same as if you just go out and do it, let people see what you can do, and let them make up their own mind.

22.

HAVE EACH OTHER'S BACK

The Story of a Good Friend's Son

"I encourage all kids to go to college, something I didn't have a
chance to do. Do all you can to stay in school and learn about taking
care of yourself by studying business or taking up a trade or finding
a passion."

—*Willie Mays*

WILLIE MAYS PAID a visit to Bobby Bonds in the final stages of his former
teammate's life.

**I went to the hospital one day, and Bobby and I talked. He said, "Willie,
you've got to take care of Barry. He's not going to listen to other people
like he does you and me. You've got to take care of him." Whatever Barry
needed, that's what I did.**

On August 23, 2003, after being treated for lung cancer and a brain tu-
mor and undergoing open-heart surgery, Bobby Bonds—a popular Giant,
three-time All-Star, and three-time Gold Glove winner—died at his Bay
Area home. He was fifty-seven years old and survived by his wife, Pat, and

four children, one of whom followed in his father's and godfather's footsteps and played outfield for the Giants.

Mays made himself available for Bonds' oldest of three sons, who had just turned thirty-nine and had four big-league seasons remaining and many records and milestones on the horizon.

As Barry Bonds slugged his way to the all-time home run record, all the while being a lightning rod for controversy and a target of boos outside San Francisco, Mays was at his side nearly every step of the way.

It was common before games to see Mays joking with Bonds in clubhouse manager Mike Murphy's office, sharing advice at his locker, or even

Bobby Bonds, left, was tabbed the next Willie Mays, a colossally unfair comparison despite Bonds' wide-ranging talents. (Ron Riesterer)

stretching him out in the middle of the room. For several decades, Mays has been a regular at the Giants' ballpark, and after Bonds' father expressed his dying wish, an extra attempt was made to be present as much as possible for the younger Bonds.

I spoke with him, and he listened now and then, and then I'd leave him alone for a bit. With Barry, you let him know you're there, but sometimes you have to back up a little bit. When he had enough, I'd move on. I didn't bother him. He was his own man. If he asked for advice, I would give it. I didn't harp on it.

This three-way dynamic began in the late '60s when Mays was on the back end of his Hall of Fame career, Bobby Bonds was a young major-league star, and Barry Bonds was a child whose playground was Candlestick Park, where his father was introducing his five-tool talents as an understudy to Mays, about the time Willie became Barry's godfather.

"I was a kid, five years old," the younger Bonds said. "I mean, I followed Willie everywhere. I would try to take his glove even though I was left-handed. I tried to put it on my opposite hand because I just wanted to wear his glove. It was cool because the Giants allowed the kids to go out on the field with the guys and shag baseballs. I went to center field and watched Willie throw the ball underhanded and make basket catches.

"I always tried to copy him, but I couldn't catch at that time because I was too little and would always fall down. Willie said, 'How are you going to make the major leagues if you can't throw the ball?' So I tried to throw as hard as I could, run as hard as I could, do everything Willie did. When he walked on and off the field, I was there with him."

Meantime, Bobby Bonds evolved into one of the game's all-time multi-dimensional threats, combining a new level of power at the plate and speed on the bases. While Mays was the first player with two seasons of 30 or more home runs and 30 or more stolen bases, Bobby Bonds was the first to do it three seasons. And four. And five.

Today, just two players are five-time members of the 30-30 club, and the last name of both is Bonds.

Pat would bring all the kids to the ballpark. Pat should be commended. I still say she was the key to the whole family. More than the other kids, Barry stayed with me. He messed around at my locker—I had cases of bubble gum—and came on the field with me. I remember him when he was five years old. Mac (Willie McCovey) helped me with him, too, talked really nice to him, didn't holler at him.

Young Barry was able to visit Mays at Candlestick for just a few years because Mays was traded to the Mets two months before Barry's eighth birthday. In that time, the kid and the Say Hey Kid created a close relationship that has lasted a lifetime.

"I was safe with Willie," Barry Bonds said. "My dad would say 'sit here.' I didn't sit there because I wanted to go where Willie went. My dad figured, 'I've got to beat this kid to death or ask Willie to watch this kid because this kid isn't going to listen to me.' Willie was like, 'Leave him alone, he's with me.' That's the only time my dad wouldn't talk back to me. Willie could've taken me to China, and my dad wouldn't say anything."

Willie Mays, Willie McCovey, and Barry Bonds combined to hit 1,943 home runs, 1,701 while with the Giants. (Brad Mangin)

When Mays was traded to the Mets in May 1972, Bobby already was an All-Star and entering his prime. He had a stronger arm and more speed than his son would develop and was a force in every way imaginable. Naturally, because he was a phenom showing all-around prowess, Bonds was billed the "next Willie Mays" by fans, media, and the industry's talent evaluators.

It was unfair, inappropriate, and just plain wrong. For both parties. But if you're good enough to be compared with the best, it's inevitable, though it did nothing but bring on unwanted pressures for the young outfielder.

He didn't like that. He wanted to leave me out. I said, "Bobby, they're not going to let you leave me out. Just go and do your own thing."

It didn't take Bobby long to bust out of Mays' shadow. The season following Mays' exit was the best in Bonds' career. He hit .283 with a .370 on-base percentage, .530 slugging percentage, 39 home runs, and 43 stolen bases. He missed becoming the first 40-40 man by one homer and finished third in the MVP voting to Pete Rose and Willie Stargell.

But a year later, after seven seasons in San Francisco, Bonds was traded to the Yankees for Bobby Murcer, who was dealing with his own pressures because he was supposed to be the next Mickey Mantle, an expectation as impossible for Murcer as it was for Bonds to be the next Mays.

Bonds had a splendid 14-year career that probably would have been far better if not for his well-chronicled battle with alcoholism. He played seven more years after the Giants traded him and continued compiling impressive numbers. Three of his 30-30 seasons came after he left the Giants. But he repeatedly wore out his welcome and never was able to stay in one spot, never able to shed his baggage. In those seven years, he played for seven teams.

I knew Bobby very well. We used to talk a lot. We had a lot of fun together. I remember helping him when they were buying their house, when they came up from Riverside. On the field, Bobby could do everything. He could hit home runs. He could run. The only thing was his drinking.

Through it all, Bobby Bonds maintained a high level of respect for Mays.

"Willie Mays was the only one who could tell my dad what to do," Barry Bonds said. "I ain't never seen anyone tell my dad what to do but Willie. Everything was about Willie for my dad. He'd say, 'Willie can do this, Willie can do that.' And, 'You grow up, you want to be the best, look at what he does.'

"To me, my dad did everything Willie could do. He could run as fast if not faster. He could go catch a baseball. He could hit home runs. He was comparable when you look at the ability. Willie used to hit to right-center. My dad would hit to right-center. They both tapped their gloves before catching a fly ball.

"My dad said, 'But Willie's a superstar.' My dad appreciated that. He was able to separate that. He was never jealous over that. He never was like, 'I have just as much ability as Willie.' He was like, 'No, Willie's the man.' He just idolized him and wanted to emulate him."

When Barry Bonds was growing up in San Carlos, a short drive south from Candlestick, his relationship with his father was tumultuous. The drinking didn't help. That his dad no longer played for the Giants created further distance.

The younger Bonds dominated youth leagues and went on to become a star athlete at nearby Junipero Serra High School, an all-boys school with a rich sports tradition that produced Tom Brady, Lynn Swann, and Jim Fregosi. Bonds was drafted out of Serra in 1982, a year after his dad's final big-league season.

The team that selected Bonds in the second round? The Giants. His dad wanted his son to go play college ball. So did Mays, who said one of the biggest regrets of his life was not experiencing the college life.

That's what I was concerned about, his education. Once you get that, it can't be taken away. Other stuff, they can take it away some kind of way. I never had the opportunity to go to college. Think about it. With an education, you can do anything you want.

I played quarterback in high school, but at that time, you didn't see black quarterbacks in the pros. Football was my first sport. Basketball, my second, but I didn't think I was tall enough to play basketball. Baseball was the way to go. They didn't have the opportunities in college for me.

When I finished my playing career and entered the business world, it was hard because I didn't have a college education. I had to figure things out on my own with help from many other people. It was a big adjustment that would have been made easier with an education. So I felt the most important thing for Barry was to go to college, play three or four years, enjoy himself, and come out a man.

While Mays received nothing further than a high school education, he's proud that he lived a life that would warrant him honorary degrees from Dartmouth, Yale, Ohio State, San Francisco State, and Miles College, which is located in his hometown of Fairfield, Alabama.

By the time his godson was being wooed by pro scouts and college recruiters, Mays was retired for nearly a decade and receiving no favors from baseball. The man who gave so much to the game was on the suspended list, thanks to Commissioner Bowie Kuhn's decision to ban him because he was employed at Bally's, an Atlantic City casino.

It didn't help the Giants' case in trying to sign Barry Bonds that they weren't exactly aggressive in negotiations. General manager Tom Haller offered $70,000 and refused to budge further even though the Bonds camp suggested slightly more at $75,000.

"That's a true story," said Frank Robinson, the Giants' manager at the time. "We drafted him and couldn't get it done. It came down to only $5,000. I was there. In negotiations, we came up. But he wouldn't come down. I asked him why he wanted $75,000, and he said that's what he felt he was worth. I said, 'Give the kid $5,000 of my salary,' and I was serious. They wouldn't do it. He was the type of player we needed in our system at that time."

Mays wasn't buying it.

"Willie just said, 'I don't care if it's the Giants or whatever, you need to go to school and grow up without ending out on the street,'" Bonds said. "In baseball, if you don't do nothing, you're kicked to the curb. If they don't like you, you're gone. There's nothing you can do. Regardless of what goes down, you go to college, you're guaranteed that education. That's how Willie and my dad explained it. You could break a leg, something could happen. What's $70,000 going to do for you? You can't even buy a house for $70,000."

I said no, no, no. That's not enough. Let him go to school. Bobby had told me Barry could hit a ball farther than I could. I said I don't think so. But if that's true, the major leagues could wait. Education was more important.

Appeasing his father and godfather, Bonds accepted a full-ride scholarship to Arizona State, a baseball powerhouse. Three years later, he was drafted sixth overall by the Pirates and signed for $150,000. By 1986, not only did he have a degree from ASU in criminology, but his big-league career was under way.

In retrospect, Bonds understands and appreciates Mays' guidance.

"I wanted to go to college anyway. I felt I needed to go step by step," Bonds said. "If there was any doubt, Willie said, 'You need to go to school.' He always put the period behind the sentence."

Bonds played seven seasons in Pittsburgh, won two MVP awards, and led the Pirates to three straight National League Championship Series, each time falling a step short of the World Series. It just so happened Bonds stopped hitting every October.

After the 1992 season, Bonds became a free agent and was seeking baseball's biggest contract. By then, Mays was back working for the Giants as a special assistant. Peter Ueberroth, Kuhn's successor, had wisely reinstated him and Mantle, who also had a casino gig.

In what turned out to be perfect timing for Bonds, Giants owner Bob Lurie was selling the team to a group of San Francisco investors led by Peter Magowan, who stepped up after a sale to a Florida group was rejected by National League owners. One of Magowan's primary goals was to sign Bonds, which he did for six years and $43.75 million.

Another was to sign Mays to a lifetime contract. Done.

Peter called and said they were trying to get Barry, and I said get him. I could take care of him, and Bobby could take care of him.

Bobby Bonds was hired as hitting coach and first-base coach, his first coaching job since he was in Cleveland five years earlier. Dusty Baker, who like the Bondses had roots in Riverside, was the new manager. Suddenly, Barry Bonds found himself with the ultimate support group and envisioned being part of an all-time Giants outfield of Bonds, Mays, and Bonds.

"I completed the cycle," the younger Bonds said. "That was important."

For Magowan, too. He knew his history, growing up in New York, watching Mays play from his rookie year in 1951, and ultimately moving west and reacquainting himself with his childhood team.

"I had known Bobby really well," Magowan said, "and Bobby had great, great respect for Willie. Barry knew Willie as a child in the Giants' clubhouse and loved Willie. I think it was great for Barry to be back in San Francisco, and I think Willie had quite a bit to do with the appeal of coming back."

Only because controversy followed Bonds everywhere, the simple task of obtaining a uniform number led to headlines for all the wrong reasons. There was an ill-conceived plan endorsed by Magowan for Bonds to wear Mays' cherished uniform number 24, which Bonds wore in Pittsburgh. Common sense prevailed, and Bonds took his father's number, 25 (Bobby wore 16 as a coach), and should have been thankful he didn't get 7, the number initially issued to him by the Pirates in the spring of 1986 as a takeoff on agent 007 James Bond, a bad idea all around.

"I said, 'C'mon man, you're tripping,'" Bonds said. "So I took 24. Everyone thought it was because of Willie, but it had nothing to do with Willie. I was born on July 24. Ever since I was a little boy, I was told by my grandmother that should be my lucky number because that's the day God gave me life. My godfather just happened to be 24, my idol, and I was born on the same day. The best of both worlds. That's the story of 24."

On the Giants, he was 25.

Now you've got 24 in the middle, 25 on the left, and 25 on the right. You've got the whole family in the outfield. Let's do that, and nobody can say anything against Barry or anyone else.

Bonds played 15 seasons in San Francisco, won five more MVP awards, broke the career and single-season home run records, and became the second player behind José Canseco to join the 40-40 club, which his father almost reached in 1973.

Now wearing the same uniform, Bonds got a chance to renew his relationship with his father, and they often showed public displays of affection, a sign that joining forces did wonders for their relationship. Nobody knew Bonds' swing better than his dad, who was in an ideal position to tutor and motivate his son, even kick him in the butt if it helped get him back on track. In large part, Barry was receptive.

Bobby's time on the coaching staff ended after his son's 40-40 season in 1996, though Barry remained open to talking hitting with his dad, and he went on to finally enjoy a big postseason in 2002. He was set to be crowned World Series MVP until the Giants blew a golden chance to clinch in Game 6 and lost to the Angels in seven.

It easily was a Hall of Fame career if just the numbers were considered: 762 homers, 514 steals, seven MVP awards, .298 batting average, .444 on-base percentage, .607 slugging percentage, 14 All-Star selections, eight Gold Glove awards, and 12 Silver Slugger awards. But Bonds' connection with the world of performance-enhancing drugs proved to be a difference maker on many levels—during his career and after—and could have challenged his relationship with Mays. Rather than distance himself from his friend's son, however, Mays grew closer.

As Bonds climbed into the revered top echelons of the home run chart and became the fourth player to surpass 600, his association with the BALCO lab in nearby Burlingame was coming into focus. By the time he was approaching Mays' 660 in April 2004, it had been reported by the *San Francisco Chronicle* that Bonds was among several players to receive steroids from BALCO, an epicenter of baseball's performance-enhancing drug scandal.

Mays continued to be at his godson's side, as he was for most every other step of his life.

Most of the time, we didn't talk about baseball. We talked about everything else. You don't want to talk baseball with a guy who's going good anyway. If I see he's in a rut, that's when I can point something out. If he went 0-for-10, the phone would ring. "Where are you?" Mostly, we talked about life.

Mays' guidance didn't go unnoticed by those who were there.

"Willie was a calming force," said Dusty Baker, the Giants' manager in Bonds' first ten years in San Francisco. "He would tell Barry the truth, and then Barry would listen. This is one of the few guys that Barry would listen to. I mean, listen intently. Barry would listen even when he acted like he wasn't listening, but when he was talking to Willie and Willie was talking to him, he *acted* like he was listening.

"What Willie was telling him superseded and was more important than what I could've told him. He was coming in with a different level of respect. It was almost like the Lord talking to him. I wasn't the Lord, not even close. But Willie was Willie Mays, man."

Bobby Bonds was able to witness his son break Mark McGwire's single-season homers record in 2001 and dominate the 2002 postseason, but Bobby died late in the 2003 season before the BALCO scandal took over the headlines. Barry needed and relied on Mays more than ever and sought his advice approaching 660—one of baseball's most sacred numbers, aside from Hank Aaron's 755 and Ruth's 714.

"That's always been the big one for me," Barry said. "I never wanted to pass him. Willie's my idol. But he's the one who encouraged me to go after it all. My dad always did, and I listened to my dad, but like I said, Willie put the period after the sentence.

"Willie always wanted you to be better than him. Like with me, if someone says, 'I'm gonna beat your record,' I hope you do because what

I've done, I've already done. Same thing with Willie. Willie was the one who said, 'Go for it. You can do it.' I never wanted to make him unhappy."

So Bonds went for it.

I wanted to pass the torch. Like my dad when he played ball. He passed the torch to me. I knew about playing every position because of my father. When we went out to play, we didn't work on just one thing. We worked on different things every day, all the positions. Just he and I. I knew how to hit, field, and throw.

So when Barry was having reservations about passing me, I told him not to worry about it. It's part of history. I passed Mel Ott for the Giants' record and National League record. You keep going and don't worry about everyone else.

I went on the road with him to make sure he enjoyed what he was doing. He didn't get much to hit in San Diego, then he came home and got 660, and I came out to greet him and pass the torch. I told him to thank the fans because they're the ones who love him and support him.

The torch was passed to Barry Bonds, literally, when he matched Willie Mays' home run total of 660. (Brad Mangin)

This torch was different. It literally was a torch, a ceremonial Olympic torch that Mays carried a few blocks in San Francisco as part of a relay before the 2002 Winter Games in Salt Lake City, and he had it encrusted with $18,000 worth of diamonds with the numbers 660, 25, and 1. As in, Bonds' jersey number and one more for 661. Clearly, Mays, who often consoled Barry Bonds in the winter leading to the fateful 2004 season, in the wake of

Bobby Bonds' death, was cool dropping to number four all time if it meant his longtime apprentice would be the one to surpass him.

When Bonds matched Mays' 660 with a homer in a game against Milwaukee, Mays handed him the torch during a brief on-field ceremony and encouraged him to keep swinging for the next plateau, Ruth's, 54 away.

It's a number, a milestone. There was no competition between us. We knew he'd get it, and I wanted to be there for him when he did.

Mays stayed close as Bonds went on to pass Ruth in 2006 and Aaron in 2007 to become the all-time homers king while baseball's drug scandal heightened. Shortly after the publication of Mark Fainaru-Wada and Lance Williams' 2006 book, *Game of Shadows,* which traced Bonds' and other athletes' performance-enhancing drug trails and cited the Giants and Major League Baseball as enablers, Commissioner Bud Selig summoned former Senate majority leader George Mitchell to lead an investigation into the use of PEDs throughout baseball.

Despite Bonds' 28 home runs and league-leading on-base percentage, all thirty teams snubbed him in 2008, forcing an unexpected end to his career. Furthermore, his road to Cooperstown was roadblocked five years later when he appeared on the writers' Hall of Fame ballot for the first time and fell well shy of the 75 percent required for election, voters leaning on the rule to consider integrity, sportsmanship, and character. In 2020, for the eighth time, he missed getting elected, giving him two more tries on the ballot.

Mays is leading the campaign. In August 2018, during an on-field ceremony to retire Bonds' number 25, Mays made an unscheduled plea not only for the Giants to erect a Bonds statue but for the writers to elect him to the Hall of Fame. Mays stole the show and concluded his six-minute, fifteen-second speech by saying, "So on behalf of all the people in San Francisco and all over this country, vote this guy in. He is very, very important to me." The speech hadn't been on the docket, but no one cared. When

Barry Bonds relied on Willie Mays, his godfather, while climbing the single-season and career home run charts. (Rick Swig)

Mays wants to speak, others defer. In this case, he was expressing his desire for Bonds to join him in the hallowed grounds of Cooperstown.

"That's my godfather," Bonds said. "Willie knows what's right. I know what's right. Everybody knows what's right. Eventually, they'll make it right. Or they won't."

In their conversations, Mays sometimes tried to work on improving Bonds' image and reputation, whether it was treating others (including teammates) better, showing restraint in front of the media, or simply mellowing out. That lesson didn't always hit home. When Bonds did try to be accommodating, kinder, and gentler, he'd see his game suffer because he'd lose his fiery edge.

"I should've handled things a little different. I didn't," Bonds said. "I was so zoned in and focused. I'm introverted. I'm a loner-type person. I don't care for all that stuff. I just wanted to go to work and go home. I didn't want to lose focus."

In the mind of Mays, who took Barry Bonds under his wing decades after he took Bobby Bonds under his wing, that shouldn't affect a Hall of Fame candidacy.

You go by the numbers, he should be in. When I was on the ballot in '79, twenty-three writers didn't vote for me. You never know. I just think he should have that honor.

23.

STAY YOUNG AT HEART

The Story of Three World Series Rings

"You want to help people. You want to help kids. If you've gone through something they're going through, you can be there for them. It can be a big difference."

—*Willie Mays*

EVERYONE HAS A Willie Mays story.

Whether it's Pablo Sandoval igniting the Giants on baseball's biggest stage like Willie. Or Buster Posey shooting a commercial with Willie. Or Travis Ishikawa getting invited to dinner by Willie. Or Brandon Belt answering a trivia question to win gear from Willie.

Or even Bruce Bochy getting scolded by Willie—back when Bochy was a high schooler trying to run off with some baseballs during a spring training workout in Vero Beach, Florida.

They're all Willie's kids, the folks who have suited up daily in the uniform he once wore, who were responsible for an extraordinary stretch of World Series championships, who welcome and cherish his dignified presence, high-pitched commentary, and infectious laughter.

The Giants are my family. I was nineteen when I signed. I came up with the Giants. I returned to the Giants. I'm still with the Giants. We've had a beautiful relationship over the years. I've enjoyed being around the kids, watching them grow and develop. It's the franchise I've been with most of my life. It's home.

Most Hall of Famers don't frequent major-league ballparks unless a promotional event warrants it, but the Giants have been fortunate the Say Hey Kid has been a regular at their park. What he has done on a nearly daily basis over the past few decades isn't seen elsewhere and usually makes for a lively, if not surreal, atmosphere.

Mays can be seen in longtime clubhouse manager Mike Murphy's office, right across the hall from the manager's office, with his assistant Rene Anderson. He sits at a small table, commonly known as the Willie Mays table (which he signs and encourages visitors to sign as well), and it's an open-door, come-in-and-chat policy. He makes himself available to everyone in the vicinity, whether it's Giants players, opposing players, former players, managers, coaches, staff members, reporters, or fortunate fans who catch him at the right time.

The same is true in spring training, where Mays visits the Scottsdale Stadium clubhouse before each home game and sits at another Willie Mays table. He shares his knowledge or exchanges playful barbs, sometimes simultaneously. Rookies often are too shy to approach, but veterans tend to be more comfortable sitting for a chat. Mays will mentor on the game's finer points, tell classic stories from yesteryear, or entertain the entire room and leave everyone busting up laughing.

"The last ten years, I've been able to interact with arguably the greatest player of all time," Posey said. "As a student of the game, I feel very fortunate. Baseball has been his life since he signed as a teenager, and he still enjoys talking the game. There's a sense people have that the game has changed so much since he played, but it's the same game. You pitch it, hit it, and catch it. The tidbits he brings back that are in his memory still apply today."

Shortstop Brandon Crawford said, "My dad grew up in San Jose, so he watched Willie. When I was growing up, he talked about the history of the Giants, so Willie was talked about a pretty good amount. Getting to introduce ourselves and meet one of the best players, if not the best player, ever to play baseball, that's special. He's there almost every night of the season and keeps up with how everybody's doing. He feels a lot of pride in the organization, and I think he was just as happy for us as anybody when we won the championships."

Mays played in five World Series, his first with the Birmingham Black Barons in the Negro Leagues (1948), three with the Giants (1951, 1954, 1962), and one with the Mets (1973). His lone championship, featuring his back-to-the-plate catch at the Polo Grounds in Game 1, was in 1954 when the Giants swept heavily favored Cleveland. They took fifty-six years to win another title, the 2010 team beating the Rangers in five games.

After Brian Wilson threw the final pitch past Nelson Cruz, Mays was teary-eyed. The Giants clinched in Texas, and he watched the game and ensuing celebration at home with friends, reflective of his many close calls as a player but mostly proud for the group that staked claim to San Francisco's first title. He was twenty-three when he celebrated in 1954, and now he was seventy-nine and feeling joy on another level.

It was an exciting night for the franchise and city and a wonderful feeling for me. It wasn't about looking back to '54 or '62. It was about what these kids did. You could see how excited they were. It was important that they enjoyed it because no one knew if they would get to experience it again.

Two years later, they experienced it again. Tim Lincecum, Matt Cain, Madison Bumgarner, and Posey were back in the postseason, and this time, the Giants ground out three elimination-game playoff wins over the Reds and three more over the Cardinals to earn a spot in the World Series.

The Giants pulled off their first World Series sweep since 1954, again beating a heavily favored team, Detroit. Much as Mays provided momentum with his dramatic catch of Vic Wertz's tremendous drive in the first game, Sandoval set the tone with his own historic Game 1 by hitting three

In 2010, the Giants won their first World Series championship in San Francisco. Willie Mays received a ring from center fielder Andres Torres. (San Francisco Giants)

home runs, a feat that had been accomplished in the World Series only by Babe Ruth, Reggie Jackson, and Albert Pujols.

"Willie means a lot to us," Sandoval said. "He's such a special human being. He talks to us about everything, including life, what's most important. I wasn't born yet when he made that catch, but every time I see it, it reminds me how important it was in that World Series. He made that catch, and they swept Cleveland. I hit those three home runs, and we swept the Tigers. That means a lot to me. It means a lot to the organization."

Mays saw a parallel, too.

I like Pablo. He's a nice kid, a strong kid. He had that big game in 2012, and it got everybody going. I remember in '54, when you look back, Cleveland had two guys on base in the eighth inning, and Vic Wertz hit that ball. Two or three runs might have scored, but we kept the game tied and won when Dusty Rhodes hit a home run in the 10th inning. So that play, to me, was the key to the World Series.

Pablo was the key to this World Series. I enjoyed that year. Buster was the MVP of the season, Pablo was the MVP of the World Series. But it wasn't a group of individuals. Everyone came together as a team, and that's the biggest thing. That's what you remember most.

In 2014, the Giants became the first National League team since the 1940s Cardinals to win three World Series in a five-year run, and Travis Ishikawa had such a historic moment that he conjured up the name Bobby Thomson, whose home run off the Dodgers' Ralph Branca clinched the pennant for the Giants in Mays' rookie year, 1951, prompting Giants broadcaster Russ Hodges to famously cry out, "The Giants win the pennant! The Giants win the pennant! The Giants win the pennant! . . ."

Likewise, Ishikawa smashed a pennant-winning homer to eliminate St. Louis and catapult the Giants into the World Series, where they beat the Royals in seven games behind Bumgarner's majestic pitching performances.

"I'm not going to take away from anything I did, but you can't compare what I did to Bobby Thomson," said Ishikawa, noting the 1951 Giants were trailing the Dodgers in the final game of a best-of-three playoff while the 2014 Giants were tied with the Cardinals in the fifth game of a best-of-seven. "He is the original. I'm just happy to be mentioned in the same breath as Bobby Thomson."

Crawford was on deck when Ishikawa homered. The fellow on deck when Thomson hit the Shot Heard 'Round the World? The twenty-year-old Mays, who sixty-three years later must have had an inkling about Ishikawa because back when the first baseman/outfielder was a prospect, Mays invited him and two other young players, Fred Lewis and Emmanuel Burriss, to his home in Arizona for dinner.

"I remember when talking with Willie McCovey, he shared stories of his rookie year and Willie Mays taking him in, buying him suits, letting him use his car, taking him to dinner," Ishikawa said. "It reminded me of the time I was sitting in my locker in spring training and Ron Garcia, who works in the clubhouse, says, 'Ishi, you doin' anything Friday night?'

'I don't have any plans.' 'Well, Willie wants to invite you to dinner at his house. I was like, 'sure.' Who's going to say no to that?

"Willie put together an amazing Southern meal for us, and I tried to eat as much as I could so I wouldn't come off as rude. I was honored that he'd even consider me. That was a small example of how generous he really is. I was a guy he didn't even know. My locker was near his table, and all I had ever done, whenever he was free, was say hello to him and ask how his day was going."

Ishikawa's homer paved the way for another World Series, this one dominated by Bumgarner. In three appearances, including a five-inning save in Game 7, the left-hander pitched 21 innings and surrendered just one run, giving him a career ERA over three World Series of 0.25, the lowest in history among pitchers with at least 25 innings.

The 2010 Series was wonderful for these kids, and they won a lot of big games in 2012. Buster hit that grand slam in Cincinnati to clinch, and then they beat St. Louis. It was a special group going back to Lincecum and Cain and Bumgarner, all those guys who did very well for themselves and the franchise. I really liked the Kansas City one in '14 when Bumgarner came in and finished the last game. That was a tremendous performance.

Mays and other franchise Hall of Famers joined the parades through the streets of San Francisco to celebrate the championships, just as Mays and his teammates had paraded through downtown in 1958 to celebrate the Giants' move to the West Coast. Mays also was part of the three visits to the White House, where President Obama honored the champions and always made a special acknowledgment to Mays, suggesting trailblazers such as Willie made it possible for an African American such as Obama to serve as president.

"When they were making this run in 2010, Willie was rooting hard because he knew what it would mean to this city if they could cash in," Giants broadcaster and former pitcher Mike Krukow said. "When we got back home and were in the parade, the players were all looking to see how

Willie would react, and he was completely moved. When you win the war, you're looking for the reaction of the king, and Willie gave the reaction they were looking for. The biggest takeaway was they got to lay their accomplishments before the king. They saw what it meant to him, that it was another layer of validation as to what they accomplished. It's so cool. I just get chills."

"Yeah," said Krukow's television broadcast partner, Duane Kuiper, "at the ring ceremony, he was just as excited as any one of those other guys standing on the field."

Kuiper and Krukow broke into the majors shortly after the end of Mays' career. Krukow was a 20-game winner with the Giants in 1986, the year Mays officially returned to the club as a special assistant, brought back under owner Bob Lurie. Mays was in his fifties, suiting up and actively involved in working with players' physical and mental approaches to the game.

"Very few retired players could maintain a leadership presence in the clubhouse after their careers end, but Mays is that guy," Krukow said. "Usually when your career ends, your voice ends. But with Willie, he'd walk into the clubhouse talking with his high-pitched voice like he was in the lineup that day. He'd bring energy as he did as a player. He'd always have something to say, and he'd go right to the guy who was struggling and say something that we all listened to. We all got better because of it."

One of the recipients of Mays' guidance in 1986 was a self-assured and extremely gifted rookie.

"I talked to Willie Mays every chance I got," Will Clark said. "I mean, good Lord, where else are you going to get that kind of information? That's the best player in baseball, and he's standing next to you. I tried to pick his brain as much as possible, along with Willie Mac. I remember Willie telling me, 'When you walk to the plate, look where the center fielder is playing, that's generally how they're going to pitch you. That was big for me. If he's on the left-field side, they'd pitch me away. Right-field side, they'd pitch in. It's pretty amazing. When you have that wealth of knowledge, and they're around you, you try to take advantage of it as much as possible. I see a lot of guys now who don't ask any questions. Willie's here all the time. Talk to him. He'll tell you exactly like it is."

Clark evolved into a six-time All-Star and .303 lifetime hitter.

"Okay, so one day in spring training, I'm hitting with Kevin Mitchell and Matt Williams," Clark said. "Willie and Willie Mac are behind the cage, and Kevin's ragging on Willie, 'Come in here and hit.' Willie keeps saying no. Kevin keeps ragging on him. Willie finally says (Clark's voice rises a couple of octaves), 'Gimme a bat.' I'm standing next to Willie, and I'm swinging a 35-33, which is fairly decent size. I hand it to him, and he shakes it around and says (again a high voice), 'I don't want that toothpick' and throws it over his shoulder. I'm like 'geeez.' Kevin is swinging a 35-35. Willie grabs that and says, 'Yeah, that's about right.' Literally, the third swing he took, he hits it over the center-field monster at Scottsdale Stadium. Oh my God. He whacks the hell out of it. I'm like, 'Thanks, Kevin, for ragging on him and letting him show us up and remind us who the best player ever on the face of the planet is.'"

In 1989, the year the Giants won their first pennant since 1962, Clark finished second in the National League MVP voting. The MVP was Mitchell, who has his own Mays story. Before he was traded to the Giants, the most homers Mitchell hit in a season was 22. In 1989, he hit 47. He credited Mays.

"I didn't consider myself as a home run hitter. It just happened," Mitchell said. "When I used light bats, I tried to muscle the ball, tried to overswing. Then Willie taught me how to hit the ball to right-center, how to use the wind tunnel at Candlestick. He changed my bats, put big bats in my hand and let it happen. You've got to respect what he says."

All part of the gig.

I love the game and coming every day and being around the guys. It's what I want to do, and the organization makes that possible. There might be a time a guy needs me for whatever reason. If someone has a problem, I know what it's like because I've done it. I don't want them being intimidated. It might take a while for some kids, but I'm there for them just in case they need something.

I don't try to tell a guy what to do. Now if he comes up to me, I can help him. The correct way to do things. Play the game properly and have fun. I might kid them, they might kid me. I like to keep the guys laughing and loose because when they're comfortable, they can perform better.

Hunter Pence, who helped the Giants win titles in 2012 and 2014, will be remembered for his pregame speeches that were so inspirational in the playoffs that he earned the nickname The Reverend. As a right fielder, Pence has played in front of the Willie Mays Wall and drawn inspiration from Mays, saying, "Having a living legend around changes the atmosphere. You feel awestruck. He's willing to talk to everybody who comes up to him, but he's most likely going to talk trash to you, in a great way. You always love the banter with Willie, but he seems to have an intention to challenge everyone with high expectations." When Pence moved to the Rangers in 2019, he was given 24, Mays' number. "Maybe the man upstairs wanted me to be that," Pence said.

A first baseman on two of the championship teams, Brandon Belt was drafted in 2009 and that fall attended a workout at the Giants' park for top prospects. As is the case with many of the team's functions involving minor-leaguers, Mays gave a lively and colorful speech, speaking of his own career and motivating those in the room to succeed themselves. This particular event included a Mays trivia contest.

"Whoever answered a question correctly got some signed Willie Mays stuff, so I studied all his stats, all his information so I could get one of those questions right and take home some memorabilia," Belt said. "When they asked when Willie debuted, I shot my hand up before they could get the question out. I gave the date and got a signed Willie Mays jersey. I was beyond ecstatic. That's my first memory of being around Willie. Three, four years later, he's hanging out and experiencing the championships with us. Pretty cool circle there."

Bruce Bochy's circle with Mays stretches further back in time. He attended high school in Melbourne, Florida, not far from Vero Beach, where the Dodgers trained. Bochy visited the workouts but not just to watch the pros.

"We would go down there and steal baseballs," Bochy, the manager for all three World Series titles, admitted. "If they hit a ball down the left-field

Willie Mays was present for the Giants' three runs to World Series titles in San Francisco, all managed by Bruce Bochy. (San Francisco Giants)

line, you could run down the hill and get the ball. Somebody would usually shout at you or chase you. We'd run off and try to get enough baseballs to take batting practice. I remember 1973, my senior year, Willie was there with the Mets. We're trying to run off, and Willie's yelling at us. It was still pretty cool for me to see him for the first time. It's like you're looking at a god. There was Willie Mays. I told him that story."

Completing the circle, Bochy had a gift waiting for him when he started managing the Giants in 2007, which he still fondly remembered as he stepped aside in 2019.

"My first day in spring training, Willie came in and said, 'I left a dozen balls I signed for you on your desk. People are going to ask you, and you can use those,'" Bochy said. "That was pretty nice of him."

Posey emulated Mays on many fronts. He was called up in late May like Willie. Won Rookie of the Year like Willie. Found himself in a World Series right away like Willie. Won an MVP award his first full season like Willie. Became the face of the franchise like Willie.

I first saw him in the College World Series and thought, "You hit like me." He can wait on the pitch and go to right-center. He has been doing it all along, but he'll pull the ball, too, so he's got a nice approach. I enjoy watching Buster hit.

Fittingly, they filmed a 2019 commercial together in which Posey drives a Toyota truck through rough terrain and comes to Mays in a full Giants uniform perched atop a massive boulder in a remote area. "Oh, great one," Posey says. "I've traveled far to ask one question: What is the secret of the game?" To which Mays says, "You drive a nice truck." A giddy Posey responds, "That's it? Awesome." And drives away. Mays says, "Wait, wait, that's not the secret." And sighs. Not bad.

"When I think back to my childhood, if you would've told me I would do a commercial with Willie Mays one day, I would have laughed you out of the room," Posey said. "So to think my children, grandchildren, and great-grandchildren theoretically will be able to access that commercial is a real neat thing. You don't take your time with Willie for granted."

Players come and go. So do managers, coaches, owners, and front-office officials. The one constant from Mays' first day with the Giants on the West Coast is Mike Murphy, a clubhouse fixture since 1958. "Murph" was a batboy those first two seasons, became visiting clubhouse attendant when the team relocated from Seals Stadium to Candlestick Park in 1960, and moved to home clubhouse attendant in 1980.

When former Giants stop by the clubhouse, from the legends to the role players, the first man they usually visit is Murphy, who not only cleaned their uniforms, ordered their equipment, and prepared their meals but became their friend. When he's visited by Mays, his all-time favorite, Murphy still takes care of him and brings him a bite to eat.

"He's like a pop to me. He's the best that God ever put on this earth," said Murphy, still on the job as the home clubhouse manager emeritus. "He came to me right away in 1958 and introduced himself, and we've been friends ever since. When he was traded, I cried my eyes out. I couldn't believe Mr. Stoneham would do that. But he had to, I guess, to

Buster Posey appeared in a commercial with Willie Mays in which the Giants' catcher addressed Mays by saying, "Oh, great one." (H&L Partners)

survive here. Mrs. Payson would take care of him with the Mets, which she did."

Immediately after the 2010 World Series, Murphy phoned Mays and said he was happy for him and now knew what he felt like in 1954. Mays told Murphy he deserved a championship for all the years he served with the team.

When I came to San Francisco, I didn't know people. Guys like Murph and (then-clubhouse manager) Eddie Logan made it comfortable for me. I was starting over. Murph's still taking care of these kids. So when these guys come back, they look for Murph. He did more than take care of them. He taught them how to be professionals. He treats everyone on the team the same, one through twenty-five, and the guys trust him.

Mike Murphy, the Giants' longtime equipment manager, first met Willie Mays in 1958, the team's first year in San Francisco. (Rick Swig)

Murphy loves to tell the story of the day Mays became the second player in history to hit 600 home runs, a pinch-hit blast in San Diego in 1969: "Rawlings had a trophy they were going to give him. Willie was supposed to get a rest that day, so the trophy was packed up. I'm playing cards in the clubhouse, and then Willie comes up and hits a home run. We had to unpack the trophy and rush down to the field. Luckily, he slowed down a little bit around the bases, and by the time he got to home plate, I had the trophy for him."

Mays laughs at the story and confirms he slowed his pace for his friend. A small gesture in a lifetime of countless gestures, countless memories, and countless laughs.

You've got to keep going. I don't feel old. You enjoy yourself as long as you can and move on and help people as you go. You do what you've got to do and don't feel sorry for yourself. Whatever the age, just enjoy yourself. I do that all the time.

24.

MAKE A NEW FRIEND

The Story of a Love Affair with Fans

"Praise kids when they do the right thing and lead by example. You do the right thing, they'll do the right thing."

—*Willie Mays*

STICKBALL EPITOMIZED WILLIE Mays. It perfectly illuminated the kid inside him that never went away. The fun he had playing a simple street game. And most of all, his opportunity to delight a bunch of children.

In Mays' early years in New York, when he lived on St. Nicholas Place in Harlem, a few fly balls from the Polo Grounds, he was the hit of the neighborhood. Kids would knock on his apartment window, an indication they wanted him to come out and play, and Willie obliged. Hours before he stepped into the batter's box at the Polo Grounds, he cherished the moments he could loosen up and hang out with kids.

In 1951, I came up during the season, my first year with the Giants, and they got me a ground-floor apartment near the ballpark. The kids came around and asked me to play stickball. Stickball? What's that? I didn't know what they were talking about when I first got there. I said, "Well, let me see it." Oh, I've been playing that all my life. In the South, we called it broomball. We got a broom or mop and cut off the end and used it for a bat. We used a tennis ball. They used a little hard ball, but I knew how to hit it.

I played once, and then I had to play every day. Guys would knock on my window, and I'd come out and play before I went to the ballpark. For bases, sometimes it was a car, sometimes a building, sometimes a sewer. Sometimes they bounced it, sometimes they threw it straight. On my block, they bounced it. If I hit it on top of the building, I'm out. That's how they penalized me. But if I hit it on the ground, I could run.

It was good for me because they'd bounce the ball to me different ways, curve it this way or that way, and I'd learn to follow it where it went. We'd play until it was time to go to the ballpark. But first, we'd go to the store on the corner, and I bought ice cream for ten or fifteen guys. Those kids loved ice cream, boy. That was a joy for me.

Willie Mays played stickball with kids in Harlem even on days he played games for the Giants. (National Baseball Hall of Fame and Museum)

Mays always was comfortable around kids and eager to give back to his communities—from Birmingham to New York to the Bay Area—through charitable endeavors, including his Say Hey Foundation, and simply in everyday practices. He never forgot he made a living playing a kids' game, and his mind-set as a player was not only to perform with passion and desire but to have fun and show he was having fun if only to further entertain and inspire others. Similar to how he lives his life.

Who exhibited more joy on the diamond? Who was more kidlike? Willie's flair and unlimited array of skills coupled with the fact it often appeared as if the game came easy for him made fans adore him and clamor for more. So he delivered and took special pride in catering to children. That never stopped.

I love to talk to kids, be around them, make sure they enjoy themselves. Sometimes I feel more comfortable around kids than grown-ups. Kids are fine. You have to let them ask the question. They'll tell you if they don't like something. They're genuine. Sometimes the grown-ups, they get ticked off about stuff. I'm there for the kids. Let 'em grow up a little bit. Kids repeat very quickly. I've got to make sure to send the right message.

When I talk to a group of kids, I don't need a script. I have to wing it a little bit sometimes and see how things develop. I never know what I'm going to do or say because you never know what *they're* going to do or say. You can't go in with a big plan, I don't care where they're from. With adults, I've got to think about it. With kids, they have their own minds, so you go with the flow. I get kids. They'll tell you what's up, and they'll ask you questions, and that'll give you an idea on what to say.

So I just maneuver around a little bit. To tell what the kids are going to do or say, you don't know. At least I don't. You have to let them tell you what's going on. And they know. They know a lot more than you think.

Mays often visits the Lucile Packard Children's Hospital at Stanford but never in the public eye. Local newspapers and radio and TV outlets aren't alerted. He simply stops by with his assistant, Rene Anderson, and Fred Menzel of the San Mateo County Sheriff's Office. At the hospital, Mays meets with ailing children and their families, poses for pictures, and hands out baseballs, his way of showing his love and shining a light on them.

If a kid is tiny, Mays will share some soothing words and comfort the parents. If the kid is older, he'll speak with him or her like they were long-lost friends. In no time, Willie's spinning tales of yesteryear and talking ball with the kid, who's cherishing the moment. "What's your position?" "How do you hold the bat?" "How's your arm?" Willie's acutely aware of when healthy siblings are in the room and realizes they also need to feel important, so these kids always are included in the conversation. "Who are you?" "A brother?" "Sister?" "Do you play ball?" While parents are in awe as they snap pictures with their phones, kids feel at home. They might not know Willie Mays the legendary ballplayer, but they know Willie Mays the larger-than-life figure who cares about their well-being, and that goes a long way.

A few other examples of Mays' many philanthropic gestures, most of which involve children:

The day before the 2007 All-Star Game in San Francisco, Mays lent his name and vision for hope to the Willie Mays Boys & Girls Club in the city's Bayview Hunters Point community, where Candlestick Park once stood. Included on the premises is a ballfield, gym, and Willie Mays Club-house, where programs are offered to satisfy the kids' diverse interests in academics, sports, and art. On a wall in the club is a giant picture of Willie taking hacks in a stickball game in Harlem.

Back in Fairfield, Willie's hometown in Alabama, Willie Mays Field is easily identifiable with its ballfield, basketball court, and playground. It was renovated in the 1970s and rededicated to Mays in 1985, and he stopped by in 2009 to donate $50,000 in baseball equipment to local youth.

After the Giants won the 2010 World Series, their first since Mays helped them win it all in 1954, they brought the trophy back to their roots in New York to share it with old-timers who were bummed their team re-located and youngsters who were learning about the franchise's New York history. During the contingent's visit, Mays visited P.S. 46, a public school in Harlem, to meet with kids, a couple of generations removed from the kids who played stickball with him. More than 200 students gathered in the auditorium to hear from Mays, and he connected with them by spinning tales of his younger days in Harlem and inspiring them to follow the right path.

Baseball fans are plenty familiar with The Catch, Mays' sensational play in the 1954 World Series, but in football lore, The Catch is Dwight Clark's last-minute leaping grab of Joe Montana's end-zone pass in the 1981 NFC Championship Game against the Cowboys, which jump-started the 49ers' dynasty in the 1980s. Clark died in 2018 of amyotrophic lateral sclerosis, also known as Lou Gehrig's disease. In 2017, Mays did a photo shoot with Clark in which each was seen holding a picture of his epic catch for a limited number of autographed lithographs. *San Francisco Chronicle* columnist Scott Ostler arranged it, and Bay Area photographer Michael Zagaris shot it, after which Dwight said of Willie, "That's the coolest dude

Willie Mays made The Catch, and so did San Francisco 49ers wide receiver Dwight Clark. (Michael Zagaris)

I've ever met." Mays agreed to participate only if proceeds would go to help support Clark.

One of Willie's favorite days of the year is Halloween, when kids (and their families) line up outside his door to get treats from the Say Hey Kid. Anderson, Menzel, and others from the sheriff's office are on hand to keep things moving. Sometimes folks who visited as kids decades earlier return with their kids. Sometimes adults find themselves stepping in front of their own children because the great Mays is in sight, though Willie respectfully brings the kids to the front and pays most of his attention to them because it's their moment.

Mays has traveled to countless fundraisers over the years and in 2015 appeared at a Palm Springs luncheon benefiting the Barbara Sinatra Center for Abused Children, the type of function that tugs at Willie's heart. During the event, which raised $300,000, he did a question-and-answer session with Marty Lurie, who hosts Giants pregame and post-game radio shows and is close to Mays despite growing up in Brooklyn a Dodger fan. Lurie, who interviewed Mays many times over the years, slipped in a question he had never asked: "What would you like to be remembered for?"

"It was one of the most dramatic moments of my life," Lurie said. "Willie loves fans and gives back to fans and can capture an audience with his great descriptions. When I asked him the question, he said, 'I performed for the fans' and started crying. That's what he said he wanted to be remembered for, being out on the field and giving his best effort. It meant so much to him to perform for people. There's such a deepness to Willie that's very sweet and sensitive."

Mays has earned a truckload of plaques for his philanthropic work, dating to his playing days. In 1971, he was the first to receive what became the Roberto Clemente Award, which annually goes to a big-leaguer for his character and community involvement. Dedicated to giving underprivileged children better opportunities and safer communities, Mays' foundation has assisted schools, children's hospitals, youth teams, scholarship programs, Boys and Girls Clubs, churches, public safety departments, homeless programs, violence prevention programs, and diabetes disease research—and what old-timer can forget his plea to kids in a 1960s public service announcement to avoid blasting caps? "Remember now, don't touch them."

Mays still receives a bundle of fan mail delivered to the Giants, the Hall of Fame, and his foundation, and the stories and memories in the letters continue to enlighten him. Over the decades, countless people were influenced by Mays, all the way back to those kids in Harlem who knocked on his window every day to play stickball with their popular neighbor.

Mrs. (Ann) Goosby was my godmother, and I stayed with her and her husband. Mrs. Goosby cooked for me and looked out for me. If someone wanted to see me, she'd stop them and make sure they were okay. "Who are you?" "What do you want?" I couldn't do anything, man. I had to be home by ten.

It was a short walk to the ballpark. I was on top of the hill on St. Nicholas Place. There were two ways to go. Either drive or walk. When I walked, I took the stairs off 155th Street down to the Polo Grounds and then walked right across the field. The clubhouses were in center field. There were always kids around, and that's why I played so much stickball.

New Yorkers take great pride in their stickball tradition. In its heyday, stickball was highly organized and pitted one block against the next for neighborhood bragging rights. In its simplest form, teams were chosen for pickup games. Open fields were limited, and equipment wasn't required beyond a stick and a ball, so it was a game for all socioeconomic backgrounds—baseball in the street with no time restrictions so long as there was daylight or streetlights. The pitcher usually would bounce the pitch or the hitter simply would bounce it himself and hit it. Sometimes rules would vary depending on the neighborhood.

"Kids still play stickball but not as much as when Willie played," said Youman Wilder, who runs the Harlem Hitting Academy, a program for inner-city youth with an emphasis on placing kids in college through baseball scholarships. "Kids would walk into each other's block like a gang, not to fight but to play. You could take a kid who wasn't a great baseball player, and he might be a great stickball player. It's unique. If you were the best stickball player on your block, it meant everything. It's more communal than anything. It was all over Harlem, and Willie was everyone's favorite player. Stickball probably made him a better hitter. You can't open up. You had to hit the ball straight, dead up the middle."

Julian McWilliams, who covers the Red Sox for *The Boston Globe,* grew up in Harlem and was one of the first to come out of the Harlem Hitting Academy. He played his Harlem Little League games at Holcombe Rucker Park, across the street from where the Polo Grounds once stood, now the site of a public housing project. When McWilliams was a kid, his grandfather spoke often about Mays and Hank Aaron, and McWilliams became so fond of Mays that he had his likeness tattooed on his right arm in 2014 when he was twenty-five, the artwork extending ten inches and depicting Willie swinging in a stickball game on St. Nicholas Place.

Underneath the tattoo are these words: "Just a kid who likes to play," directly inspired by Willie's Say Hey Kid nickname.

"Willie Mays was a giant to me, not just the team he played for but the icon he became," McWilliams said. "I used to hear stories about how he dominated at the Polo Grounds. When I used to look across the street as a child, I used to think, 'Willie Mays probably hit it as high as that project window on the twenty-fifth floor and onto Harlem River Drive Parkway.'

"I wanted to be Mays. His flair for the dramatic and the fact he had such an impact on the Harlem community made him feel more like my guy. The stickball games he played in Harlem, I keep near to me. He just epitomized so much more than baseball. He also represented to me where I was from. I heard so many stories of how he immersed himself within the community, and that really stuck with me."

Plenty of other folks in the sports media world swear by Mays, and perhaps there's no better example than Tim Kurkjian, who discovered him as an eight-year-old while watching the 1965 All-Star Game on his family's black-and-white TV in Bethesda, Maryland. Mays led off the game with a home run, scored twice, and played all nine innings in the National League's 6–5 win.

Willie Mays has been an advocate of public safety officials and worked with agencies through his Say Hey Foundation. (San Francisco Giants)

"I was dazzled," Kurkjian said. "Willie Mays immediately became my favorite player even though I lived 2,900 miles from San Francisco. He had the perfect body of a baseball player, so athletic, so fast, so strong. Watching him run the bases, his cap flying off, was breathtaking. I was captivated by his flair for the game. I had never seen anyone make a basket catch. My friends and I would imitate him."

Fast-forward to the 1999 Hall of Fame induction, and Kurkjian found himself interviewing Mays for ESPN: "I was trembling. I got to speak to the game's greatest living player and, for me, after Babe Ruth, the greatest player of all time. I shook his hand, and like everyone else who meets him for the first time, I was struck by how big and powerful his hands were. It was the highlight of my professional career, a chance to interview my baseball hero."

Rock superstar Huey Lewis was influenced by a variety of blues, jazz, and soul musicians along with a young ballplayer named Willie Mays. Born in Manhattan, Huey was five when his family moved to the Bay Area in 1955, three years before the Giants moved west. He spent countless hours as a kid at Candlestick, where he and the rest of Huey Lewis and the News later performed the national anthem many times, before both Giants and 49ers games. Huey and the News also sang the anthem for a Say Hey Foundation fundraising dinner in 2001.

"I remember the World Series team in '62, a Giant-Dodger game, Mays ran from first and came all the way around to home, the throw beat him, and he slid and kicked the ball out of (John) Roseboro's glove," Lewis said. "Mays was my favorite ballplayer. Then I got to meet him, and he was the nicest, sweetest guy you ever met. His youthful exuberance was just unbelievable, and he's like that today.

"We'd play golf, and he'd be coaching me and rooting for me. I saw him in the Giants' clubhouse a year or two ago. He asked me to sign the card table he was sitting at. Willie Mays asked for *my* autograph. Unbelievable. That's the definition of making it, isn't it? Who needs the Rock and Roll Hall of Fame when Willie Mays is asking you for your autograph? He's still a kid. So youthful, and you don't want to admire anything he owns, because he'll give it to you, the shirt off his back. What a pure, pure guy."

Artist Thom Ross, who has painted iconic American figures and events to portray their deeper meaning, is a San Francisco native who painted a sequence of five life-sized cutouts of Mays making his famous World Series catch and placed them at various locations around New York City including the site of the Polo Grounds on the fiftieth anniversary of The Catch, September 29, 2004.

"This wasn't just a really fine defensive play in a crucial ballgame," Ross said. "It was some kind of standard that was beyond the reach of every other man who had ever played the game. I, as an artist, wanted to do art that would stand in relation to other works of art at that same level. Now, have I done it? Hell no. I try, and I will continue to try, and if credit for that determination goes to Willie Mays, then I could not be prouder of the inspiration. I realize and accept that I am not Willie Mays, but he inspires me to keep trying. I think that is the proper role of a hero in one's life. To view your heroes in a light that isn't so much about being them, but rather to live a life that they would approve of."

Scott Boras grew up near Sacramento, an hour and a half from Candlestick, loving Mays. He played minor-league ball with the Cardinals and Cubs and one time in high school met Mays when a Reds scout got him into the Giants' clubhouse. Years later, after becoming the most powerful agent in sports, Boras learned of Mays' role in the development of the players' union. It came during a meeting Boras had with Marvin Miller months before the union's founder and former director died in 2012, seven years before he was elected to the Hall of Fame.

"I called Marvin and said I wanted to spend two days with him to talk about how he dealt with players and got players' trust, back when players trusted no one," Boras said. "We met in New York, and he told me, 'I'll tell you how I built the union. I built it with two players, and don't forget this: It's the greatest of players who will lead without voice. I served as the voice, and players' intentions served as the rule.' I said, 'Who were the two players?' He said, 'Willie Mays and Mickey Mantle.'

"Marvin went to Willie and said, 'I want to get a pension plan for all these players.' Willie was making $125,000 at the time, Mickey the same. Willie said, 'That's wonderful. I want to see all those boys get their pension.' Marvin went to the other players and said, 'Willie will strike so you'll get your pensions, so if he's giving away his $125,000, you can give away your $8,000.' Mickey said, 'If Willie's doing this, I'll certainly do it.'

"So our union exists today because of Willie Mays. Truly, Willie Mays did it all. The greatest player in the game, and he built the union. My hero."

Boras, who negotiated $814 million in contracts for Gerrit Cole, Stephen

Signing autographs has been a constant for Willie Mays, especially when kids are the recipients.
(San Francisco Giants)

Strasburg, and Anthony Rendon at baseball's 2019 winter meetings, said Mays would command a record deal in today's game.

"He'd probably be worth close to $50 million to $55 million a year," Boras said, "because he would be the person to compare all others to. 'He could hit like Willie but . . .' 'He could play defense like Willie but . . .' 'He could run like Willie but . . .' All of them will have one or two tools like Willie Mays but none of them will have all of Willie Mays' tools. There are people who have great layers, but no one has as many layers as Willie Mays."

Doing the math for Boras, and realizing the longest baseball contract was for 13 years . . . well, 13 years at $50 million a year is $650 million. At $55 million a year, it's $715 million.

Early in Mays' rookie year with the Giants, a father took his nine-year-old son to the Polo Grounds, early enough to watch the young center fielder in pregame drills. The boy was inspired by Mays, who became his favorite player, and forty-one years later spearheaded a group of investors that bought the Giants and quickly handed Mays a lifetime contract.

"Willie stood in deep center field," Peter Magowan recalled, "and threw about twenty balls in a row to third base, where Alvin Dark had his glove out over the bag, and each of the throws was a perfect one-hop to the base. It was unbelievable. It's probably like watching Steph Curry warm up before a game and make twenty three-pointers in a row."

Bob Lurie, after several failed attempts to replace Candlestick with a new ballpark, had agreed to sell the Giants to a Florida group that would relocate the team in St. Petersburg. National League owners nixed the deal to allow local investors to step up and keep the team in San Francisco, and Magowan paved the way. He was credited with saving the Giants, though his early inspiration and introduction to the game came from Mays. So perhaps Willie, in a roundabout way, had a hand in keeping the team in San Francisco—the Giants finally left Candlestick and moved to their current location: 24 Willie Mays Plaza.

Out front is a bronzed statue of Mays, commissioned by Magowan and his wife, Debby, and surrounded by twenty-four palm trees. It was dedicated in March 2000 before the ballpark's opening. Mays is depicted following through on a swing, "a triple to right-center," Magowan said.

"His feet are already starting to move." Inscribed at the statue's base are these words: "Given in honour of Willie Mays and his fans, wherever they may be."

"They may be in New York," Magowan said nearly two decades later. "They may be in San Francisco. They may be scattered across the country. They may be in heaven. Wherever they are, this was for them."

Willie nodded when hearing the story of a young Magowan in awe of watching his pregame work in 1951.

I used to try to do that all the time so fans could have that opportunity. That's what I used to like to do when I warmed up. I didn't like to throw all over the field. I'd concentrate on one thing. Obviously, I didn't know Peter as a nine-year-old boy, but I liked the fans to understand they could come to the field early and see something different. Later, I appreciated everything Peter did for me. I had never heard of a lifetime contract. He was there for me.

A few years after Magowan first saw Mays in person, another young boy, from Midland, Texas, had that opportunity. His grandparents lived in Greenwich, Connecticut, and his dad's brother, "Uncle Bucky," brought the boy to the Polo Grounds in the mid-1950s, his first big-league game, and Mays was patrolling the outfield and dazzling in all facets.

"Willie had it all. I mean, this guy could run, he could hit, he could throw, he could catch. He was electric. That's when my infatuation with Willie Mays took hold, and from that point forward, I followed his career closely," said George W. Bush, the forty-third president of the United States.

The New York Giants became Bush's childhood team, and in an interview for this book, he recited the lineup of the World Series champion 1954 Giants. Bush vividly recalled Mays' famous Game 1 catch, along with Dusty Rhodes' key pinch hits in the Series, and noted that season "really established Willie's reputation as a great player." Bush also recalled the end of the 1962 World Series when Mays was stranded on second as Willie McCovey lined to Yankees second baseman Bobby Richardson for the final out of Game 7—"it nearly took Richardson's hand off."

Back in Texas, Bush was a catcher in Little League and cherished his games of catch with his dad, who played first base for Yale in the 1947 College World Series, four decades before George H. W. Bush became the forty-first president. The younger Bush's stories of playing catch with his dad are reminiscent of Mays' stories about his own father.

"It's a coming-of-age moment and also a father-son bonding," Bush said. "Playing catch is a way for a son to realize how much his dad loves him and cares for him. That's very inspirational. The fact that Willie kind of began to find his way as a result of the inspiration of his father is a long story of humanity. Fathers can influence their sons in positive ways, and it sounds like what happened to Willie certainly happened to me."

Bush's great-uncle, George Herbert Walker, was a minority owner of the 1962 expansion Mets, whose majority owner, Joan Payson, traded for Mays a decade later. "I saw how unique it was for him and how excited he was," said Bush, who later was part of a group that bought the Texas Rangers. "His enthusiasm for being an owner kind of spilled over to me."

Bush played on Yale's freshman team as a "mediocre middle reliever" before moving to rugby his last two years of college. As Rangers owner, Bush befriended Nolan Ryan and attended the pitcher's 1999 Hall of Fame induction in Cooperstown, where the then-governor of Texas met his childhood idol, Mays. As president, Bush twice hosted Mays at the White House, in 2005 for a black-tie presidential dinner party and 2006 when Willie was honorary commissioner at a T-ball game on the South Lawn, an annual event by Bush to promote baseball and softball and encourage kids to exercise through team sports.

"A lot of these kids had no idea who Willie Mays was, but I'm sure the adults and parents said, 'Wow, you're going to meet Willie Mays,' and then when they did, he didn't disappoint them," Bush said. "He's got a vibrant personality. When you're a kid, you're inspired to play like Willie Mays. When you're an adult, you find he's kind to people and cares for kids."

In one of Bush's defining moments as president, he took the mound at Yankee Stadium to throw the ceremonial first pitch before Game 3 of the 2001 World Series, weeks after the terrorist attack on New York. Had it

President George W. Bush sits with First Lady Laura Bush and Willie Mays to watch a T-ball game on the South Lawn at the White House. (Rick Swig)

not been for the bulletproof vest, 55,820 in attendance, and horror of the attacks fresh in everyone's memory, Bush may have felt in his childhood element, throwing a strike to his dad while envisioning being Willie Mays.

"Let me tell you something, that was the most nervous I ever was during the presidency," Bush said. "It was a memory I'll never forget. It was an unbelievably, emotionally packed moment, and New York City rose universally in defiance of the attackers, and the World Series was a part of that. I hadn't realized it at the time, but looking back at it, it was part of a healing moment, and baseball's got the capacity to heal. When I get to be a doddering old guy drooling in the corner, memories will fade, but that one never will."

When I visited the White House, it wasn't about politics or government. It was about doing the right thing for the country and the kids. That's

why I went a lot of times. The Little League game with George Bush, that was a nice day, watching the kids play ball, some with special needs, all having fun. It was their day, and I was fortunate to be a part of it and thankful the president invited me.

The other time, it was more formal. When we were coming into the room, I noticed the president's tie was crooked and reached over to straighten it, and a Secret Service agent came to me. I said, "Okay, okay, I'm just tying his tie." He said, "Oh, yeah, thank you very much." I got to know father and son very well. They've been nice to me.

These days, Mays has a close-knit group of friends who hang with him at his home and sometimes the ballpark, where he has a suite above the left-field line and entertains friends, associates, and youth groups.

Phillip Saddler has known Mays all his life. His father, J. D. Saddler, a dentist, was Willie's good buddy from their New York days in the 1950s and later settled in the Bay Area, where he became Berkeley's first African-American dentist. Phillip followed his father into dentistry, and Mays bought him equipment so he could get started and advised him on where to set up his practice, also in Berkeley.

"I wouldn't be where I am without Willie," Saddler said. "When I was a kid, he came by the house all the time. I didn't know Willie as a baseball player but as my dad's friend who had a nice car, a pink Chrysler. Years later, he helped me get my practice. One thing he says, always check the checker. If there's someone working for you, make sure you have someone check him. He'd have one lawyer and then hire another lawyer to check on the first lawyer, and he'd ask both the same question. From that, he found the truth. I listened to him."

Another friend, Dan Sanchez, accompanied Mays to the 2015 All-Star Game in Cincinnati, where Major League Baseball honored the four greatest living players (voted upon by fans): Hank Aaron, Johnny Bench, Sandy Koufax, and Willie Mays. They walked onto the field together with their arms interlocked, a sign of affection and respect (as well as age). All four of them. Five, actually. The fifth was Sanchez, who called himself the fifth Beatle. On the left, Aaron used a cane for support. On the right, Mays had Sanchez.

It was just a few months after Mays cracked a rib in a fall, which caused him to miss spring training for the first time in decades, and Sanchez was there for support. Four months later, Sanchez was among several friends and acquaintances to accompany Mays to the White House, where he received the Presidential Medal of Freedom from President Obama.

"I've known Willie thirty-some years, and I'm an average Joe. That's how he flies," said Sanchez, who met Mays in the 1980s when installing a security gate at his house and can cite all of his statistics. "My joke at the All-Star Game was, between the five of us, we hit 1,800 home runs. Major League Baseball wanted just the four out there and didn't want me around. Willie said, 'No, Dan's going with me.' In the Green Room, I'm a kid in a candy store. Koufax was smooth. He said, 'Let's all clinch our arms and walk out in stride,' so we clinched our arms and walked out. My phone was pinging off the hook.

Willie Mays posed for a picture after receiving the Presidential Medal of Freedom. First row: Harry "Ace" Bell, Jack Morrissey, Jeff Bleich, Malcolm Heinicke, Dan Sanchez, David Rapaport, and Phillip Saddler. Back row: Pam Baer, Larry Baer, Lee Mendelson, President Obama, Mays, Michelle Obama, and Rene Anderson. (Official White House Photo by Pete Souza)

"I'm a fan and lucky to have Willie trust me, and I never take that trust for granted. I'm a gate salesman from Millbrae, California, and I'm walking out with these legends at the All-Star Game and meeting the president at the White House. Only Willie Mays can make that happen."

David Rapaport is a high school teacher who as a kid lived in Mays' San Francisco neighborhood of Forest Hill and used to stop by to hear stories and eat cake and ice cream. On Halloween, Rapaport recalls, Willie would give out Baby Ruth bars and Oh Henry! bars—"all while complaining with full tongue in cheek that there wasn't a Willie bar"—and sometimes silver dollars and half-dollars taped to the candy. A long time later, they became good friends, and it came after Willie saved Rapaport's son's life.

"I wanted to live my life in a special way because I had Willie Mays, the best baseball player in history, in my life," Rapaport said. "Willie was my neighbor—generous, warm, friendly—and I didn't want to do anything that would reflect poorly on that. I always felt there was some reason the man touched my life. Four decades later, I knew the reason. My son was ten when he came down with a rare form of hepatitis. He took medication that tasted terrible, like oil. For months and months, he took it. Then he stopped. It can be fatal without the medication, and we had nowhere to turn. He wouldn't take it.

"For some reason, I thought about getting back in touch with Willie to tell him about my son. He said, 'Bring him over tomorrow.' Willie and my son talked. Willie said he took medication himself and encouraged my son to do the same. It worked. My son is now fully recovered. Willie not only inspired me but carried it to another generation. He wasn't just the most intelligent man on the field, but he's sensitive socially and reads people beautifully, especially kids."

Jeff Bleich, one of Mays' friends who serves as one of his attorneys, shares a story of how Willie resolved a potentially steamy issue and made friends along the way. In a phone call with his airline to handle an important matter, Willie was treated rudely, and when he requested to arrange a meeting because of his preference for conversations in person rather than over the phone, he was told, "We don't meet with the public." Nevertheless, with Bleich's help, Willie set up a meeting with the airline's general counsel. Once he arrived, as he was passing by a junior lawyer's office on the way to a conference room, he noticed some baseball photos and memorabilia on the wall and entered. Of course, the lawyer was stunned when Mays began telling him stories about the images on the wall, one of which was of himself.

"Some of the other staff started drifting closer, and before you knew it, pretty much the entire floor was crowded around Willie in this little office as he regaled them with stories," Bleich said. "Willie said the room was way too crowded and, 'Why don't you all come with me to the conference room?' With that, Willie arrived to meet the general counsel with all the man's lawyers already by his side. The general counsel chuckled and said, 'I can already see how this discussion is going to go.' Willie won the day. As we were getting ready to leave, Willie said, 'Now that is how you treat people. You keep your word, and you show respect. How hard is that?' Then he signed a baseball for the junior lawyer who had let him come into his office to reminisce. Willie makes friends with everyone, even people who are on the other side of a transaction. The only things he won't abide are people not keeping their word or treating someone unfairly."

Mays once brought another friend, attorney Malcolm Heinicke, to a Hall of Fame induction, where Heinicke experienced firsthand how revered Mays is in Cooperstown. At Willie's invitation, Heinicke brought along his brother-in-law and a buddy. Once at the Hall, when Willie asked if they needed anything, Heinicke said he was fine. He didn't want to wear out his welcome. When Willie insisted, Heinicke wondered about meeting other Hall of Famers. So Willie told him to find four folding chairs and bring them to the cash register at the Hall's gift shop. Heinicke had no idea why, especially because of the extra chair, but soon learned that Willie would sit there and make it possible for them to meet some baseball legends.

"One by one, each Hall of Famer got to the register," Heinicke said, "and one by one, they were all thrilled to see Willie. They each asked for a photo with him, and he said, 'Sure, as long as you do the same for my friends here.' Indeed, the line of Hall of Famers to see Willie grew long, and it was truly a surreal moment when Tony Gwynn tapped me on the

On and off the field, Willie Mays has had a knack for lighting up people's lives. (Osvaldo Salas/Collection of Rick Swig)

shoulder and said, 'Excuse me, sir, would it be okay if I took a photo with Willie, too? I'm a big fan.' Tony said that to *me*. Here was Willie, the king in his castle, and what was he concerned about? His friend and his guests."

When Mays went to the White House to receive the Presidential Medal of Freedom, Saddler, Sanchez, Rapaport, Bleich, Heinicke, and Anderson joined him, along with minor-league teammate Harry "Ace" Bell, TV producer Lee Mendelson, and Jack Morrissey, Heinicke's father-in-law who hooked up Willie with Bell, plus Giants CEO Larry Baer and his wife, Pam.

Unlike other friends of Mays, Martha Whetstone isn't into baseball.

"Willie is my dear, dear friend, but I see him differently with different eyes," Whetstone said. "I see him from a female perspective, and I see the effect he has on people that I don't know if guys see. When traveling, people light up. It's just wild to see the reaction from people. Even the president of the United States asks him for an autograph."

Whetstone should know. She was a presidential appointee of Bill Clinton, a friend from Arkansas, and introduced Mays to the president.

"I put together the president's golf games," Whetstone said. "He likes being around athletes, talking sports, and asked if Willie would play golf with him. I told him, 'You're the friggin' president of the United States. Are you out of your mind?' Even for him, it was hard to realize Willie Mays would play golf with him. I called the Giants on behalf of the president, but I guess they didn't believe what I was saying because Willie said later he never got word. Anyway, I eventually introduced them, and they played golf a few times."

Yes they did.

"One time, we played in San Francisco," said Clinton, who began idolizing Mays as a ten-year-old when his family bought its first black-and-white television. "Willie was playing pretty well. It was 2001, my best year as a golfer. I got down to a 10 handicap. I could still hit the ball a long way. Willie was playing with clubs that were twenty years old or more. One of the woods he was playing with was kind of cracked, and he had it taped up with masking tape. I said, 'Willie, when I was president, people gave me all these golf clubs. I've got them up the wazoo. Why don't you let me give you a new set of clubs? You've still got a good swing, and you're strong.'

"He said, 'No, I'm comfortable with them. They remind me of my life.' I didn't know if it was pride or whether it really was that he thought his life had reached a different stage and he wanted to take his clubs with him. That's understandable. I get that. I've still got a rescue club I got in 1992, and I know it's going to execute the shot."

Mays appreciated the presidential golf outings, of course, and one in particular is more memorable than others.

Bill hit the ball off the first tee. Second hole, I hit it toward a tree. He was in the fairway, then he hit a ball in the trap and said to his guy, "Give me another ball." Someone asked me, "Are you gonna say something?" I looked up, and there was a guy in the tree with a long rifle. "No, I'm never gonna say nothing to that man." We all start laughing. It was a lot of fun, man.

Bill has been good to me. Really nice guy. He's helped me with my foundation. You've gotta respect these guys, and that's what I did. Always try to talk to them with respect. If they ask for something, I try to get it because I feel they'd do that for me. But like I said, I don't talk politics. They get tired of it anyway. They'd rather talk about baseball.

Clinton planned to attend a Giants game early in the 2000 season with his daughter, Chelsea, who was at Stanford at the time. The game was rained out, however, and Clinton spent hours talking baseball with Mays, Bobby Bonds, and Barry Bonds, "one of the most thrilling baseball experiences I ever had."

Among Clinton's prized possessions are three framed Mays jerseys from the New York Giants, San Francisco Giants, and New York Mets. All gifts from Willie.

"That was very touching," Clinton said. "I wouldn't trade them for the world. I almost couldn't speak. I was so moved. Every time I'm with Willie, it's like I've been with him my whole life because from the time I got that TV until the present day, he's just been this looming presence of the combination of greatness and joy."

The Say Hey Kid did what he could, in retrospect, which was quite a bit. He inspired people through the generations with his five-tool accomplishments, matchless elegance between the lines, and off-field persona that captivated the public from all parts of the map. He has been a leader, pioneer, trailblazer, unifier, and peacekeeper who tried to make an impact in baseball and society while keeping a special place in his heart for children.

I love kids. I love baseball. There is a connection, and I've tried to make a difference with both. I've tried to inspire others, and I know many people have inspired me. There are so many people who helped me do so many things. It started with my dad, but also my aunts, Piper, Leo, Monte, and many more throughout the years who took care of me and protected me. In baseball, in business, in life. So many fans were behind me, so many kids inspired me. I feel grateful and fortunate, and to all those people, I say thank you.

BONUS INTERVIEW FOR BARNES & NOBLE EXCLUSIVE EDITION

WILLIE MAYS AND John Shea spent more than 100 hours together for this book project, mostly at Willie's home, and the material in their conversations was wide-ranging, insightful, inspirational, educational, emotional, and often amusing. Here's a sampling:

Willie, now they have all these shifts in baseball, defenses moving across the diamond depending on who's at the plate.

I don't buy that kind of stuff.

Wonder how they would've shifted you.

If they did, I'd bunt, get four hits, steal second, steal third, and score. They didn't do that to me.

They wouldn't have shifted you because you'd have hit the ball to right field.

Wherever the ball was pitched, that's where I hit it.

You remember they did it for Ted Williams and Willie McCovey. The last few years, more and more, they've been doing it for pretty much every-body, especially lefties.

Because they hit the ball a certain way.

The spray charts in their computers tell them to do it. Positioning fielders to one side of the field creates better odds to get outs. If you're a lefty who tends to hit the ball to the right side, they stack the right side with defenders. Your numbers drop. That's the theory.

The only time I remember they shifted a little on me was when Junior Gilliam played third. He dared me to bunt, so I bunted and got on base.

For lefties, grounders up the middle now are outs. Suddenly, the field narrows for these guys. It's why they keep doing it.

Okay, did they have computers when I played?

Not like they do today.

I hit the ball all around. Homers to right-center, homers when I pulled the ball, whatever was needed.

You never tried to hit home runs.

Nah. Every now and then, you try to hit home runs. The key to hitting, I think, is hitting the ball hard. Regardless of where it is. You hit the ball hard, it'll go over the fence. You've never seen me hit a ball to right field?

Oh yeah. You and Roberto Clemente.

No, Clemente hit the ball to right field more than I did. At least that's what I thought. He was my teammate in winter ball. He could throw, he could run, he was a very good hitter. He could hit, man. He hit the ball to right in all kinds of ways.

Now they encourage an uppercut swing. Back in the day, they taught everyone to hit down on the ball or swing level. Now, uppercut.

Look at all the guys who hit .300 every year. Which way do they hit?

Generally, all fields.

Then why shift?

Some guys keep hitting into the shift, so why change? The sluggers who keep pulling the ball, for instance.

If you can hit, it doesn't matter where they play. Just hit it over the fence. I'm kind of lost on that one.

Not everybody is Willie Mays. You know what else has gone away? The two-strike approach. Choking up with two strikes just to make contact.

If you choke up, now you're playing their game. If you make contact, the ball will be dead. No, I kept my bat the same all the time.

Then you'd fit in today . . . which is an understatement.

I don't know how you guys are writing about the game nowadays.

We evolve. Your games were two hours. Now they're an hour longer, sometimes more. Outfielders stand out there for twenty minutes.

Not me. I'd go get some water. "When you guys get ready to play, let me know."

Willie, what's the greatest part of baseball?

What's that mean? You hit the ball, you run, you catch the ball, you throw the ball. Now what else? It's all the greatest part of baseball.

I thought you'd say defense.

I told you a long time ago, to play baseball, you have to have a good defensive team. That's what I think. I don't know what other people think. I learned how to play baseball by playing defense, all the time. How many errors do you think I made every year?

You made a few. Four, five, six. As many as nine. But you took chances. You had the most outfield putouts in the history of the game, more than 7,000. So yeah, you made errors. You were aggressive. Vin Scully told me you played center field like a shortstop. He said Duke Snider was too conservative on base hits at the Polo Grounds, not wanting the ball to skip by him and go to the wall.

The ball got by me one time at the Polo Grounds, and Duke hit the ball. I made five to eight errors a year, but maybe three or four or five on throws. Not fly balls. I may miss one every year, maybe.

Sometimes you had to cover for the corner guys.

You didn't know that when I played. I always told them, "Do the best you can, don't worry about it, all I want you to do is hit the ball. You hit it, we're going to score runs some kind of way."

When did you start playing shallow?

We played accordingly, based on who's pitching and who's hitting. How're you gonna play deep on everybody who comes to the plate? First of all, you have to talk to the pitcher before you consider the batter. The pitcher is the key to playing the outfield. Some of the guys have good stuff, and you play accordingly. Sometimes you know he's not gonna hit it that far. If he does, you better get yourself back. I never did worry about stuff like that. I just played and enjoyed myself.

When you were a rookie with the Black Barons in '48 and Norm Robinson got hurt, you became the regular center fielder. You didn't know to play shallow right away, did you? You were a teenager.

I had already played center field in Chattanooga, Tennessee. I knew how to play center. I knew how to play everything because of my father. Every position. I know you don't think so.

I don't doubt you.

After the Black Barons, I signed with the Giants and went to Trenton. Then all the way up. A lot of guys tried but couldn't get the ball over my head.

Evidently.

The harder they tried to hit it, the easier I caught it.

Like you said, the pitcher and batter determine everything.

The pitcher more because he has to throw the ball. (Juan) Marichal had a good screwball, an overhand curve. Gaylord (Perry) had a . . . I don't know what he had.

You don't want to know what Gaylord had. He and Marichal talked about your three-minute meetings with them when they took the mound.

Yeah, before the game. When I got the three minutes, we'd go over the hitters.

Who was the toughest pitcher you faced? You talked about the tall reliever from Boston, Dick Radatz, who was tough in All-Star Games.

The guy in Cincinnati, Gary Nolan, struck me out four times one game. I didn't know who he was. Next time, I got him. You don't hit .300 every year and have to worry about that. Sometimes I might be 1-for-4 or 1-for-5, and then you get four hits the next time. What do you mean struggle? Get no hits off them?

Well, yeah.

Who do you have me not hitting?

Jim Bunning: .213 in 89 at-bats.

He knocked me down all the time.

Yes, but you got out of the way. You were one of the best at doing that. Guys would throw at you but not hit you. In fact, nobody hit you more than twice. Bunning was known for hitting a lot of guys. He hit you just once. How about Bob Gibson? One of the most intimidating pitchers ever. You hit just .196 off him in 92 at-bats. He never hit you.

Gibson never threw at me. I just wanted him to see me. Bill White brought him by my house, and Gibson had glasses on. I said, "Bill, who's that guy with you?" He said, "Bob Gibson." "That's not Bob Gibson." "Yes, it is." I didn't know who he was. "You mean he can hardly see?" Dang, I didn't know he needed glasses. I told Gibson, "Next time you pitch to me, put your glasses on." Couple of days later, when I faced him again, I told the umpire, Shag Crawford, "I'm not hitting until that guy out there puts his glasses on. I can see him. He can't see me." I faced him, but I had to make sure when he threw close to me, I could get out of there.

Then there's Don Drysdale. You hit him well, .330 in 227 at-bats. Going down the list of guys you faced the most: Warren Spahn, .305. Robin Roberts, .312. Larry Jackson, .351. Lew Burdette, .311. Amazing. The more you faced guys, the better you hit them. Of the twelve pitchers you faced the most, you hit .300 against eleven of them, and these are big names. Bob Buhl, Bob Friend, Curt Simmons, Harvey Haddix, Vern Law, Johnny Podres . . .

You bring up all these numbers. Did we win the game? That's what I worried about. Sometimes I'd go to bat, we're up five, six runs, what good is me hitting a home run? It won't mean nothing. I never worried how I did against a guy. I worried about the team hitting and winning. If we won the game, I didn't care how I hit.

Like the four-homer game in Milwaukee. If you lost, it wouldn't have been one of your favorite games.

All these guys you're talking about, you gotta look at two things. One, were we winning big when they got me out? Two, I could get one hit off them, and we could win the game. That's more important to me.

You worked hard to be so good, obviously. I hear people say you're a natural, that the game comes easy to you. Does that bother you? Is it unfair considering they're overlooking all the hard work?

No that's a tribute. I think it is. I didn't just go out there and start playing now. You have to go through a lot of stuff to get in position to catch a fly ball, and I had to catch fly balls that the left fielder and right fielder couldn't get to. They knew I'd catch it. I learned early. When I was fifteen, I was playing with guys who were twenty-five.

Did you ever play to make your father proud?

Why? He was always proud. We didn't do that in the South, man.

You love baseball. You love kids. What would you want to be remembered for?

No, no, no, no. You can't talk about yourself. I think you have to talk about other people, okay? It's like with this book. You're not writing the book because of you. You're writing the book because of the people. People don't want to hear about me all the time. They get tired of that stuff. I'd rather talk about a combination. When I talk about a combination, I mean I helped this guy, I helped that guy. Well, did those guys help the next guy? That's a combination. You don't want to talk only about yourself in a book.

Well, I interviewed more than 200 people who shared their thoughts for the book. Many of them said they learned from you or were inspired by you.

I tried to show guys early on. You've got to help them. They also helped me. Guys in Birmingham, guys in Trenton. It was a combination of those guys helping me to fulfill whatever I needed. You can't harp about what you do when you've got eight more guys on the field. It's not about one guy. You've got to help each other. You mean to tell me when you talk to a guy, you only talk about things I did? No, no, no. You talk about things they did. When I was playing, I didn't want to talk about me. I wanted to talk about the other guys. I helped them more than I helped me. Sometimes I didn't have to tell them. I just had to show them.

You watched out for the younger guys. In your final years, you took George Foster, a young outfielder, a fellow Alabama native, under your wing. He idolized you growing up. The Giants traded him to Cincinnati in '71, and he went on to win an MVP award with the Big Red Machine. He told me he felt accepted with the Reds because you had called Pete Rose and asked him to "take care of the kid." He said when you no longer were teammates, you continued to check in on him, have him over to your place, and help his game. He became the first player to hit 50 home runs since you twelve years earlier, and he told me it justified what you did for him.

George was a good kid. He could throw, he could run, he could hit. He had a lot of power. I don't know why we got rid of him. I tried to help those guys. You knew they could play. They just needed a chance. I remember talking with him quite a bit about that, and you'd talk more than just baseball. Even though you're no longer teammates, you still want to take care of them.

And when you were young, the older guys took care of you. The guys at Birmingham, for example.

They showed me. Places I was able to go, they hadn't been able to get in the door. I was very lucky and fortunate. All the guys on that team helped me some kind of way. Not to catch a ball, not to throw a ball or run or anything like that. They helped me with real life, all those guys.

I asked what you wanted to be known for, and you said it's more about helping others. So you did that all the way up. With this book, you're still doing that. It's not about you. It's about what this message could do for others.

It's like if you were an announcer and said, "Willie, come on the air," you don't want me talking about myself all the time. If someone wants to know, we go in a corner and talk. I don't go out and brag about all that kind of stuff.

It's interesting, Willie. You never talk in clichés. You talk straight ahead. I can't ask a lazy question. "How do you feel about . . ." You'll say, "Ask me the dang question." That's the beauty of this book. I'll ask you specifically about moments in your career or the Black Barons or racism or Monte Irvin or Hank Aaron or Mickey Mantle, direct questions, and you'll give me direct answers.

I told you about all those guys.

Beautifully.

I'd rather talk about them than about myself. Every guy.

You do that, and the other people talk about certain games you guys were in, certain relationships you built.

Let them talk.

Exactly. Willie, you played other sports. Football and basketball as a kid. Later in life, golf. So many people I interviewed for the book said you were a very good golfer.

I was four or five handicap. I hit it pretty good. I could play a little. I tried to hit 80 down. I'd hit in the 70s, the pros would hit in the 60s.

I imagine you could improve your game playing with the best in the world.

If I wanted to know something, they'd stop the game and show me. Whatever it was. They showed me everything. Each one of those guys had a different game. Some could hit. Some could putt. I really enjoyed playing with the pros. They were all good guys, funny guys.

You played with Lee Trevino.

Trevino talked a lot. As he hit the ball. He was funny, man.

Jack Nicklaus.

Nicklaus was the other way around. You've got to keep quiet when he's hitting.

Chi-Chi Rodríguez.

Chi-Chi showed me how to hit the ball up high and get it near the hole.

Arnold Palmer.

Palmer was a stats guy. I remember we played in Palm Springs. Par five, Palmer shoots a five. I hit it right by the green in two. I chip it and putt. "Oh my God, I made four." He says "no, no, no, no." "What do you mean, no, no, no, no?" "You double hit." That's the first time I heard "double hit." I hit it twice on one shot. "I just made four, man." "No, you made five like me."

You golfed with celebrities, too.

Oh, yeah. You name him, I played with him.

Frank Sinatra? Dean Martin?

Leo (Durocher) introduced me to Frank, and that's how I knew those guys. I played with Dean. He was okay. He just liked playing and talking. He enjoyed the game. When he had his program on TV, he'd work on Sunday and go play golf during the week. I remember him telling me one time, "Can you imagine they want me to rehearse during the week?" He said, "I ain't doing no rehearsal. Just tell me what to do, and we'll do it." He didn't like to rehearse. He played golf and enjoyed himself.

You befriended trailblazers in other sports. So many African-American athletes in the '50s, '60s, and '70s can't be commended enough as pioneers. A lot were your friends.

Arthur Ashe, we played softball in the wintertime down in Doral Beach in Florida to raise money for the kids. Arthur played second, I played short, (Ed) Kranepool played first. Quiet guy. A lot of times, I guess he had to be quiet. At the time Arthur played tennis, they didn't have a lot of African Americans in there. We need more black coaches in the communities to get these kids playing all the sports. That would lead to scholarships and opportunities like we have in other sports. I knew Althea Gibson, too, and Charlie Sifford, the first African American who played on the PGA tour. All of them went through a lot.

Many people don't know this, but you appeared on a bunch of TV talk shows back in the day. Ed Sullivan, Dick Cavett, Johnny Carson, Della Reese, Joey Bishop, Merv Griffin, Jack Paar, Steve Allen. Also sitcoms. There was a classic *Bewitched* episode with Elizabeth Montgomery, the actress who played Samantha Stephens, who sees you from across the room and says, "Say hey, Willie." You respond, "Hi, Sam." You were a warlock. Samantha knew it. Her husband, Darrin, didn't. At least until he saw you disappear.

They jumped me back to the ballpark. Elizabeth Montgomery, a nice lady. All these people helped me. They got me involved. Donna Reed put me on her show and helped me quite a bit. Dinah Shore, too. I needed a few thousand to buy some furniture. "Come on the show." When I needed a dollar, they got it for me, right quick.

Game shows, too. *What's My Line?* You were the mystery guest, and four blindfolded panelists had to guess who you were by asking you questions. You were on multiple times several years apart, and the same actress kept guessing you. What was that all about?

Arlene Francis. "Are you Say Hey Willie Mays, the ballplayer?" She was a good baseball fan. She listened to the voice, I guess.

How about *The Dating Game*? Three bachelors behind a screen, and you were the one chosen. You went to the Bahamas.

Judy Pace, the actress. Curt Flood saw her on the show and ended up marrying her.

Willie, in Harlem, you hung out at a couple of nightclubs, the Red Rooster and Smalls Paradise. What was that vibe?

The one I went to all the time was Red Rooster. George Woods, he's the one who took care of me. He was one of those who put me in my car every night about nine o'clock. "Go home." You could eat there, you could drink there, meet a lot of people. Smalls was bigger, right near Roy Campanella's liquor store. Everybody went to those two places. All the time. If I told you "meet me at Smalls," you'd know what I was talking about.

Your drink of choice?

Coke. Coke and a cherry. They never gave me alcohol, are you kidding? I couldn't do anything in New York, man. Everyone took care of me, and I tried to take care of others.

ACKNOWLEDGMENTS

When I first approached Willie Mays about collaborating on this project, he said, "I'd like to see this book in classrooms." The inspiration for an inspirational book was established, and we mapped out a plan to engage readers of all ages. We wanted to write a Willie Mays book unlike any other. No bibliography. No borrowing from old magazines, documentaries, or microfiche. None of the same quotes that have been handed down from book to book. All fresh and exclusive material, all new interviews that provide readers original looks at baseball's greatest and most exciting ballplayer.

The book, which could be listed under several categories—history, race, baseball, sports, inspiration, self-help, children's, photography, biography, autobiography—came to fruition not only because of the more than 100 hours I spent with Willie for the project but the more than 200 people I interviewed, from the dozens of Hall of Famers to the teammates, opponents, managers, commissioners, executives, broadcasters, friends, and associates. Also individuals who were influenced at an early age by Willie and made their own mark in life, whether they're from the world of art, music, journalism, or just ordinary folks who befriended the Say Hey Kid.

Oh, and presidents. I was privileged to check in with three. Bill Clinton and George W. Bush were born in the South in the summer of 1946 and became the first baby-boomer presidents, and both shared with me during lengthy interviews why they called Willie Mays their favorite player from childhood—they weren't alone, as Willie highlighted the first generation of black superstars following World War II—and how they became friends with him after moving into the White House. Clinton is invaluable in these pages for explaining Mays' contributions to the civil rights movement. When he told me, "Willie Mays made it absurd to be a racist," we had our chapter 17 title. Bush opened up about drawing inspiration playing catch with his father, George H. W. Bush, much like Willie did with his own dad: "What happened to Willie certainly happened to me." As for President Barack Obama, he offered full support of the book and had assistants provide everything he said publicly and privately about Willie in and around his administration, including along the campaign trail and when Willie visited the White House and rode aboard Air Force One.

Some of my most treasured conversations were with Willie's Negro League teammates, including Bill Greason, Artie Wilson, Jim Zapp, and Sammy C. Williams. Plus the great Monte Irvin, who started in the Negro Leagues, became one of the Giants' first two African Americans, and mentored a young Mays. I visited with Irvin in Houston and Greason in Birmingham, two of the most amazing men I've ever met, and spent time with Greason, Wilson, Zapp, and Williams in Beverly Hills when Mays and his four teammates from the 1948 Birmingham Black Barons were honored at a baseball scouts dinner.

Hank Aaron was instrumental in telling stories of his relationship with Willie and the hardships both fought and overcame while following parallel paths to greatness. Joe Morgan explained how Willie counseled young black players and emphasized the importance of passing the knowledge down. Rickey Henderson, whose autobiography I wrote—what an honor to be biographer of both the greatest player in Giants history and greatest in A's history—commented on growing up a Willie fan and wearing his idol's number. Willie McCovey, Orlando Cepeda, and Felipe Alou told enlightening stories of their time as Mays' younger teammates in baseball's most diverse clubhouse.

All these folks, along with so many others interviewed, had something in common with me. They loved telling Willie Mays stories.

The co-MVPs of this project were editorial consultant Kurt Aguilar and photographic researcher Brad Mangin, whose goal was to make the book as excellent as possible with the right words and pictures. They're two of the best and most respected professionals in the publishing industry who happen to be historians of baseball and Willie Mays. The subject and content are dear to them, and they contributed invaluable research and keen recommendations. I thank Kurt not just for his contribution as my personal editor and sounding board but for wisely suggesting *24* as the title and Brad for his skillful eye and tremendous contacts to help assemble the rarest and most comprehensive collection of Willie Mays photos in one publication, more than ninety in all.

Rene Anderson was a level higher than an MVP. Willie's trusted assistant does more than anyone knows and is masterful with everything she does. I can't thank her enough for her kindness and support. That goes for Willie's close friends, some of whom are featured in chapter 24, including attorneys Jeff Bleich and Malcolm Heinicke, both influential in making the project materialize. Another friend of Willie's, Rick Swig, was kind enough to offer the world's largest collection of Willie Mays photos, which includes his own exclusive shots from places no other photographers were permitted.

We're blessed to showcase so many rare pictures from Pete Souza, the chief White House photographer for Presidents Reagan and Obama, the great Cuban photographer Osvaldo Salas, and the renowned William Jacobellis, Michael Zagaris, Jean Fruth, Ron Riesterer, and Brad Mangin. John Horne was instrumental in giving access to the Hall of Fame's photo library, Daniel Murphy contributed personal shots of Willie, Guy Watkins furnished a different perspective of The Catch, and many unique photos were unearthed deep in the Giants' archives.

During my visit to Willie's roots in Birmingham and Fairfield, I met with many wonderful people, starting with Bill Greason and childhood friend Charles Willis, who invited me into his home, where he and Willie hung out as kids, and showed me mementos from their youth. Clarence Watkins guided me around historic Rickwood Field, the country's oldest existing professional ballpark and Willie's home with the Black Barons, and let me study his abundant records and photographs. The folks at the Negro Southern League Museum were gracious with their time and knowledge, including former Negro Leaguers Jake Sanders, Willie Walker, Samuel Bruner, and Ernest Fann. Thanks also to the staffs at the Fairfield library and school district and Jonathan Nelson, general manager of the Birmingham Barons.

The love of history runs deep in this project, and I'm indebted to everyone at the National Baseball Hall of Fame and Museum, especially former president Jeff Idelson, his successor Tim Mead, curator Erik Strohl, publicists Jon Shestakofsky and Craig Muder, and researcher Bill Francis, who kindly directed me to the Willie Mays file. Also: Negro Leagues Baseball Museum president Bob Kendrick, Dodgers historian Mark Langil, Mets PR legend Jay Horwitz, and the late Giants beat writer Nick Peters and his wife, Lise, whose Mays file rivals the size of the Hall's. I absorbed all their information in a bid to ask the right questions.

I was honored to receive advice from distinguished authors and journalists Jane Leavy, Howard Bryant, Scott Ostler, Larry Stone, Bill Madden, Claire Smith, Mark Fainaru-Wada, Chris Haft, Steve Kettmann, Tyler Kepner, and Tim Brown. Speaking of respected journalists, Julian McWilliams reflected on his childhood in Harlem and his Willie Mays tattoo, and he did a wonderful job narrating Willie's words for the *24* audiobook. Bill Madden hooked me up with legendary Yankees and Dodgers. Lyle Spencer turned me on to Don Newcombe. Scott Ostler supplied a never-before-published Bill Rigney interview. Terence Moore provided Hank Aaron insight. Kevin Kernan connected me with Robinson Cano.

I thank the fabulous group of journalists at the *San Francisco Chronicle,* where I hold my dream job and where miracles happen every day, courtesy of Audrey Cooper, Al Saracevic, Jon Schultz, Mike Lerseth, Henry Schulman, Susan Slusser, Scott Ostler, Bruce Jenkins, Ann Killion, Steve Kroner, Ron Kroichick, Carlos Avila Gonzalez, Bill Van Niekerken, Pete Wevurski, and so many others. A special thank you to Glenn Schwarz, who gave me the opportunity of a lifetime when he hired me, and all my other editors through the years.

Kudos to talented Giants beat writers who keep the tradition alive, including Henry Schulman, Andrew Baggarly, Alex Pavlovic, Kerry Crowley, Maria Guardado, Manolo Hernandez-Douen, and Janie McCauley, along with my pal Chris Haft, whose knowledge of Giants history is unparalleled. I began compiling a list of all the talented and dedicated baseball writers I admire, and it was much too long (in the hundreds) to fit in this space, so I'll simply say it's a pleasure to share press boxes with all of you.

I was delighted to learn so much from Bill James, the godfather of baseball's analytic movement, and an All-Star cast of writers/historians/statisticians: Rob Neyer, Eno Sarris, Tom Tango, and Bill Arnold. Special thanks to Eno, who helped make perfect sense of all our advanced data in the book.

Chronicling the eloquent prose of many fantastic broadcasters was a privilege: Jon Miller, Mike Krukow, Duane Kuiper, Greg Papa, Marty Lurie, Ray Fosse, Ken Korach, Tim McCarver, Dick Enberg, and especially Vin Scully and Bob Costas. Bob's foreword in these pages shows he's not just a wonderful broadcaster but an incredible writer.

I was touched when the late Peter Magowan, the Giants' owner, told me in his final interview that he was thrilled to be part of this Willie Mays book. Thanks to Giants officials Larry Baer, Staci Slaughter, Mario Alioto, Shana Daum, Matt Chisholm, Maria Jacinto, Mike Passanisi, Erwin Higueros, Megan Brown, Joan Ryan, Mike Murphy, and Tom Zorn, and a special recognition to director of photography and archives Missy Mikulecky for opening the vault.

Let's not forget the folks with the Oakland A's, starting with Fernando Alcalá, Steve Vucinich, and Mickey Morabito, along with the commissioners I interviewed and Major League Baseball officials I queried: Pat Courtney, Mike Teevan, Matthew Gould, and Steven Arocho.

None of this would have been possible without my agent, Kimberley Cameron, whose vision and compassion made for a smooth and rewarding journey. Thankfully, Kimberley connected me with Peter Wolverton, my editor at St. Martin's Press, whose creativity and professionalism helped turn a dream into reality.

I can't overlook my many close friends, a few of whom I mention here for their presence and generosity throughout the project: Dave Collins, Rick Lewis, James Wren-Jarvis, Jon Stein, Kim Terasaki, Rick Linvill, Kevin Kirkman, and Pat Quinlan.

Thanks also to Angel Ureña, Charles Branch, and Meredith Bohen, assistants for Clinton, Bush, and Obama, respectively. Hall of Famers Ernie

Banks, Bob Feller, and Tom Seaver, whose Willie stories early in the process were an inspiration. George Theodore, former outfielder who had the foresight to do an extensive video interview with friend Herman Franks. Bill Gould, Stanford professor and Red Sox historian. Andre "Pee Wee" Taylor, who's at Willie's side throughout spring training. The PR departments of the Dodgers, Angels, Red Sox, and others. All the talented players, managers, coaches, and executives I've been fortunate to cover through the decades. And so many others in the game who were gracious with their time and recollections, not all of whom made it in the book. The websites Baseball Reference, Retrosheet, and FanGraphs were invaluable sources of information, and I referenced my own articles at sfchronicle.com.

My mother, Ann Byrne Shea, a constant source of inspiration, died midway into the project, and her love, faith, and encouragement kept me going. In her final weeks, bedside, I told her I'd dedicate the book to her, and I'll never forget her response. "Oh, no," she said, suggesting it should be dedicated to my wife, Zdena, and daughter, Tereza. I told her I was going to do that, too. She held my hand and whispered, "That's beautiful." Three generations of inspirations. My son, Jan, his wife, Jenny, and their beautiful children, Jordan and Johnny, get props as do my four brothers, Terry, Mike, Dan, and Frank, cousin Rose, and all the wonderful relatives who rallied together in challenging times and vowed to live the kind of lives that would make my mother proud.

Of course, a major thank you to Willie Mays, who gave me far more access than anyone else who wrote a Willie Mays book. In his home. In his stadium suite. In spring training. At public and private functions. In his hotel room with his former Black Baron teammates when they were honored at a Beverly Hills scouts dinner. In the green room before Bob Costas interviewed him and Hank Aaron at New York University. In the broadcast booth for his visit with Vin Scully during the final weekend of Scully's career. I transcribed all the hundreds of hours of interviews myself in order to grasp the vibe and inflection of Willie and others and more accurately capture their feelings and soul. I put the ball on a tee for Willie, and he hit it out of the park—far more than 660 times—with his memories, opinions, and laughter. For his time, dedication, and loyalty, I'm eternally grateful.

INDEX